DYNAMIC LIGHT AND SHADE

DYNAMIC LIGHT AND SHADE

BY BURNE HOGARTH

WATSON-GUPTILL PUBLICATIONS/NEW YORK

Artwork appearing on pages 67, 96, 114, 132, 133, 146, 152, 154, 155, and 156 is based on Edgar Rice Burroughs' *Jungle Tales of Tarzan* and is used courtesy of Edgar Rice Burroughs, Inc.

Paperback Edition
First printing·1991

First published in 1981 by Watson-Guptill Publications,
a division of VNU Business Media, Inc.,
770 Broadway, New York, NY 10003
www.wgpub.com

Library of Congress Catalog Card Number: 81-11390
ISBN 0-8230-1580-7
ISBN 0-8230-1581-5 (pbk.)

Manufactured in U.S.A.

16 17 18 19/07 06 05

Cover design by Bob Fillie, Graphiti Graphics

Edited by Bonnie Silverstein
Designed by Bob Fillie and James Craig
Set in 9-point Palatino

It is with deep love I dedicate this book to my children, Ross, Richard, Michael, and his child, Stephanie; and also to Don Holden of Watson-Guptill for his intelligence, insight, and warmth, a human being in the best sense.

Acknowledgments

I wish to acknowledge the capable and generous assistance of James Craig, Virginia Croft, Bonnie Silverstein, and Don Holden (who was there from the very start), all from Watson-Guptill, for their direction and guidance in the details of design, editorial, promotional, and manufacturing needs of this book.

For photographic backup, I thank Yousef Habhab of Mastandrea Studios in Mount Kisco, NY, and Dan Demetriad, who both gave unstintingly of their time and expertise. Special mention is made to Jerry Robinson for use of his *Moon Trip* (Putnam) illustrations; to Don Ivan Punchatz for permission to use his American Hero painting; in memoriam, to Herbert Morton Stoops, for the illustrations of western life; to Kaethe Kollwitz, for the powerful, moving etching of the "Schlachtfeld"; and to the ukiyo-e masters, Hiroshige and Koryusai, for their striking and elegant woodcuts of Japanese landscapes.

Special acknowledgment is given to Marion Burroughs, Vice President, and Edgar Rich Burroughs, Inc., of Tarzana, CA, for their permission to publish illustrations created by the author: four panels from the newspaper syndicated Sunday page, *Tarzan* (Copyright 1947, 1949, 1950, Edgar Rice Burroughs, Inc., All Rights Reserved); and seven illustrations, appearing in Chapters 6, 8, 11, 13, and 15, based on the book by Edgar Rice Burroughs, *Jungle Tales of Tarzan* (Copyright 1976, Edgar Rice Burroughs, Inc., All Rights Reserved).

I also affirm an obligation and heartfelt thanks to those artists and printmakers, living and dead, before and after photography, who set forth in pictorial record the experiential events of the numerous problematical phenomena of light and shade which, in their totality, lie beyond the province of any one person to amass, know, or express.

CONTENTS

INTRODUCTION

We see the way our social order *lets* us perceive. To put it another way, our perceptions mirror or symbolize the behavior of a specific culture. It is through art that these perceptions are expressed; art sets forth the *visual* form of our social experience. Thus art is an expression of the perceived values of a socio-cultural process at a given time in history. The following story, which I read several years ago though I don't exactly recall where, illustrates this point.

In the eighteenth century, a British naval mission was dispatched to the Far East to open diplomatic relations and trade with China. To introduce his sovereign to the Chinese emperor, the British admiral presented a portrait of King George III painted in the grand style of the Baroque era. The painting was handsomely executed—a three-quarter view with dramatic chiaroscuro that plunged one side of the face into deep shadow.

The Chinese emperor perused the picture, pausing to study the dark tone on the shadow side of the face. Turning to the admiral, the emperor politely commented on the British king's disability. Was he, in fact, missing an eye, and was one side of his face so badly discolored? The admiral did his best to explain that his sovereign was in no way disabled, and that the portrait was an excellent likeness.

The Chinese emperor ordered his own portrait brought before them. Like the European painting, the Chinese portrait was skillfully done, but it was a frontal view, showing the features in bilateral symmetry, with flat color and no suggestion of light and shade. Pointing to the clear skin and the intact features, the emperor declared that the portrait was a perfect likeness of a sovereign in good health. "Why," he wondered, "is the king's portrait so dark and discolored if the British Lord is well?"

The portraits, in this apocryphal story, represent two irreconcilable viewpoints about painting—and specifically about the function of light. The difference is *not* in the paintings, but in social values—the way in which each society trains its members to *see*. What *we* know as light and shade, and the way in which our culture comprehends light and shade in a picture, is simply *our* way of seeing. Other societies do not always conceive or express light and shade as we do.

As Max Friedländer, art historian and author of *On Art and Connoisseurship*, has said: "The light that strikes the eye is not the same as the light that strikes the mind." In short, we see in the way that a social order trains us to perceive.

In our day, westerners like ourselves approach the universe with an empirical, analytical, scientific viewpoint, stemming from early Greek civilization, and rediscovered in the Renaissance with the birth of modern science. We are interested in art that describes deep space (through linear and atmospheric perspective), anatomical form, and the effects of time, seasons, and weather. Western artists and their audience are concerned with light that illuminates these specific phenomena in nature.

Thus, the purpose of this book is to show the objective, naturalistic properties of light and shade—the visual appearance of the world as modern western man is trained to perceive it. The book will also explore the expressive qualities of light and shade—the realm of mood, affect, and subjective phenomena.

We will begin with light and shade in their primary, most basic form: the concept of figure and ground—the silhouette as *form* on the white *ground* of the paper. Then we will examine a series of silhouette forms that imply spatial recession on the white ground. We will discuss reverse silhouettes and silhouettes of various sizes that create the illusion of space, near and far.

We will explore the ways in which minimal light (or highlight) reveals form, and we will see the effects of five fundamental categories of light and shade: single-source light; double-source light; flat, diffused light; moonlight; and sculptural light.

We will investigate spatial light—how values create space; environmental light—the effects of weather, atmosphere, time, and the seasons; textural light—the way in which light reveals surface qualities; transparent light—the effects of light on transparent, translucent, and reflective materials; fragmentation light—which conveys disintegration of form in motion; radiant light—the intense light of the sun or an artificial light source; and finally, expressive light—the psychological and poetic power of light.

These phenomena are illustrated with a wide range of drawing media: pencil, charcoal, carbon, pen-and-ink, brush-and-ink on a variety of drawing surfaces, ranging from conventional papers to exotic textures like linen. The reader is encouraged to experiment with diverse media as a means of researching the problems of light and shade—and a means of spurring the reader's awareness of the solutions.

CHAPTER 1

BLACK-AND-WHITE SILHOUETTE

The Picture Plane as a Field of Light

When an artist sits before a sheet of white paper to make a drawing, he sees the picture plane—whether consciously or intuitively—as a field of light. In the same way, he sees any mark, stroke, or scribble within that picture plane as a form, a presence—something inside that field of light. In short, the bounded area of the paper has become a *place*, and the mark, no matter how crude, has become a *thing*.

Picture Plane

This rectangular area—which may be a sheet of drawing paper or a canvas—is a simple picture plane. If you think of this rectangle as a *space*, the picture plane becomes a void, a ground, a field of light that may contain some kind of mark that represents a form.

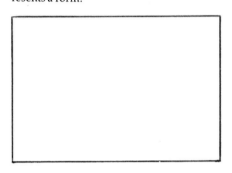

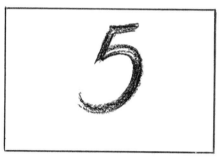
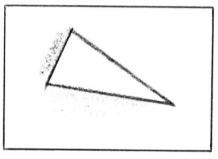

Figure and Ground

When this rectangular space is filled with a mark, a number, a triangle, a tree, there is now a presence in the void. We now have what psychologists call "figure and ground." The ground is the bare rectangle, while the figure is a mark that interrupts the void. If you can recognize a specific form in that bare rectangle—such as a tree—then you are convinced that a "thing" can be said to "exist" within that space. No amount of argument will dissuade you from knowing that you are seeing a figure in its ground or field of light, that you are seeing an image inside the picture frame. The idea leaps to your mind that *you are looking into a real space.*

The Silhouette as a Form in Space
Once we have accepted the white space as a field of light—a background on which things may happen—then *any form* that interrupts the field of light becomes something "real." It becomes a "figure" on a "ground." The simplest example of a figure on a ground is a silhouette on a piece of white paper. A silhouette is a profile view of an object, the simplest essence of a form in space, recognizable as a dimensional object within the field of light.

Geometrical Silhouettes
Some silhouettes are ambiguous and some are not. In the first column at the left, the three squares are ambiguous because they do not suggest specific three-dimensional forms. It is not clear whether they represent cubes, a head-on view of a cylinder, or the rectangular base of a pyramid. The middle column represents a slight shift in viewpoint, with less visual confusion: the three silhouettes do, in fact, suggest a cubic form, a cylinder, and a pyramid. But the three silhouettes in the right-hand column are clearer still, particularly in the case of the pyramid, which now obviously rests on a square base.

11

The Silhouette and the Third Dimension
If we are to understand the silhouette as a real presence in the world, we must see some suggestion of the third dimension, as seen in the foregoing examples. A clear, unambiguous silhouette depends on finding the right viewpoint—a view of the object that gives a sense of perspective, a grasp of the whole form. To achieve this sense of perspective, the drawing must communicate the presence of a ground plane on which the form rests.

Balancing Figures
This action silhouette is believable because the feet of the lower figure seem to rest on a base line. The athlete's legs communicate a firm sense of the ground. Throughout the two figures, there is also a clear sense of the vertical line of gravity.

Objects on a Table
The silhouettes of the bottle, wine glasses, cork, and box all imply the presence of a table top. The objects not only seem to exist in a field of light and space, but also communicate a definite front-to-back relationship. At the right, the overlap of the wine glass and bottle signals the fact that the glass stands behind the bottle. As for the cylindrical cork that lies on its side, the right side seems nearer to you than the left side. All this happens because the silhouettes imply perspective and the presence of a ground plane—the table top.

12

House

Seen in perspective from above, this silhouette shows us a large house with wings attached to the main structure. Look at the topmost line of the roof: does the rooftop recede from left to right or from right to left? Looking at the total silhouette and studying the visual logic of all the other structures, you know that the form of the roof recedes from left to right. The back of the house is at your right.

Objects on a Drawing Board

The pen, brush, ink and paint bottles, eyeglasses, eraser, leads, and coffee cup are not parallel to one another but are all at odd angles. Yet they seem "right" because each silhouette makes us feel, without question, the presence of the firm, flat surface of the drawing table on which the objects rest. For each object, the best viewpoint—the best angle—has been chosen to suggest that the white paper is not just a field of light, but a dimensional space. Note the left lens of the eyeglasses. The magnification of the temple piece *through* the lens and the patch of light *on* the lens are powerful visual signals that convey the illusion of the third dimension.

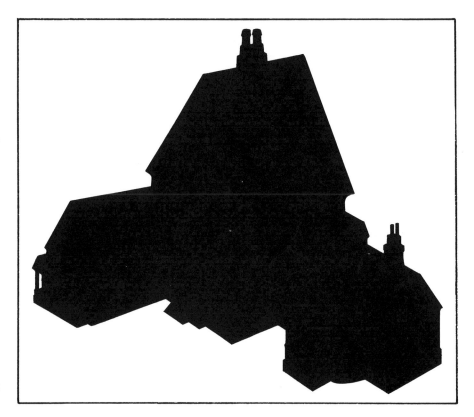

Silhouette Figures in Space

The silhouette of the human figure presents problems because we do not have precise geometric forms to work with, as we do in the preceding example. And there are still more problems when we deal with the soft, plastic form of the human body in groups. The figure requires new perceptions.

Fight Scene

Here is a scene with many figures in various stages of action. Study the actions and the shapes carefully, and do not be put off by the multiple arms and legs, which are meant to show *action sequences* in some figures. Start with the tense, angular, straight-legged figure who moves diagonally upward from the lower right, holding and heaving a figure at the upper left. From here, the design moves downward, counterclockwise, to the left. As you look at each figure, try to imagine front views, back views, twists in the torsos, right and left legs. As your eye moves, you will perceive space and depth. The horizontal figure in the lower right—a back view, is it not?—establishes the much-needed ground plane or base line.

More Figures in Action
There is an important difference between this group of fighting figures and the group in the preceding illustration. In this rotating design, the central figure and one or two others move *toward* us and *away* from us. If you study the silhouettes of the arms and legs, and especially the fingers and toes, you will become acutely aware of how the details of the silhouettes convey depth. Contrary to what you may think, the silhouette does not necessarily lie profiled on the flat paper like a skinned animal rug on a floor, but has rich possibilities for conveying three-dimensional space.

Silhouettes Can Convey Degrees of Light
Although we have only the white paper to
communicate the brightness of the light,
the silhouette can actually suggest differences in the amount or degree of light—
greater or lesser *intensity* of light.

Jungle Scene
As a large tree boa emerges from a jungle
setting, the network of leaves, vines,
fronds, and tropical verdure along the
edges seems *darker* than in the central,
open area. The central space appears
bright, indeed; else, why would the ser-
pent appear so sharp and clear in contrast
with the murky, indistinct shapes of the
surrounding jungle? Let your eye move
back and forth from the center to the
edges to confirm this impression. Along
the edges, the dense concentration of dark
silhouettes somehow makes black ink
look blacker! Spatial question: Look
around the boundary and ask yourself
whether the boa is moving *away* from you
into the picture or outward *toward* you.

Leopard

In contrast to the foregoing illustration, this view of a leopard in a tree is generally dark throughout. Most elements of the picture are in the foreground, but there is still a sense of depth and spatial definition. See how the tail of the animal curls, and observe the overlapping leaves at the top as well as the curling tree trunk and branches.

Jungle Man

A dark foreground is implied in this image of a figure in a tree, accompanied by monkeys and surrounded by dense tropical growth. The silhouette of the figure communicates a foreshortened top view. To analyze the action of the body, look at such details as the twist of the torso, the forward thrust of the left arm, the hair of the eyelash, and the upraised little toe of the left foot. Do you feel that the pattern of light and dark in the drawing begins to suggest *color*—cool tonalities of green, blue, and purple, with a sunny contrast of yellows and greens where the lion travels across the open ground beneath?

Different Silhouette Sizes
Create Perspective

A change of size in known elements—that is, in objects whose size we already know from experience—will communicate a sense of deep space. The bigger shape looks closer, while the smaller one looks farther away.

Cowboy in Action

As the cowboy ropes the steer and drops him to the ground, we have a clear sense of the foreground plane where the animal falls and the background plane where the cowboy rides his horse. Several changes in scale are at work here: the difference in the sizes of the animals, near and far; the diminishing sizes of the plants in the foreground and distance; and the rise and fall of the shapes of the ground. And notice how the lariat grows thicker as it moves from the cowboy's hand to the rear leg of the steer.

Reverse Silhouettes

Silhouettes can become even more complex to create a particularly complicated sense of three-dimensional space. One possibility is a *dual system* of what might be called "reverse silhouettes," black-on-white *and* white-on-black. The combination can be so subtle that we hardly notice.

Warriors on Horseback

The silhouettes tell us that the *nearer* horseman is at the right, while the fallen horseman at the left is slightly *farther* away. The rumps of the horses are the key: we feel that we see them from behind, and this seems consistent with the three-quarter back view of the horseman raising his ax. The confirmation, subtle as it is, appears in the black-and-white silhouettes of the grass. The upright rear leg of the striding horse is in *front* of the grass, while the body of the fallen horse is *behind* the grass, which we see in white silhouette against the dark body. Note the silhouette of the head of the fallen horse; we seem to see the head from under the jaw. The message: Never lose an opportunity to relate facts in a silhouette.

19

A Frieze of Leopards
A three-stage design of black-on-white and white-on-black produces an interesting spatial effect. In the upper left, the white shape of the leopard's head appears to be in the immediate foreground. Then the black shapes of the running cats—against the white background—become the middleground. Finally, the white-on-black panorama of trees, grasses, and verdure—behind the black cats—functions as the background, against which we can see the foreground and middleground without confusion. The design is both decorative and functional.

Swamp
In another three-stage silhouette design, the planes are not separated, as in the previous illustration, but overlapped and interconnected. The immediate foreground is represented by the black silhouette of the swampy growth at the bottom of the picture. The black shape quickly overlaps the white silhouette just behind, representing lush, swampy growth, a leaping hare on the land, and a jumping frog on the water. This white silhouette, in turn, overlaps the black silhouette of the rocks, turtle, sapling, more elaborate tropical growth, and the startled heron about to take flight. Such a drawing demands careful planning and painstaking execution. There are virtually no shortcuts. But the reward is an effective and "colorful" work in black-and-white that has all the earmarks of a satisfying rendering in full color.

CHAPTER 2

MINIMAL LIGHT

The Primary Definition of Form
I shall never forget painting a studio still life in my student days. I was struggling to get some *form* into my painting of a big, green bottle. But the paint lay on the surface like dead matter. The instructor walked by, squinted at my painting, and said: "There are two things you do with form. First, you push the object *into* the surface—you send it back in depth. Then you get it *off* the surface, free it, force it out!" So saying, he picked up a brushload of white, made a curving slash on my green bottle, and the form swelled, leaping from the canvas with the most beautiful highlight I have ever seen.

You have seen that the *silhouette* is the first and simplest impression of the total contour of a form in space. The simplest essence of a form in *three dimensions* is in the *highlight*. Although the highlight is the most minimal light possible, that highlight signifies the outward thrust of the form as it advances from the picture plane toward the viewer. Attached to the silhouette, which defines the contour of the form most clearly, the highlight adds the third dimension and communicates the object's outward movement into space.

Varying the Direction of the Light
Do not be troubled by the recurrent use of a single-light direction—from the upper right—in these drawings or in your own. Sometimes the continued use of a simple, logical solution reinforces your performance. But if you need a new light source, just hold these drawings up to a mirror and you will see how the light works when it comes from the opposite direction. Or rotate the drawings as you please—even turning them upside down—to discover new light directions.

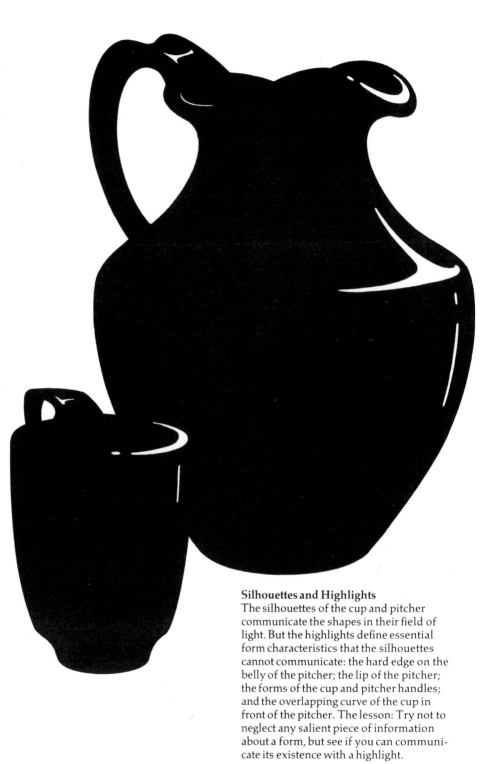

Silhouettes and Highlights
The silhouettes of the cup and pitcher communicate the shapes in their field of light. But the highlights define essential form characteristics that the silhouettes cannot communicate: the hard edge on the belly of the pitcher; the lip of the pitcher; the forms of the cup and pitcher handles; and the overlapping curve of the cup in front of the pitcher. The lesson: Try not to neglect any salient piece of information about a form, but see if you can communicate its existence with a highlight.

Highlights on Edges

These hard-edged, rectangular forms are explained by highlights that follow the vertical and horizontal edges of the planes. The highlights all start from the projecting corners. Note the direction of the light, which moves into the corner of each box form and then tapers away along the receding edges of the planes. The choice of the light direction is entirely arbitrary—selected to show the form most clearly. If your choice of light *reads well*, let no one tell you that it is wrong!

Matching the Highlight to the Form

For each form, the highlights are chosen to explain the shape most clearly. On the pyramid, all that is needed is a linear highlight on the forward triangular corner. For the chess pieces, a light source has been placed slightly above and to one side, and the highlights tend to repeat the external contours. In each case, the form is explicit and discernible.

Variations within the Highlight

Note that the highlight thickens at certain points. This accent or stress within the highlight clearly denotes the point of the form that is closest to the light source. Where the highlight tapers and gradually disappears on a curved or receding surface, the narrowing highlight suggests places where the highlight becomes diminished or vague. The needle and thread obviously need no additional light to explain the form; they exist very clearly as simple, pristine silhouettes.

Inward and Outward Curves

The two cosmetic bottles, one large and one small, show convex and concave curves, both in their silhouettes and in the highlights that follow these silhouettes. Once the silhouette is explained by the simplest means—by the simplest and most explicit minimal light—there is nothing more to be done.

Making Forms Recognizable

Just as it is essential to choose the silhouette that shows the object in its most recognizable, unambiguous contour, you must choose the highlights that reveal the form most clearly. In this drawing of spherical and disk-shaped objects, the problem is to show the essential changes in the forms as revealed by the highlights. Although they are *not* drawn from actual models, these silhouettes and highlights communicate effectively for two reasons. First, all the lights come from one direction—from the upper right, at an angle of roughly forty-five degrees. Second, the minimal lights (highlights) within the silhouettes tend to repeat the nearest external contours.

Inventing Light Sources

In this drawing of disparate objects on a drawing board, the minimal lights (highlights) do not reflect a single, consistent light source. The direction of the light varies and the highlights have been invented to express the salient forms with maximum clarity. Where the brush hairs emanate from the metal holder of the disk eraser, for example, the highlight is designed to reveal the series of tiny indentures that clamp the hairs. This invented highlight is simple and convincing. Never overlook a necessary form; a lazy statement is worse than none.

**Edge Light—Another Use
of Minimal Light**
Simple, minimal light—the highlight—is
the most economical means of revealing
three-dimensional form within a silhouette. Edge light is another, secondary
use of minimal light that may be combined with the highlight to enhance three-
dimensional form. This combination is especially effective in drawings or paintings
of the figure.

Combining Highlights and Edge Lights
These two figures, shown largely in silhouette, show minimal highlights within
the forms. On the right figure, there are *islands* of minimal light on the features of
the head, on the neck and chest, and on the
hand that holds the staff. The left figure
shows similar droplets of light on the but-
tock, fists, left shoulder, neck, and other
areas. These highlights are used selec-
tively to clarify or express certain forms or
actions that are essential to the drawing.
For the same purpose, edge lights have
been introduced (largely on the tops and
right sides of the forms) to show muscle
stress on the shoulders; tensions within
the tendons of arms, hands, and feet on
the ground plane; pulls within the chest
and legs; and the overlap of the crossed
staves.

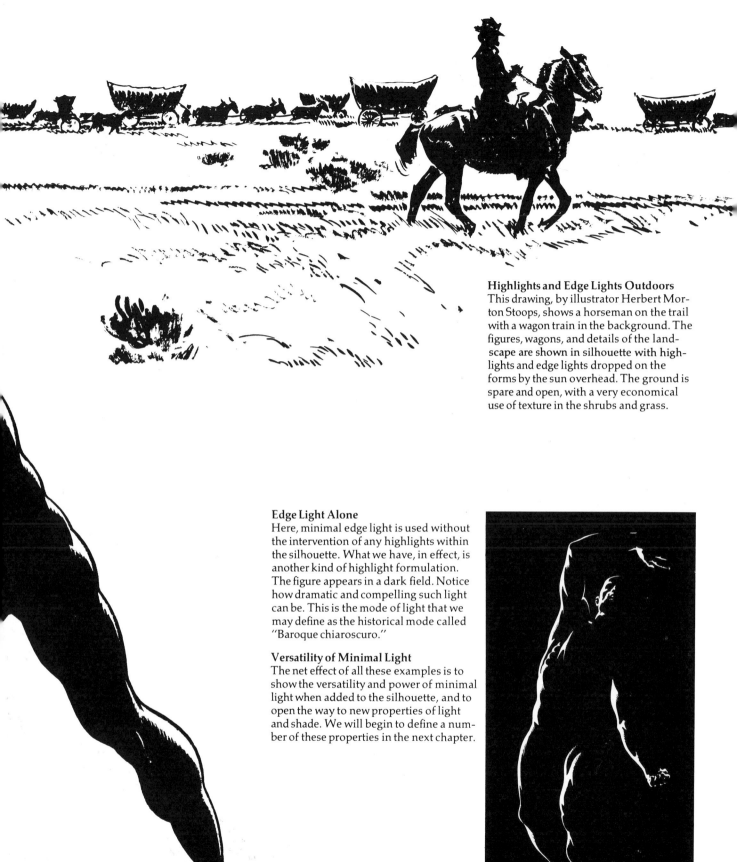

Highlights and Edge Lights Outdoors
This drawing, by illustrator Herbert Morton Stoops, shows a horseman on the trail with a wagon train in the background. The figures, wagons, and details of the landscape are shown in silhouette with highlights and edge lights dropped on the forms by the sun overhead. The ground is spare and open, with a very economical use of texture in the shrubs and grass.

Edge Light Alone
Here, minimal edge light is used without the intervention of any highlights within the silhouette. What we have, in effect, is another kind of highlight formulation. The figure appears in a dark field. Notice how dramatic and compelling such light can be. This is the mode of light that we may define as the historical mode called "Baroque chiaroscuro."

Versatility of Minimal Light
The net effect of all these examples is to show the versatility and power of minimal light when added to the silhouette, and to open the way to new properties of light and shade. We will begin to define a number of these properties in the next chapter.

CHAPTER 3

FIVE CATEGORIES OF LIGHT AND SHADE

Five Kinds of Light

For the purposes of the artist, I believe that there are five kinds of light—and their corresponding kinds of shade—that tend to fit almost all the light conditions that we are likely to draw or paint: single-source light; double-source light; flat, diffused light; moonlight; and sculptural light. I will introduce them briefly in this chapter. Then, in the following chapters, I will explain and illustrate each type of light and shade in greater detail.

Single-Source Light

The simplest kind of light comes from a single source, such as the bright light of the sun on a warm summer's day, in the late morning, at midday, or in early afternoon. This single-source light—or *direct* light—may also occur in an interior setting, where there is a bright, artificial light coming from a fairly high, overhead source. Whatever the season or time of day, and whatever the setting, indoors or outdoors, the net effect is a bright light with a correspondingly deep, sharp-edged shadow. Thus, *direct, single-source light* can also mean bright light illumination by photo flash, fluorescent tube, flame, arc, fireworks, dynamite, lightning, and so forth.

Single-Source Light from the Upper Left

In this two-figure group, the direct, single-source light comes from the upper left—almost overhead. Compare the soft-edged *flesh shadows* on the volumes of the bodies with the hard-edged *cast shadows*. The falling light has thrown cast shadows on the neck, chest, and legs of the upright figure, which has, in turn, thrown a strip of shadow on the prone figure. The cast shadow on the ground combines the shapes of the two figures in simplified form. There is a critical difference between the two kinds of shadows. *Flesh* or *body shadow* is integral to the figure and expresses the particular qualities of the form. *Cast shadow*, on the other hand, does not belong to the figure, but is *imposed* on the form.

**Single-Source Light
from the Upper Right**
This sketch of a part of Rodin's *John the
Baptist Preaching* shows the effect of a high
light source in the upper right, somewhat
in front of the figure. Even in such a spontaneous sketch—with the tones quickly
applied in the shaded areas—the shadows
clearly follow the linear edges of the
planes.

Artificial Light Indoors
This figure is brightly illuminated by an
artificial light source, such as a spotlight,
within the interior space of a room. The
light source is virtually overhead, and the
background recedes immediately into
darkness. Note the hard-edged cast
shadow of the arm falling across the chest.
The thigh emerges from a hard-edged
dark into the "hot" light. But see how
some of the fleshy forms emerge from the
darkness more slowly and subtly; study
the feathered edges of the tones.

Double-Source Light

The second category of light and shade is a combination of two light sources: strong, direct light from one source; and a secondary, lesser light from some opposite source, away from the strong, primary light source. Thus, we now have major and minor light, or direct and indirect light. And this kind of light and shade can occur either outdoors or indoors, whether the light source is natural or artificial.

Double-Source Light Outdoors

The young woman's head, drawn outdoors, shows the *primary* natural light coming from the upper right. This light direction is confirmed by the direction of the cast shadows under the nose and lower lip, and on the neck below the chin. The light is not harsh, but muted and atmospheric, suggesting an outdoor setting among a grove of trees or some wooded area that will reflect and diffuse the light. Thus, the *secondary* or minor light hovers softly on the left side of the face. The dark area within the center of the head falls between the *major* light on the right and the *minor* light on the left.

Double-Source Light Indoors

Now we see this dual light system on a figure indoors. On the left side of the form is the major, direct light. On the right side of the form is the minor, indirect light, thrown on the figure from some distant part of the room. The cast shadows under the left arm and on the upraised right arm—created by the obstructing head—tell us that the primary, or direct light source is at the lower left. Observe how the secondary, indirect light at the right tends to repeat the outer contour of the figure—and remember the discussion of this phenomenon in the preceding chapter on minimal light.

Flat, Diffused Light

Flat, diffused light occurs on overcast days, beneath cloudy skies, and tends to be cool, cheerless, and dreary, rather than bright, warm, and sunny. Indoors, such light has a screened, low intensity, averted character. There is a tendency toward overall shadow in this low key, moody light, projecting solemnity and melancholy.

Flat, Diffused Light Outdoors

This kind of light tends to reduce forms to simple planes, flat and semiabstract shapes that deny the third dimension. The murky light seems timeless: the time could be early morning without sun, late afternoon, twilight, a rainy day in early spring, or a damp day in late fall. The mood is oppressive and downcast.

Flat, Diffused Light Indoors

Caught in half light from the right, possibly a reflected light or a light from a remote window, the vague darks keep the figure from emerging clearly. The general tendency of flat, diffused indoor light is to reduce the form to a shadowy presence. Merging into darkness, the forms and contours lose their clarity, except for the faint accents of light on the skull and the right shoulder. Bear in mind that these are not the only possibilities of flat, diffused light. Others will be discussed subsequently.

Moonlight—Single and Double Source

Moonlight is essentially single-source light—for example, a clear sky with a bright moon illuminating a wide, unobstructed space. But moonlight in a closed or restricted space—a lane surrounded by trees, a city street, or an outdoor passageway—may be reflected or bounced from various surfaces. Thus, we may have the *direct*, primary light of the moon and the *indirect*, secondary, reflected light. In moonlight, the environment is generally dark; shadows and silhouettes preponderate. It is also important to remember that moonlight is, in itself, reflected light—light received from the sun and then reflected off the surface of the moon. Thus, moonlight cannot be as bright as anything that gives off light from its own internal combustion, such as a torch, or even a match. The light of the moon is cool and silvery.

Moonlight Outdoors

Generalized darkness prevails in this moonlit landscape. The foreground trees, buildings, shrubs, and grass are seen mostly in silhouette. Against a darkened background, the trees are unclear, and the whole foreground tends to be vague, except for the detail defined by the lights within the building. The deep tone of the sky recedes behind the silver disk of the moon, while a halo of light rises behind the hills, suggesting a cool night mist. The drifting mist in the valley—in the middleground—also catches something of the moonlight.

Moonlight Indoors

Here we have a figure in an interior space that catches the direct light of the moon from one direction, and also produces a secondary, reflected light from another direction. The direct, major light comes from the moon in the upper left, casting the brightest light on forms that tend to be perpendicular to the direction of the light—such as the top of the skull, the shoulders, and the calves. The indirect, minor light comes from the right. The background is dark, of course, but has an airy feeling.

Sculptural Light

This light system is one of the most interesting and compelling ways to define form. I use the word *system* because this is not a light that you actually see, but an arbitrary light that you *invent* to explore every aspect of the form, explaining everything, leaving out nothing. It is tempting to call this *tactile light* because you run the light over every turn and detail of the form. And like a fingertip, the light feels and records every detail of its volume. The light starts at the front of every form, then grows fainter as the form turns away from the light and recedes into darkness. Thus, the centers of the forms are brightly lit, while the edges turn away into shadow. The system assumes a middling-bright, daytime light source. And the lights and shadows are invented quite arbitrarily for maximum comprehension.

Sculptural Light on a Figure

This downward view of a female figure may look as if it is lighted from above, but it is not. In reality, each form receives the maximum light at the high point of the bulge; then the receding forms bend away into darkness at the edges. Within each form, the gradation from light to dark corresponds to the turning of the shape from high to low. Thus, the head is light at the top, dropping off to darkness at the back and sides of the skull. Following a similar strategy, light and dark contrasts are used to signify the fact that one form is higher or lower than another. Thus, the dark bulge of the head rises above the lighted chest. In the same way, the lighted thigh rises above the shadowy belly, which turns downward into darkness. This is not a logical kind of light that you can see in nature. It is an arbitrary, invented light—a sculptural light that is based on your sense of touch, your tactile awareness of the form as it moves toward you and away from you.

Sculptural Light on a Head

At first, the light seems to come from above the head, and this seems to be confirmed by the cast shadows under the nose, cigar, lower lip, and neck. But the dark areas on the hair disavow top light. And the features seem to receive their light from directly in front. For each form, a light has been invented to reveal that form with the greatest clarity, generally beginning with bright light at the center of the form and then working around to shadow at the margins. This *could* mean chaos, but the drawing is held together by the precise drawing of the contours and the tones that follow these contours on all sides. Thus, *each form* is visualized as a sculptural entity, and so this collection of particular forms becomes a unified, coherent whole.

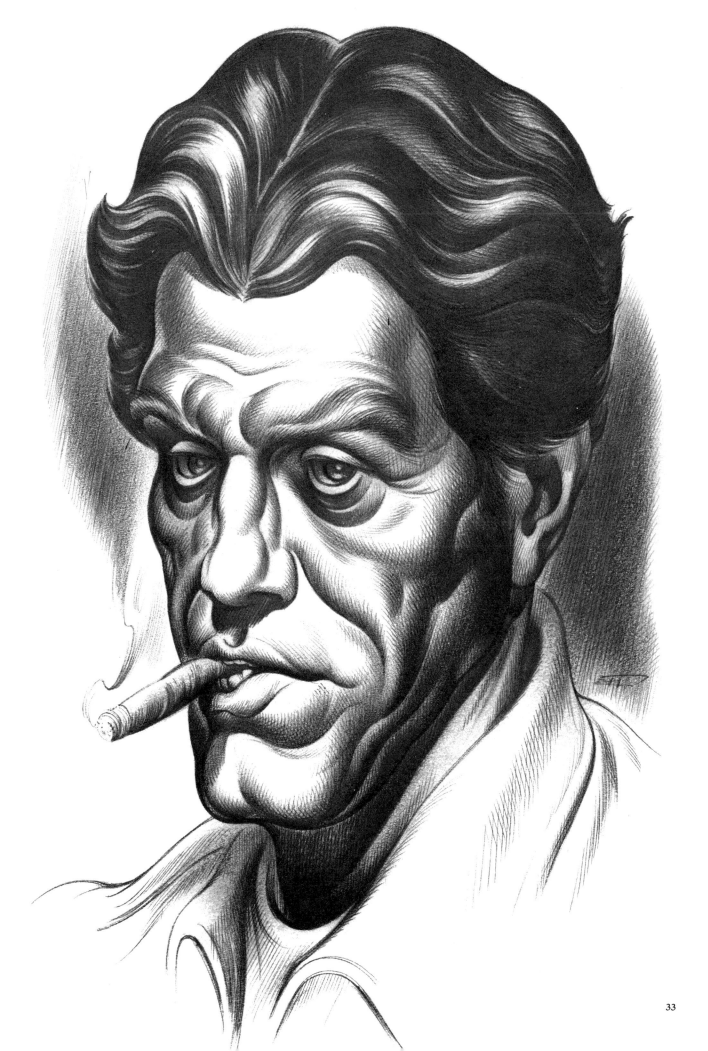

CHAPTER 4

SINGLE-SOURCE LIGHT

Equivalent Light and Shadow
In the previous chapter, you have seen that direct, single-source light can be warm, bright sunlight or strong artificial light, such as a floodlight or a photoflash might produce. Such illumination normally implies the presence of strong shadows as well. In fact, we may say that lights and shadows are *mutual;* that is, a shadow must correspond to the light in degree of brightness or intensity. Simply stated, strong light means strong shadow, and weak light means weak shadow.

Chiaroscuro
In the history of art, direct, single-source light with its strong, concomitant shadow has come to be known as *chiaroscuro*. It is familiar in the work of such masters as Caravaggio, Rembrandt, La Tour, and other painters of dramatic lighting effects. Such light is also used in theater and film, where intense, focused light enhances powerful emotions, passionate moods, and tragic plots.

Single-Source Light on Head
In this straightforward brush drawing of a head, the contrast is evident between the bright light and the corresponding dark shadow. The firm, dark edges of the features contrast powerfully with the white paper to elicit the effect of strong light. On the left side of the face, the black background intensifies the lighted contour. This illuminated area, in turn, matches the dark value of the facial mass at the right.

Head in Outdoor Light
Unlike the spotlight of the previous illustration, this head is illuminated by warm sunlight, with some other reflecting surfaces nearby. The soft-edged, airy shadows, the play of secondary reflected lights at the left, and the lesser values of the ear, jaw, and the back of the head, all suggest atmospheric outdoor light. The barely noticeable outline at the right completes the impression of the warm light of a summer day.

Head in Reduced Light
When direct light is reduced, whether indoors or outdoors, there is less intensity and less contrast, as you see in this example. Here, as the light loses its brightness, the shadows become paler, and the entire effect of the drawing is distinctly paler. If the reduction of the light continued, the next stage would be flat, diffused light. Flat light will be discussed in a later chapter.

Figure in Direct Side Light

This athlete, plunging toward the water, is illuminated by an overhead light source that strikes the figure from the right. The light produces a consistent bright edge on the right-hand contours of the forms, leaving most of the figure in deep shadow. The strength and brilliance of the light is verified by the cast shadows: the shadow of one foot on the other; the shadow of the shoulder on the back of the head; and the darkness of the lower arm, which is in the shadow cast by the head and chest.

Figures in Edge and Front Light

The acrobats are illuminated by a light source that is high and to the left. On the back of the woman aloft, we see edge light, but we see more light on the front of the male figure. The strength of the light is evident in the cast shadows on the woman's right shoulder and arm, and on the man's shoulder and face. Because this is an indoor theatrical event, with performers in costume, we perceive the light source to be bright artificial light. Conversely, because the subject of the diving athlete in the previous drawing is obviously an outdoor subject, we infer that the light source is sunlight. Our *experience* tells us what kind of light we are seeing.

**Figures in High,
Direct Light**
The edges of these two figures
are illuminated by a high light
source at the right. Depending
upon the movements of the
forms and their relationship to
the light, some forms are in
deep shadow (such as the torsos), while other forms (such as
the arms) show an intricate
play of light. Cast shadows are
eliminated to let the positions
of the feet create a convincing
sense of the ground plane.

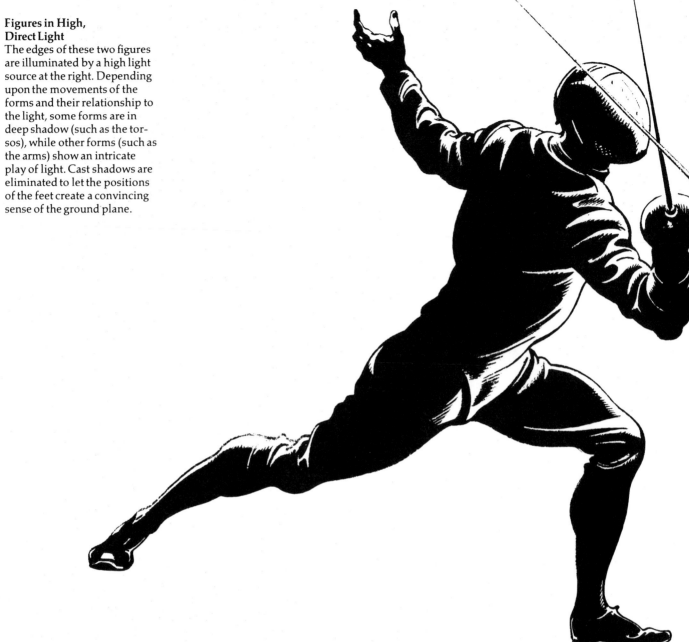

Indoors or Outdoors?

The dark background and the minimal rim light at the back of each head suggest a closed interior space. Surely, we know that the minimal rim light comes from some nearby reflecting background surface. But the strong light that comes from the upper left, producing cast shadows and soft-edged darks on the forms, suggests sunlight—as if the figures are emerging from some closed space into bright sunlight outside. What do *you* think?

Seaside in Direct, Single-Source Light

It is daytime at the shore, but cool and chilly, with a feeling of the dreary end of summer. The high, single-source light produces edge lights on the birds as they fly into the wind, projecting darkly against the sky. The fence in the foreground, edge-lit like the birds, is silhouetted against a field of light that is obviously not warm, not bright. The oncoming dark to the rear, close to the ground, suggests overcast weather, a drop in temperature, perhaps rain. The distant fence is a white silhouette that emerges from the wind-driven grass like the pale bones of some creature, bleaching in the salt air.

Single-Source Light with Dark Background

Direct, single-source light from the right illumines a racing yacht, scudding home against a brisk, darkening sky. Edge lights appear on the sails, lit by the low sun that glows on the curves of the billowing canvas. Light also breaks atop the wave patterns that sweep swiftly by. The sky above the water is still brightened by the fading sun; but higher up, the oncoming clouds tell us that the light will soon be overtaken by a stormy night and booming seas.

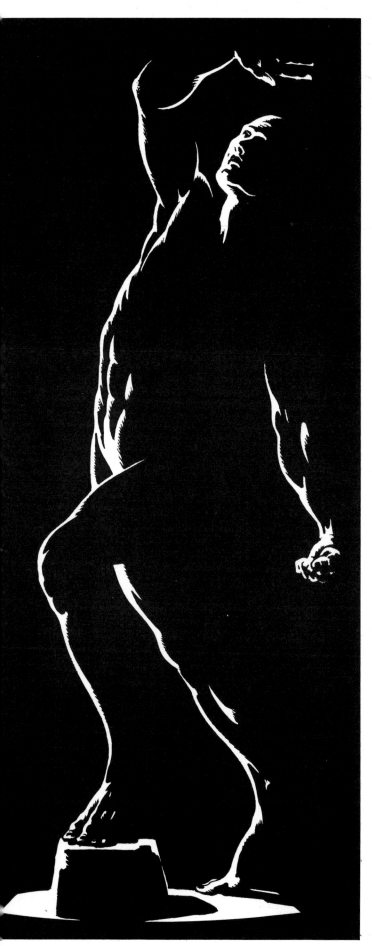

Chiaroscuro—Upper Left

This drawing and the next four are examples of high-contrast edge light, the dramatic and powerful effect known as *chiaroscuro*. Translated literally from the Italian, the word means "light-dark," and describes the characteristic lighting of much late Renaissance, Mannerist, and Baroque painting. The interior light on this figure comes from the upper left side. The vivid illumination produces extreme contrast. Because there is no secondary light source to create reflected light on the dark side of the figure, the contours on the right side have slipped away, undefined in the Stygian darkness.

Chiaroscuro—Right

Like the previous drawing, the figure is strongly edge-lit, but the light comes from the right—from a midpoint about halfway up the form. The other side of the figure is in absolute darkness once again. It is instructive to see how such a complete form can be developed in minimal light.

Chiaroscuro—Lower Right

Now the edge light comes from the lower right-hand side. Note the wider expanse of the light on the under forms of the figure: the calf muscles, thighs and buttocks, chest, and back of the skull. Also study the clenched hand in the lower right, the higher extended arm, and the open fingers of the raised hand in this low side light.

Chiaroscuro—One-Third Front

The light shifts to expose one third of the front of the figure. The light source is high. You can verify this by examining how the right side of the head, the right chest area, and the right thigh are illuminated. Other forms are partially lit on the right, except for the open palm, which is fully lit above the head. The left contours remain in darkness, since the room interior is dark and there are no reflecting surfaces to bounce light into the shadows. But there are some minor *underlights* beneath the high arm and on the left of the face; these are reflected lights that bounce off nearby parts of the figure itself. Thus, the left side of the head catches reflected light from the biceps nearby, but throws its own cast shadow on the shoulder.

Chiaroscuro—Two-Thirds Front

Still another light shift illuminates two thirds of the front of the figure. Again, the light source is high. As you did when you looked at the previous illustration, study the lighting on the face, chest, and upper leg at the right, and identify the bounced underlights.

Overhead Light
Strong light from directly over-head creates deep pools of shadow in the major under-planes of the head. A network of deep shadows spreads over the head, connecting the shad-ows with one another and with the background. The dark eye sockets slip into the cheekbone depressions, which interlock with the darks of the jaw, neck, ear, hair, and background be-yond. When strong, hot light produces correspondingly deep shadows, the lighter tones tend to be overridden and may seem to disappear altogether—as they often do in the paint-ings of Caravaggio and Ribera.

Less Intense Light
Less intense light, suggesting more air and atmosphere, pro-jects a gentler, less dramatic mood. The light source is high and strikes the front of the head, as we can verify by find-ing the cast shadows under the nose and lips, and on the neck beneath the jaw. The soft, transparent, atmospheric light lets us see *into* the forms that are overlaid with transparent shadow, so that the surface forms of the skin are soft and palpable.

Muted Light
This head is suffused with a muted, low-key light that comes from above the middle of the face. The main light centers on the nose. From here, a system of *graduated lights* recedes in all directions—upward, sideward, downward—becoming less intense, and supported by corresponding darks. See how the sharpest contrasts are at the center of the head, where the most vivid light prevails. Then see how the light and shade grow softer and fuzzier as they move away from the center, becoming somewhat lost and vague in the region of the base of the chin and the rear of the head.

Bright, Restricted Light

This profile head, illuminated from a high source, displays the effect of bright light that is restricted in its coverage of the form. The narrow light falls on just a few areas, but produces deep shadows on virtually all the oblique and vertical planes of the head. Note how a shadow drops straight down from the nose to the lip and forefinger. Take time to observe an interesting detail: the lower edge of the eye is partially illuminated by a minor light, possibly bouncing off some lower form, such as the nose or a finger.

Atmospheric Light △

When the light is not vivid, strong, or bright, it takes on an aerial or atmospheric quality. Linear elements disappear. Firm, hard-edged forms give way to pliable, fluent, or vaporous forms. In this partial head, there is hardly a line. The tones are airy, powdery, like gases of varying densities.

Atmospheric Light—Another Example

Like the preceding head, this figure tends to exist in a misty environment. The semi-transparent light seems to filter through a haze—with occasional accents here and there on the forms. Contours and details are minimized in this dusty, atmospheric light. Forms appear and disappear in a "lost-and-found" fashion. Some forms seem quite close to one another, while others seem distant. The nose is clearly up front, while the neck, shoulders, and hair seem far away.

Low Light Source

Direct light from a low source usually implies firelight in a darkened environment, whether indoors or outdoors. Such light suggests romance or melodrama—and this kind of light is obviously impossible during the day. This figure is lit from the lower left by a strong, artificial source like a photoflood. The light emanates outside the lower left leg, creating shadows that run up the length of the body. Certain obstructions produce cast shadows on the right thigh, chest, neck, and head. Against the unyielding darkness, see how warm and bright this light can be.

Low Light Disrupts Form

The low light source is near the lower face. Illuminating just a few low-lying planes, the hot, hard light sets up a field of darkness that disrupts the forms of the head. With two thirds of the head in darkness, the encroaching background tends to merge with the forms to suppress information about the contours. Note the islands of light within the dark areas. This is hardly enough information to elicit meaningful forms. But your drawing will be convincing if you plan the structure carefully and if your lighting is logically related to the planes.

Firelight

The warm glow of firelight in cold weather, outdoors, creates a soft, airy illumination from below. The air is not coldly clear, so we see some crystalline diffusion of the light, with soft-edged forms emerging from the surrounding darkness. The forms are rendered with oblique strokes that follow the light upward from the lower right toward the upper left.

49

CHAPTER 5

DOUBLE-SOURCE LIGHT

Major and Minor Light

As you have already seen in Chapter 3, double-source light is produced by a major source and a minor source. The major or *direct* source is almost always hot and luminous, such as sunlight, electric light, or firelight. The minor or *indirect* source is normally thrown from a reflecting surface that is opposite the major or direct source. The indirect or minor light is usually less intense than the major light—unless we get a *mirror reflection* of the major source.

Outdoors and Indoors

Double-source light occurs in both exterior and interior environments, particularly in closed spaces where there are many possible reflecting surfaces. In a natural, outdoor setting, we see these paired lights in groves, arbors, lanes in woods, ravines, caves, hollows, ledges, and similar formations. Indoors, double-source light is common in room interiors, corridors, and especially in studios where artificial lighting—such as floodlights and spotlights—may be combined with reflectors to manipulate direct and indirect light.

Intensity

In contrast with the warmth and brilliance of the major light source, light that projects from a reflecting surface tends to be cool and reduced in its intensity. However, it is important to observe that the major light, despite its greater intensity, may not necessarily illuminate a larger area than the minor, reflected light. Indeed, the minor light may sometimes cover a greater area.

Front and Back

On this figure in a closed interior space, the major light source illuminates the side of the body and much of the front. The minor, reflected light comes from the right rear—with the minimal light following the edge of the form and repeating the contours of the body.

Right and Left

When the figure is turned almost fully to the front, we see an interesting play of contours. The major light comes from the right, revealing a smaller area than the previous drawing, while the minor light comes from the left and covers more of the body. It is particularly easy to comprehend the forms in this light. For example, see how clearly the light explains the complicated hookup of the shoulders to the chest and thorax. If you want to learn the subtle network of the figure and its forms, use double-source light to reveal the richness of the interior contours.

Low Major Light Source
Like firelight or footlights, the light source comes from below and in front of the body, striking the legs, belly, chest, neck, jaw, and raised forearm. By contrast, the cool, reflected light on the opposite side of the form tends to retreat into the dark background, serving to reinforce the brilliance of the primary light source.

High Major Light Source
When the primary light source shifts to a high rear location, we see a sequence of active forms on the right. On the opposite side, a cool, subdued, indirect light reveals the front of the figure. Although we see more of the figure's left side in this minor light, the luminous major light source is still dominant. Compare these last two illustrations. See how much hotter the light looks in the previous drawing, and how much cooler it looks in this one.

Black and White
Although these performers are drawn entirely in black ink, leaving the paper to represent the light, we can see the major and minor light on the figures. Looking at the female acrobat's face and the male acrobat's back, we know that the major light comes from the upper left, while the minor light comes from the right.

53

Another Black and White
Without the subtle grays that define the lights in earlier drawings, this ink drawing affirms that the major light source is at the right. This is evident in the face, hands, and knee of the rider, and in the head and forelegs of the horse. The direction of the horse and rider reinforce this conclusion about the direction of the light.

Shadow in Double-Source Light

When you draw a shadow in double-source light, remember that the darkest edge of a form is next to the brightest light on that form. Study the shadow on the side of the nose. The tone is darkest where it meets the light plane on the front of the nose *and* where it meets the lighted cheek. Between these two darks, the shadow on the side of the nose grows pale, as if it contains a minor reflected light. Observe a similar effect on the shadow side of the face, where the dark edges of the brow and cheek meet the lighted frontal planes of the forehead and face.

Another Example of Shadow

In this study of a head, the brightest light comes from the right to meet the stressed dark edges of the shadows on the side of the nose, brow, cheek, jaw, chin, and neck. Once again, note the lesser values within the shadows, suggesting secondary, reflected lights. Without the accented forward edges of the shadows, the head would lose much of its strong feeling of three-dimensional form.

Dominant Reflected Light

Indirect light can be remarkably versatile. Here, the minor light comes from the left and dominates the head, while the supposedly major light actually plays a lesser role. It is in the soft, indirect light that we see the animated eye, the detail of the cheek and corner of the mouth, and the wrinkles of the brow. The major light from the right tends to conceal detail by its very brightness, and also plunges the adjacent area of the face into profound darkness, leaving this side of the head almost neutral of expression. Again, note that the darkest shadows are on the right, next to the areas of brightest light.

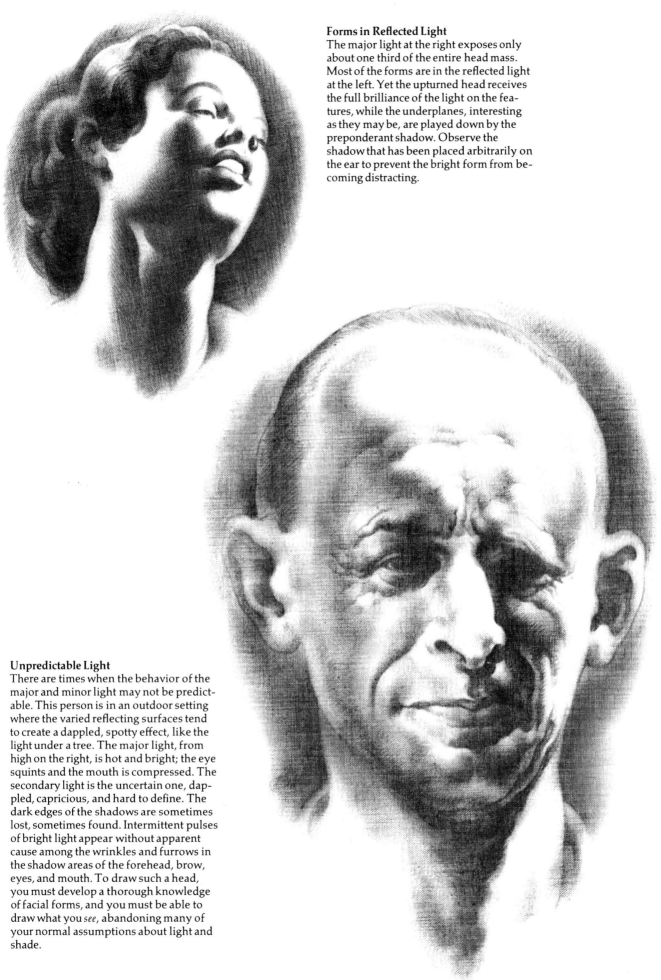

Forms in Reflected Light

The major light at the right exposes only about one third of the entire head mass. Most of the forms are in the reflected light at the left. Yet the upturned head receives the full brilliance of the light on the features, while the underplanes, interesting as they may be, are played down by the preponderant shadow. Observe the shadow that has been placed arbitrarily on the ear to prevent the bright form from becoming distracting.

Unpredictable Light

There are times when the behavior of the major and minor light may not be predictable. This person is in an outdoor setting where the varied reflecting surfaces tend to create a dappled, spotty effect, like the light under a tree. The major light, from high on the right, is hot and bright; the eye squints and the mouth is compressed. The secondary light is the uncertain one, dappled, capricious, and hard to define. The dark edges of the shadows are sometimes lost, sometimes found. Intermittent pulses of bright light appear without apparent cause among the wrinkles and furrows in the shadow areas of the forehead, brow, eyes, and mouth. To draw such a head, you must develop a thorough knowledge of facial forms, and you must be able to draw what you *see*, abandoning many of your normal assumptions about light and shade.

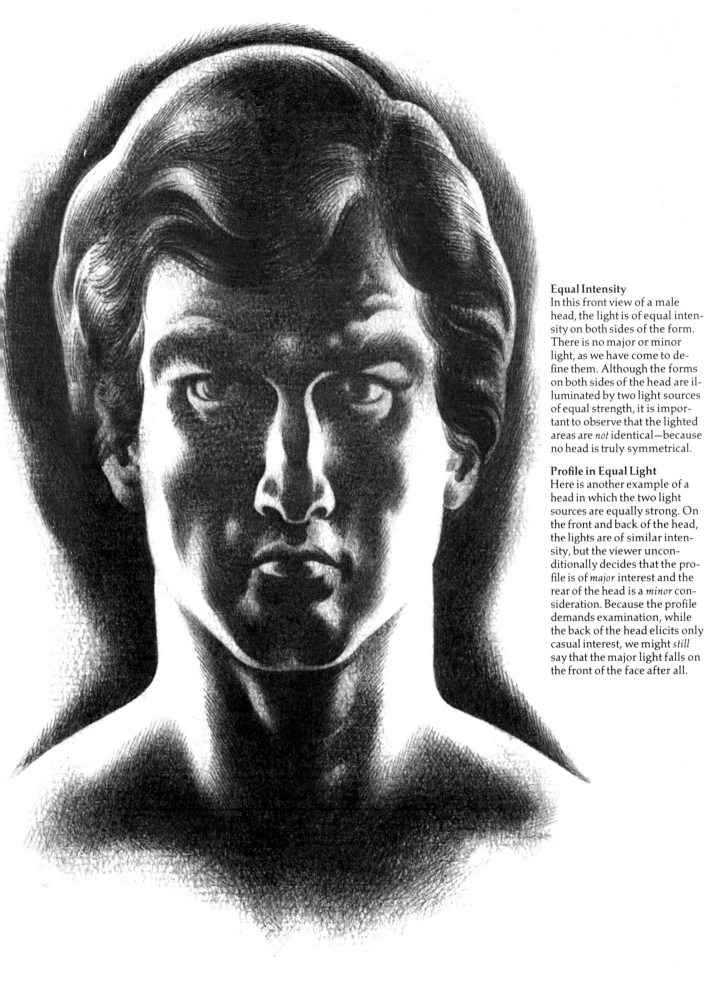

Equal Intensity

In this front view of a male head, the light is of equal intensity on both sides of the form. There is no major or minor light, as we have come to define them. Although the forms on both sides of the head are illuminated by two light sources of equal strength, it is important to observe that the lighted areas are *not* identical—because no head is truly symmetrical.

Profile in Equal Light

Here is another example of a head in which the two light sources are equally strong. On the front and back of the head, the lights are of similar intensity, but the viewer unconditionally decides that the profile is of *major* interest and the rear of the head is a *minor* consideration. Because the profile demands examination, while the back of the head elicits only casual interest, we might *still* say that the major light falls on the front of the face after all.

Soft Light, Soft Shadow

The major light at the right is comfortably bright, but not brilliant. Thus, the corresponding shadows in the balance of the head are soft-edged and airy. The accented dark edge of the shadow is next to the brightest light on the right side. The minor light at the rear sets off the shape of the hair and admits some light to define the ornament above the ear. Study the background tone, front and back. See how the tones become darker or brighter to contrast with the contours of the head, which are also sometimes darker and sometimes brighter. The pencil strokes are angled to follow the direction of the light from the upper right to the lower left.

Incidental Light

This elderly black man has a lustrous skin surface, like burnished copper, that creates a complex light effect. The major light is at the upper left, above the ovoid crown of the skull, which glows with a high luster. As the light descends, it glows on similar forms, like the tip of the nose, the wing of the nostril, and the lower lip. On the right side of the head, observe the pale reflected lights that also fluctuate on the contours. Throughout the head, reflected light seems to gleam as it is caught in crevices and projections, producing what might be called *incidental light*—light independent of the major and minor light sources.

61

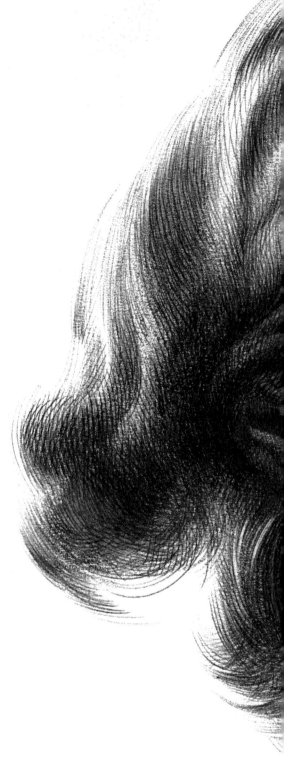

Wrinkled Skin

Wrinkles and furrows in aging skin create another complexity when you draw a head in double-source light. This older woman displays a network of wrinkles, flickering across her face. What is the best way to draw this head? In this drawing, the solution is twofold. On the right side, the shadow is condensed and solidified to minimize detail. On the left, the shadow remains open and transparent, revealing the details of the skin. Thus, complexity is balanced by simplicity. There is just enough detail to convey the character of the sitter's skin, but not enough detail to overwhelm the viewer and shatter the image.

Dark Against Light
Covering seven-eighths of the head, the shadow is condensed, solidified, and simplified to include the hair, face, and beard. The details within this shadow mass are defined by minimal amounts of reflected light. The mass of darkness is balanced against the active, exciting forms of the lighted side of the face, which are revealed by a very limited amount of light from the major source. Learn to make creative use of double-source light, balancing bright and dim, large and small, active and passive areas of light and shadow.

CHAPTER 6

FLAT, DIFFUSED LIGHT

Diffused Light Is Flat

A cloudy or overcast sky normally produces diffused light. It is also created by haze, mist, fog, smoke, dust, and incipient rain or snow. These conditions produce flat light because they reduce the contrast between light and shadow—shadows become pale, vague, and ill-defined. They even put the direction of the light source in question. Thus diffused light tends to flatten forms, often producing patterned shapes and silhouettes that become gray and ghostly in rain, snow, and dense fog. Diffused, flat light is cool, not warm or sunny, and is an excellent device for producing a mood of solemnity, melancholy, or despair.

Pre-Dawn Light ▷

The pre-dawn light filtering through a hazy, overcast sky, creates a classic case of flat, diffused light. The illusion of spatial recession is produced by the sequence of tones, from the dark clarity of the nearby rocks to the pale, vague contours of the distant mountains, which diffuse in the haze and drifting clouds. Notice the flat character of the shapes, with little or no distinction between light and shadow planes, and the pale reflections in the water.

Two-Dimensional Shapes

This drawing contains a series of silhouette-like, two-dimensional shapes in flat, diffused light. Although the contours are clearly defined and the details are drawn precisely, the sense of volume or the third dimension is held to a minimum. Tonal differences alone—the pale tone of the figure, the darker tone of the flora, and the still darker tone of the background—divide the pictorial space into near, intermediate, and far.

Line and Flat Tone
This Japanese woodblock print by Hiroshige renders flat, diffused light with linear contours and flat colors. The qualities of air and light are rendered without countours, but each form—whether figure or landscape—is enclosed in its specific outline. The ambience is serene and cool, and the image is developed in a series of flat, posterlike shapes.

Subdued Light
In another woodcut by Hiroshige, the fading light is rendered in flat, subdued tones to tell us that the day is coming to a close and the evening is coming on. Like the preceding print, this landscape depends upon the tonalities of flat, patterned, posterlike shapes to tell its story. The mood is communicated by the lightness or density of the flat tones, which are enclosed by precise outlines.

Distance
Still another print by Hiroshige shows how the flat, patterned layers of the landscape create a sense of space. From foreground to distance, the silhouettes of the forms become grayer in the mist, so that the receding tonalities communicate the effect of aerial perspective. This masterwork is an exceptional example of the simplified use of flat, diffused light.

Line Drawing

This line drawing—with dry-brush effects for incidental tone—defines the contours of all the forms to communicate the flat pattern of diffused light. We are aware of a cast shadow here and there, but the contour is pervasive; nowhere does it relax or disappear. There is no tone to suggest depth or spatial recession. We are aware primarily of *shapes.* The drawing depends upon design, so that the eye roams over the surface pattern. This design flow is achieved by visualizing all the elements in flat, diffused light.

Sandstorm
The camel riders are heading into a blinding sandstorm. It is broad daylight under a cloudless sky, but the sweeping sand begins to blot out all knowledge of the source of the light. Note the difference in values between the foreground and the distance. In the distance, the storm is coming on with a vengeance, and the values are paler. The near riders, drawn with stronger contrasts of tone, have yet to feel the full impact of the storm.

Underwater
Under bright sunshine, water is permeated by light. But, below ten feet, the failing light becomes flat and diffused—a twilight zone that darkens as we go deeper. As the swimmer moves through the turgid, murky water, the light plays on the whorls, air bubbles, and drifting weeds. The flow overrides the figure, which seems to dissolve, appearing and disappearing in the diffused, uncertain light. Notice how the head, lower arm, and other parts of the body tend to flow away into the darkness.

Uneven Light
As we have seen in the preceding example of underwater light, diffused light can be uneven. Such light is still flat in the sense that there remains very little difference between light and shadow. But the tones may vary with the caprice of the atmosphere—or the water. This medieval craftsman sits in a recessed, shady area not illuminated by direct light. The values are generally low in contrast, so that most of the forms of the figure and background seem to melt together. But random patches of light break through from overhead, brightening minor areas on the head, hands, legs, and foreground. At these places, there is marked contrast, suggesting touches of warm sunlight.

Dust-Laden Air
As a cowhand makes his way
across the wasteland, a cold,
late afternoon wind blows up
dust, sand, and grit. In the dust-
laden air, the flat, diffused light
becomes uneven. We are
aware of form and shadow, but
nowhere do we feel the warm
effect of strong light or the
hard-edged contrast of the
shade against the light. Horse
and man fight their way into
the uncertain gloom.

Above the City
Over a great city of steel and
stone, veils of smoke, ash, dust,
and pollution block the sun to
produce flat, diffused light.
Around the daredevil climber,
scaling one of the world's
tallest buildings in New York
City, we see a vaporous mist
that obscures the buildings below. The canyons of the city
take on an unreal, airy presence, hardly rooted to the
ground. The small plane, glid-
ing by for a closer look, is reduced to a ghostly presence in
the ephemeral light.

Rain
In the open landscape, the
downpour of the cold, sleety
rain is already beginning to feel
like wet, driving snow. The
gusts in the formless darkness
tend to obscure and dissolve
solid form. The background is
swallowed up in the deluge.
We see just a few feet ahead. In
this turbulent scene, all elements take on flat silhouettes
of different values—typical of
flat, diffused light.

Expressive Light
Cloudy daylight can be an expressive tool, conveying a mood of sadness, alienation, anguish, and dispair. In this figure, the intense head and powerful arm become depressed and pallid in the sallow half-light. The flat, diffused light is the key to the contradictory mood.

Somber Mood
Here the entire figure expresses wretchedness and desolation. There is only one strong contrast—the light on the figure's back against the dark background. The remaining tones are flat and diffused, with the values deepening on the lower forms. The design is circular and convoluted, suggesting that the figure has turned away from the world to an inward retreat. The mood is enhanced by the diffused light, which creates an atmosphere of grief.

CHAPTER 7

MOONLIGHT

Pale Light, Dark Field

Moonlight is a silvery, pale light in a field of darkness. This dark field is the distinguishing characteristic of moonlight. In a moonlit environment, the volume of darkness is always greater than any area of light. There are large, indeterminate regions of darkness. The moon is a massive reflecting surface for the sun's light. Thus, the moon is not really a direct light source like the hot, yellow-white light of the sun. But because the moon is the only source of light in that dark field, for all practical purposes, we define the moon as a direct light source. As a greatly diminished light source, moonlight tends to produce a range of *restricted light*, usually from a position *high overhead*. Silhouettes are dominant.

Full Moon and Crescent Moon

The silver disk of the full moon is capable of spreading a pale, silvery, bluish light everywhere on the forms of the landscape. But when the moon is reduced to a scimitar-shaped sliver, the available light is dim, indeed, and the landscape is profoundly dark. The full moon is capable of casting shadows. Unlike the shadows cast by the sun, the shadows created by the moon are dark pools with soft edges, and the details on the forms are generally unclear. (Leonardo da Vinci called these smoky-soft tones *sfumato*.) When the environment contains reflecting surfaces, we frequently see double-source light—major and minor light—like that described in Chapter 5, although far less intense.

High Light Source

The high moon illuminates the figure from the rear left. The major light is on the upper horizontal planes of the head and extended forearm. The minor light is on the vertical surfaces. Some large, frontal reflecting surface produces this secondary light on the left side of the chest until the forms bend away into the darkness at the right.

Frontal, Overhead Light
The moon is overhead, striking the front of the figure. The full moon is bright enough to produce cast shadows, which drop from the extended arm to the chest, and from the jaw to the neck. The cast shadow of the torso falls across the extended thigh and obscures most of the arm at the right. Two thirds of the figure is in darkness—a virtual silhouette. The ambience of the night tends to melt the forms into the surrounding darkness.

Double-Source Light
This moonlit figure, seen from the rear, is in double-source light. The bright, full moon comes from the right, strikes some reflecting surface on the opposite side, and bounces in from the left to create secondary light on the forms that face away from the moon. Like the figure in the previous drawing, this figure is shown in an open air space, suggesting an uninterrupted, deep void.

Landscape Filled with Moonlight
Night is settling in this Hiroshige wood-cut. The full moon has risen in the sky be-hind the mountain pines, while a mist set-tles into the valley at the right. The light is flat and diffused, as described in Chapter 6. The general tonality of the picture is in a subdued value range that tells us of the oncoming night. The moon lurks behind the trees—which are becoming sil-houettes—and pervades the landscape with its silvery light.

Figures in Moonlit Landscape

Against the brilliance of the moonlit water—under the full, rising moon—the figures are dark, distinct silhouettes. The disturbed surface of the swift water is filled with random reflections of widespread, uneven light. The sharply defined moon throws clear, inverted shadows of the rocks on the water and the figures on the shore. Halations of light bounce from the tops of the rocks in the middle distance, but the nearer rock in the lower left foreground is close enough to let some light define the edge of the form. Looking at the random light on the water, we see that the general direction of the full light is *vertical*, progressing straight down from the moon. Thus, all shadows are directly below the forms. The water darkens to the right and left of the moon's vertical zone of light.

◁ Moonlight and Reflections

The moonlight appears on the water as a light vertical band, while the shadowy reflection of the tower is a vertical band of darkness, directly below the tower. The low-lying houses on the shore also produce shadowy reflections that are aligned vertically with the architectural shapes. You may wonder why the dark shapes of the tower and the houses—as reflected in the water—are all *vertical*, not *diagonal*, even though the only light source, the moon, is at the left. Since regardless of where the light comes from, the reflection is a *mirror image*, vertical reflections are correct.

Scattered Moonlight

When the moonlight is scattered by the cloud streaks, reflections develop over a wide expanse of sea. The brightly lit area of the water is again directly beneath the moon, but there are also lesser lights bounced off the clouds onto the choppy ocean. Between the dark silhouette of the ship in the foreground and the vessels at the horizon, the tones grow gradually paler. The dark sky overhead also grows paler at the distant horizon. The sea and sky are like the two halves of a clamshell, meeting at the distant rim of the horizon.

Pure Silhouette

Rising over the jungle, the moon creates a backlight that shows no three-dimensional forms. All the forms—trees, vines, jungle plants, and figure—are pure silhouettes. Yet, flat as the forms are, there is an effect of great depth. One spatial device used here is the overlapping of the vines on the disk of the moon—a signal that "something is in front" and "something is behind." But a greater sense of depth is produced by the three values of the pictorial design: the black foreground detail, the gray sky, and the white moon. The three values suggest the division of space into near, intermediate, and far. Value creates the illusion of space—a phenomenon that you will read more about in later chapters.

Moon in Mist

The moon is framed by the dark shapes of the sea birds in flight. While the birds have sharp contours, the perimeter of the moon is blurred by the hazy night air. The contrast in contours—between the halated outline of the moon and the precise outlines of the birds—creates an illusion of deep space, enhanced by the diminishing sizes of the birds.

Expressive Moonlight

Moonlight is particularly expressive in images that evoke feelings of romance, mystery, loneliness, terror, or death. Moonlight turns our thoughts inward to the realm of symbolism. In this sketch for a projected painting, the cut stump of a great tree awakens at the onset of energy from the rising moon, which appears through the mist over a desolate landscape. The forms tell us that life will not be denied.

CHAPTER 8

SCULPTURAL LIGHT

Sculptural Light Reveals Form

Sculptural light is concerned primarily with three-dimensional form. Such light alludes to the sense of touch in that we become aware of solid, space-occupying forms in-the-round, forms that we can hold and explore with our fingertips. Thus, sculptural light is often called arbitrary light, universal light, or absolute light because it is an artificial creation—consciously designed to reveal form most effectively, and consciously avoiding the evanescent light effects we normally see. When we draw an object in sculptural light, we imagine an airless space where all forms are clearly seen and all accidental lighting effects are avoided. Such a drawing is no longer a mirror image of nature, but represents an ideal world of pure, unchanging, finite form.

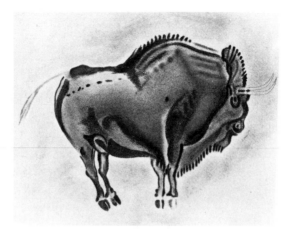

Cave Art

Sculptural or *form light* is as old as art itself. In this prehistoric cave painting from Altamira, in Northern Spain, there is no specific, single light source. Lights and darks are placed where they are needed to reveal the presence of forms and details with maximum clarity. Each form is given a precise identity by careful outlining and toning. Elements are shaped by tones that literally model the forms. See how this is done on the hump, body bulge, and rump.

Modern Poster

This contemporary poster represents the forms of the animals in essentially the same way as the prehistoric cave painting. The contours are clearly stated and easily understood. We can quickly identify every detail—fangs, brow and muscle wrinkles, the highlights on the fangs, even the whiskers. Note how the larger forms—such as legs, shoulder blades, spinal column, tail—are given solid shapes by the advancing and receding light and dark values. As each shape bulges outward, it receives more light; as it curves back, it moves into shadow. See how the *invented* halo of light behind the left ear makes the form easier to read and the spots on the little cub curve with every form.

Renaissance Art

In the figure of Adam from Michelangelo's Sistine Chapel frescoes, sculptural light expresses weight, density, and mass. The contour is clearly defined. Where the center of each form thrusts forward, the form catches the light, as you can see in the chest muscles and the shapes of the legs. Where the edges of the forms turn away, delicate shadows appear. Thus, the shadows follow the outer contours of the forms. This is not a realistic light, but an invented light that is designed to reveal form.

Torso in Sculptural Light

The weight and mass of this torso is the product of sculptural light, which emphasizes bulk and volume. As in the Michelangelo fresco, the bulging centers of the forms receive the strongest light, while the receding edges curve away into shadow. This is not a light effect that we normally see, but a kind of lighting that must be invented or designed by the artist to show each three-dimensional form with the greatest possible clarity and solidity.

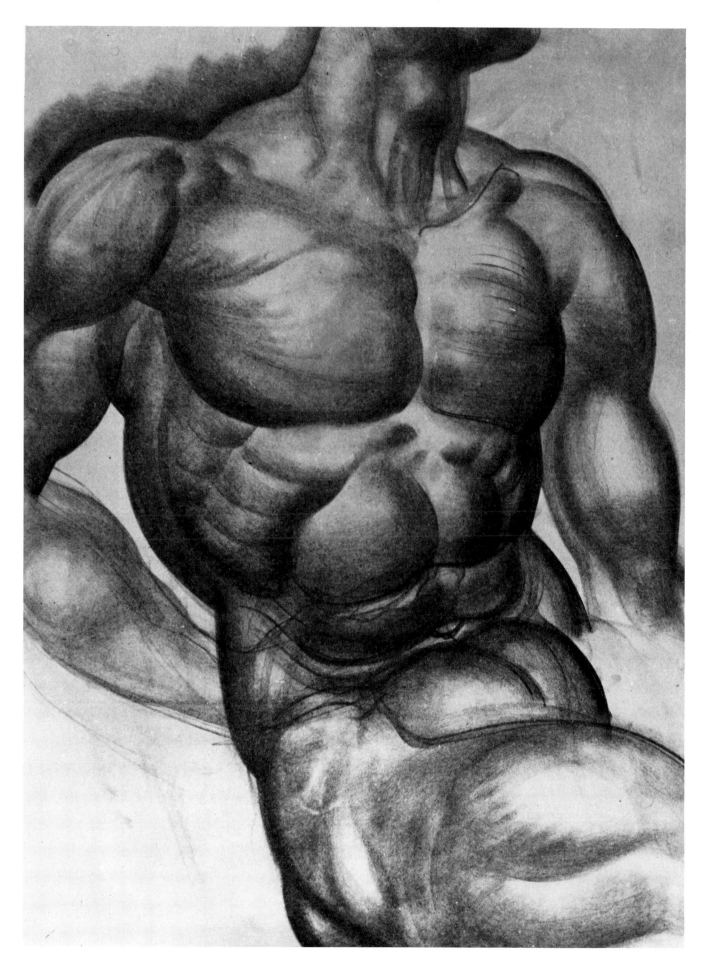

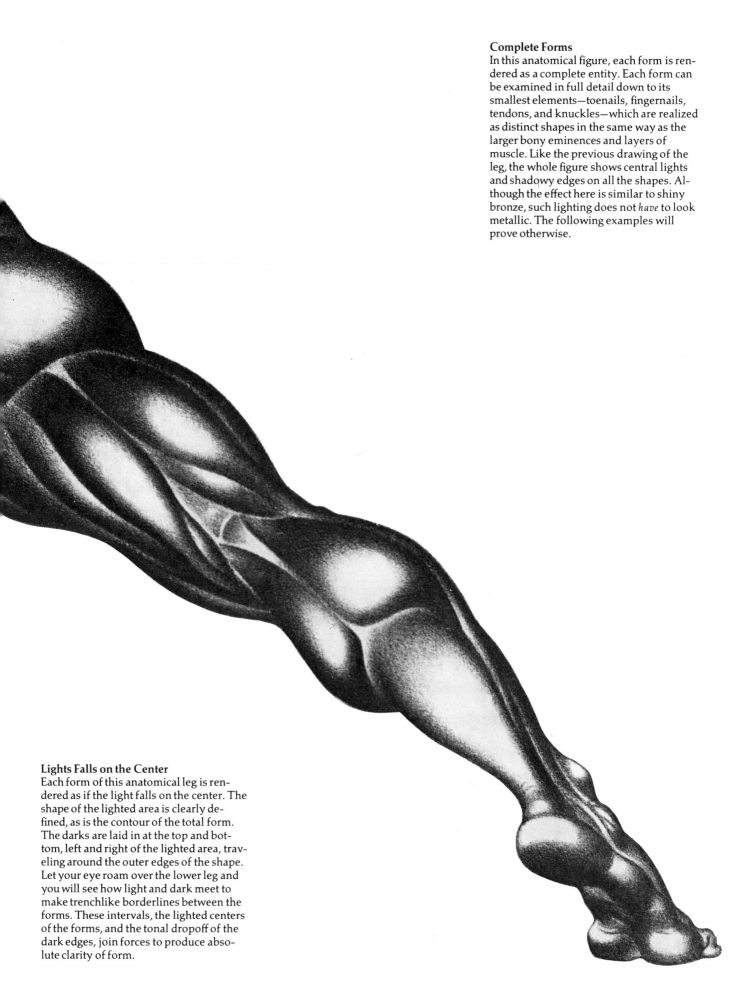

Complete Forms

In this anatomical figure, each form is rendered as a complete entity. Each form can be examined in full detail down to its smallest elements—toenails, fingernails, tendons, and knuckles—which are realized as distinct shapes in the same way as the larger bony eminences and layers of muscle. Like the previous drawing of the leg, the whole figure shows central lights and shadowy edges on all the shapes. Although the effect here is similar to shiny bronze, such lighting does not *have* to look metallic. The following examples will prove otherwise.

Lights Falls on the Center

Each form of this anatomical leg is rendered as if the light falls on the center. The shape of the lighted area is clearly defined, as is the contour of the total form. The darks are laid in at the top and bottom, left and right of the lighted area, traveling around the outer edges of the shape. Let your eye roam over the lower leg and you will see how light and dark meet to make trenchlike borderlines between the forms. These intervals, the lighted centers of the forms, and the tonal dropoff of the dark edges, join forces to produce absolute clarity of form.

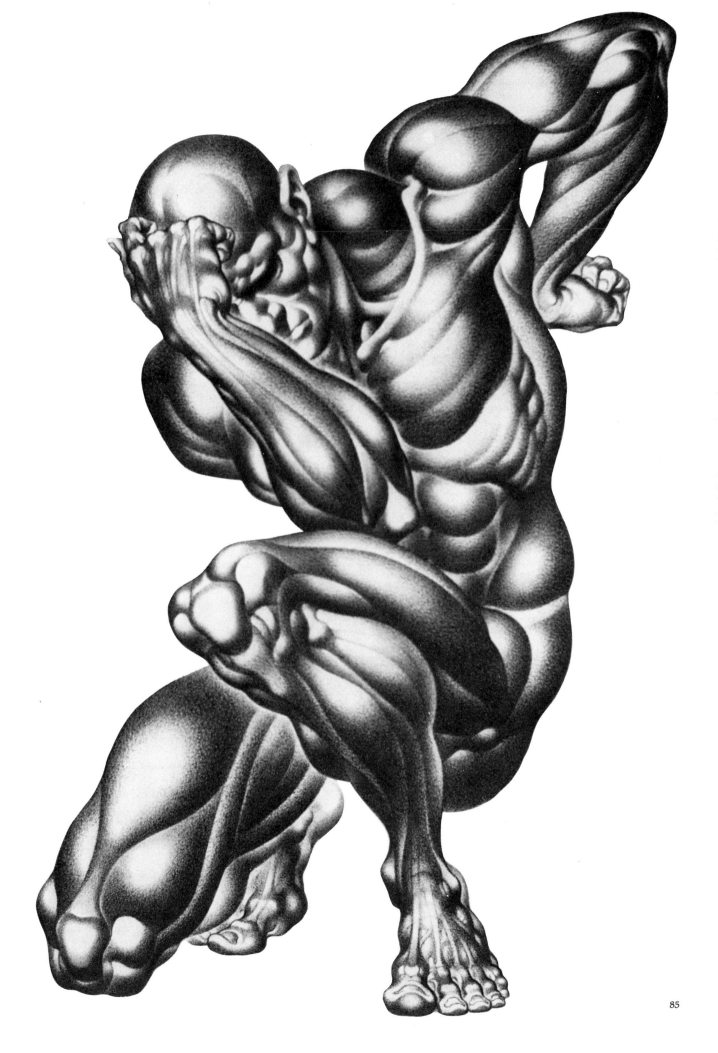

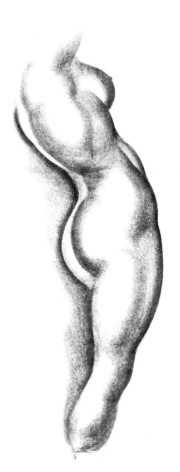

Female Torso in Sculptural Light

The softer forms of the female torso tend to obscure the taut, hard musculature that is more obvious in the previous anatomical drawings. But the sculptural light still records the shapes in the same way. Notice the central lights and edge darks on the breasts and chest forms, the abdomen, and the hips. Even such tenuous and subtle details as tendons and collarbones can be revealed by this pure light.

Drawing Method

This simple side-view figure will explain the method of rendering forms in sculptural light. You may, if necessary, begin by sketching the outlines of the forms. (If you like, start by copying this drawing.) With soft chalk, Conté, or compressed charcoal—held so that the side of the stick contacts the paper—lay in large areas with big sweeps of tone. Move the arm rather than the hand, to encourage confident, uninhibited movements. Work around the edges, accenting the outer contours with subtle pressure on the edge of the stick, and leave the lighted centers of the forms untouched. This drawing is not really finished. There is more to do. See how far you can carry it.

Form Conceived in Tone

This figure is carried to a greater finish. Once the forms are laid in—as shown in the previous drawing—the broad lay-in and buildup of tones can proceed. The power and solidity of such a drawing is based on the fact that the drawing is conceived in *tone*, not line, so that the shapes can be modeled for the greatest three-dimensional volume. As the subtle, sculptural form emerges, you begin to sense the soft, pliable flesh. The brightly lit center of the hip tells us that this is the nearest frontal form, while the subdued light on the other forms tells us that they all recede inward.

No Aerial Perspective

The overlapping forms show us the positions of the shapes in space, starting with the elbow and forearm overlapping the head as the nearest parts of the figure. From here, the thorax, arm, hip mass, and legs are arrayed successively backward in space. But, as the forms claim their positions in space, they do not become lighter or darker; that is, they do not obey the "laws" of aerial perspective, which tell us that forms grow paler and less distinct as they recede. Remember that sculptural light exists in an airless world, an imaginary world without atmosphere, where the air does not intervene to make forms vague as they recede. The illusion of forms in space is created entirely by the overlapping of forms and the rendering of light and shade to create volume—to create forms that we believe we can *touch*.

Overlapping Forms

Here is another example of the combination of sculptural light with overlapping forms to create a bold sense of three-dimensional volume. Observe how forms are forced into overlapping positions to enhance what the Italian Renaissance artists called *contrapposto*—the opposition of forms. The background darks are used to elicit contours, instead of suggesting spatial depth.

Dense Sculptural Light and Shadow

The dense tonal range exaggerates the sculptural light and gives the figure a monumental sense of volume. This quickly laid-in tonal sketch uses as many arbitrary overlaps as possible to make the forms project and recede. Thus, the figure has the strong tactile feel of a solid form in space.

Bas-Relief Form

The subtle sculptural light on this horse suggests a bas-relief instead of a massive form in the round, yet the same drawing principles are evident. The contours are clearly defined. The convex centers of the forms move forward into the light, while the receding edges turn away into shadow, which follows the contours of the outer edge.

Scribble Drawing

Sculptural light does not always demand a severe, precise drawing style. As this scribble drawing suggests, an expressive, improvised approach is also possible. The direction of the light, striking the full face from a central source, gives the key to all the shadow elements throughout the head. The forms are put in casually. Only a modicum of outline suggests the limits of hair and head. Despite the loose technique, the overall effect is not casual, but thoughtfully designed to create the illusion of sculptural form. Typical of forms in sculptural light, the stubborn nose, and hard-set mouth and jaw protrude into the light, while the receding side of the face turns away into shadow, as do the eyes in their deep, shadowy sockets.

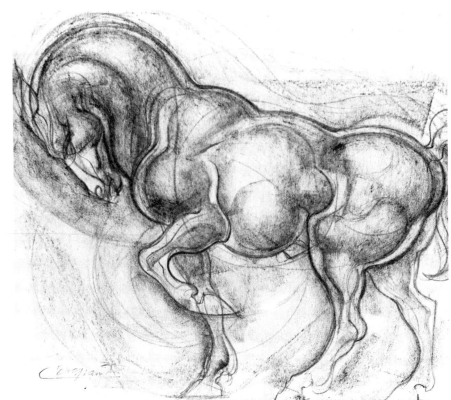

Clearly Defined Forms

In this study of a man from the Gulf of Papua, the pure, sculptural light reveals every detail of the features—the forehead creases, the narrowed eyes, the assertive nose, the protruding lower lip, and the jutting jaw. Equally clear are the artifacts and decorations that give distinction to this proud, dignified warrior. The tones are worked up with multiple, cross-hatched lines that create a full range of tones, surrounded by firm, contoured edges. Each shape, no matter how small, has its own contours and its own gradation from light to shadow.

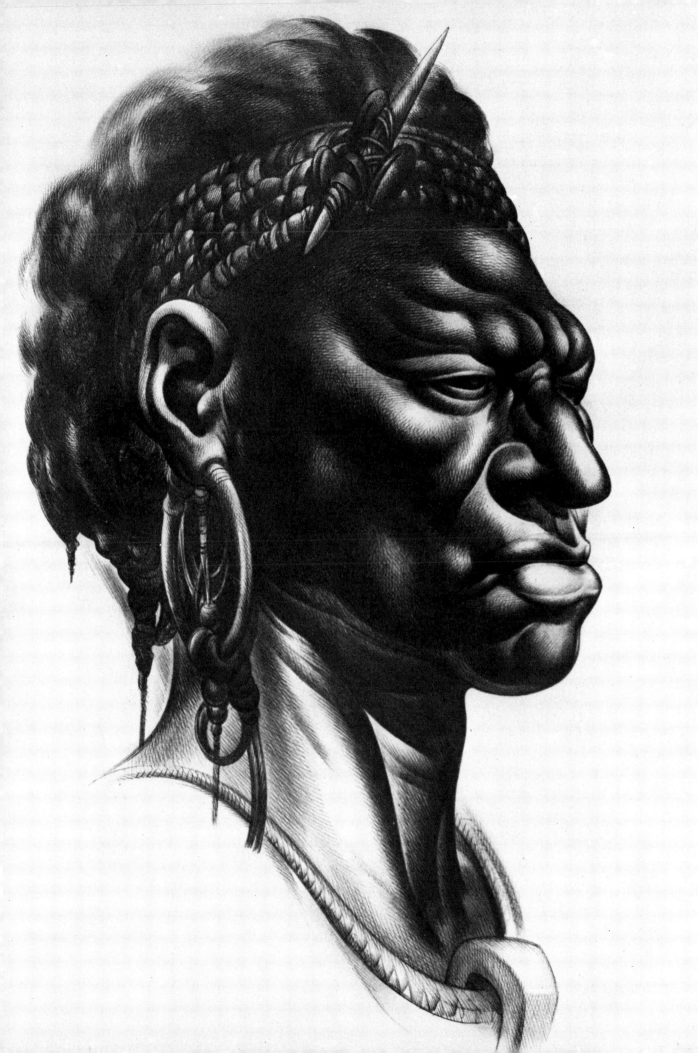

Every Detail Plays Its Part

This poster design of a bullfighter, driving home his sword between the shoulders of a charging bull, exploits the clarity of sculptural light to create a sense of tension and danger. The light reveals every detail, every form, so that all essential elements are visible. The dark mass of the animal with its muscular forms; the eye of the bull under the cape; the hair at the tip of the tail; the matador's "suit of lights" with its agitated play of creases; his tense hand, determined face, and slick hair; even the bows on the slippers, the shiny sash at the waist, the shoulder tassels, the pointed barbs—all are shown in sharp focus. If you care for drama revealed in precise detail, this is the light to use.

90

CHAPTER 9

SPATIAL LIGHT

Values Create Space

We know that perspective is essential in conveying the illusion of three-dimensionality within the picture plane. But by organizing the objects within the picture into a carefully worked out system of values, the artist can make the relative lightness and darkness of objects lead the eye in and out of the picture, suggesting space and communicating near and far distances. This schema of values is based on a rational and logical system which I define as *spatial light.* Spatial light can create a sense of distance, move the eye into and around the picture to create a visual focus and force the eye to concentrate on a given place within the picture plane, sometimes called the *center of interest* or *area of dominant impact.*

Phototropic Principle

The principle of spatial light is based on the fact that the eye is phototropic—that it will always seek out and focus on the *lightest* area in a picture, which represents the brightest value. This is typical of the way our eye focuses on real objects—in that we tend to be attracted to the most brilliantly lit areas of a scene—and it is also the way we respond in a realistic drawing. So if there is a light form in the foreground of a drawing and the area behind it is a darker tone, the dark-toned area will become a receding background plane in our minds. The net effect of the dark background, then, is to force the light form forward. But if the situation were reversed and the lit object were in the background while the foreground forms were dark, the effect of this distant light would be to lead us *back* into the pictorial space.

Figures in Interior: First Version ▽

This interior with figures is clearly divided into foreground, middleground, and background. You will see this picture in three different versions, all identical except for the disposition of values—and the shifts in spatial focus that will be created by those changes in value. In this first version, because brightest light is on the nearest figure, the light focuses your attention on the foreground. Other areas recede because they are toned with darker values. The result is an outward movement from back to front, created by the concentration of the bright light in the foreground. The diminishing size of the figures has nothing to do with where the eye focuses in the pictorial space. Spatial focus is defined only by the light.

Figures in Interior: Second Version
The pictorial elements are the same as in the first version, but there is now a radical shift of interest to the background, where the light is now illuminating the personnel who scan their computer screens. The rest of the picture is in black and a medium gray. Again this proves that the eye is drawn to the light, no matter where that light may be and regardless of the subject or the narrative. The placement of the light can be arbitrary as long as it has optical appeal and as long as the eye finds it convincing. *What the eye accepts as logical is pictorially permissible.*

Figures in Interior: Third Version
Now the light shifts to the seated man in the middleground. All other elements in the picture are black and medium gray. The eye moves inward and outward, locating the bright light in a central position between the extremes of near and far. To test the force of these three light positions, turn the three pictures upside down and look at them again. When the subject matter no longer interferes, the shifts of the lighted areas—and their magnetic effect on the eye—will become more evident.

Light in the Foreground

In this jungle setting, the emphasis is on the boatmen who sit in a patch of light at the river bank. This result is reinforced by the dark silhouette of the foliage that frames the immediate foreground. Across the water, the opposite shore and sky are held to an overall medium gray tone. The eye is attracted to the foreground, seeking the region of strongest light.

Light in the Near Middleground

In this night scene of a village celebration, the eye is drawn to the near middleground. Surrounded by the darks of the foreground building and lesser architectural structures in the distance, a bright bar of light sweeps across the middleground, moving across the plaza, rising on the celebrants, and then bouncing up to the front and back of the tower. Everything else in the picture is reduced in value. This picture also shows that the spatial light does not necessarily have to be located on the ground, but can move vertically as well as horizontally.

Light in the Middleground

The light divides this pictorial space virtually in the middle. In the shallow space of the entrance to the stable, a central light from an unseen high source drops midway into the interior, falling on the man and the horse. All other pictorial elements are held to reduced, dark values. The eye focuses on the middle distance. The spotlight effect carries the eye to the center of interest like an arrow to a bull's-eye.

◁ Landscape with Light in Middleground

In another version of the bull's-eye design, the light carries the eye to the middle distance, where the action occurs. The lighted middleground is framed by the darker foreground tones of the trees, vines, jungle verdure, rocks, and water. The subdued values of the background force the eye forward into the lighter midregion. The spatial light is less obvious, more delicate and discrete.

Light Past the Middleground

Now the focus of the light is past the midpoint of the pictorial space. The fisherman casts his line in shallow waters as twilight settles, and the dim light sends dappled reflections across the surface. The rocks and water in the immediate foreground are already darkening into dusk. Farther back, the light surrounds the fisherman. In the distance, the reduced values convey a misty, vaporous sky above an unclear horizon. The eye moves past the darkening waters to focus just beyond the center.

Light in the Background

The eye moves into the picture as the spatial light focuses our attention on the background. The foreground is held to black and medium gray on the warrior and the surrounding rocks. The thrust of the eye is to the rear, where we focus on the distant cliff and the curling smoke. This rear space is the lightest value and the center of visual interest. The pictorial design reinforces the inward movement of the eye: notice the angular thrusts of the spear, the sword, and the folds of the cape, all carrying the eye to the right rear.

Light in the Remote Distance

A brilliant patch of moonlight on the still water draws the eye to the far horizon. The eye is drawn inward—through the dark foreground—by the bright light in the distance. The design of the pictorial space is like a tunnel: the shapes of the foreground tree and rocks create an elliptical passage that carries the eye to the rear light. Thus, the light becomes a target—like the bull's-eye effect of previous examples. Notice how the alternating black and gray bars in the middleground slow the eye as it moves toward the background light. Without these bars, the deep space would shorten and collapse.

CHAPTER 10

ENVIRONMENTAL LIGHT

Environmental Light Is Circumstantial
Thus far, you have seen special kinds of
light—such as single and double-source
light, flat light, and moonlight—that are
determined by limited causal factors, such
as the source and direction of the light. But
environmental light is not a specific kind
of light, but is the product of atmospheric
circumstances such as warm and cold, or wet
and dry weather. Environmental light also
reflects the time of day (sunrise, sunset,
nightfall, moonrise) and even the time of
year (spring, summer, fall, and winter).

Varieties of Environmental Light
Environmental light encompasses not
only visual effects, but sensual modes and
feelings. Images of environmental light
can convey balminess and lambent
warmth; cold rain or frigid drizzle; blus-
tery snow and icy wind; rain, murk, and
night wind; and twilight afterglow or overcast gloom. Such images can also capture
the atmosphere of varied locales such as
grassland, woodland, mountain, valley,
forest, and tropical or arid places. In short,
environmental light evokes time, place,
and atmosphere.

Dawn
Over the scrubby growth, dawn appears
and lights up a fast-disappearing, overcast
sky. Dark night clouds are scudding
away. From behind the clouds, a pale, rosy
light reaches across the streaked formations in the sky. In the foreground, a broad
stretch of mud flats, flanked by weeds
and grass, reflects the oncoming light,
heralding the approach of a cool, bright,
early summer day. Notice how the dark
band of the land area is isolated by intermittent bars of gleaming light, above and
below.

Mist

Early morning mist stirs from a ravine and begins to drift as the warming air rises. Streaks of mist emerge and float away in shredded layers. The sun has not yet appeared over the craggy pinnacles of eroded sandstone, but the thermal airflow already begins to dissipate the misty atmosphere that shrouds and softens the distant shapes of the landscape.

Morning Sun

The midsummer morning sun rises over a reservoir lake surrounded by scrub pine, shrubs, and stunted undergrowth. It is the beginning of a hot, humid day. The ground is parched. There has been no rain and there is no rain to come. The sky has been cloudless for a fortnight. The sun penetrates the haze, burning through the moist air with stabbing rays that radiate in all directions like subtle spokes. On this bright, sunny day, the entire picture is constructed with dark silhouettes—from foreground to distant background—supported by a hazy sky, toned gray and streaked with white. Just three values—black, gray, and white—express the hot, clammy light.

Midday in Midwinter

Cool, bright contrasts appear under the clear sky of a midwinter day. Clear air and flat light display every detail in sharp relief against the snow-carpeted whiteness of the land; brittle grasses, denuded saplings, scattered evergreens, even the faltering stream that threads its uncertain way down the gentle slope. Beneath the larger undergrowth we see pale shadows, but they are largely overruled by the darker tones of the big trees and the stream. White snow and clear, wintry air reveal every element in the landscape with singular contrast and clarity.

Coastal Fog

A bank of fog shrouds the seacoast with dense, misty atmosphere. It is midmorning, but the summer sun has difficulty dissolving the mantle of fog that sweeps in from the sea. Some light works through and glows dully in the air and on the water. The light also finds its way through places of lesser density—around the sailboat, for example—and a patch of light, higher in the sky, heralds a clear day later. The rocks close to shore have some weight, some connection with the laws of gravity, but the boat and the distant sea seem to be lost in a misty, nongravitational space. This effect is produced by the falloff of values from the dark, fairly distinct rocky foreground to the uncertain, unclear background, which suggests a deep, endless space.

Winter Gloom △

Here is another vision of winter that is quite different from the Japanese mode. It is afternoon among a grove of trees that have been lightly dusted with snow. The wind is bringing heavy clouds and damp, cold air, presaging more snow. The murky sky, streaked and ominous, settles close to the ground and darkens the background with a cheerless pall. The white snow is caught on twigs, branches, and bark. Compare the bone-chilling atmosphere of this drawing with the Japanese winter of Koryusai. The Japanese woodcut is pleasant and soothing, detached and aloof, appealing to the mind, awakening a tranquil mood of meditation and contemplative enjoyment, while the drawing evokes cold gloom.

Snow in Flat, Diffused Light

Gentle snow is falling as a lady readies herself, with the aid of a servant, for a walk in snow that is already deep on the ground. The sky is overcast. In the flat, diffused, gray light, heavy flakes course downward through the still air. The diffused light tends to emphasize the contours, patterns, and flat shapes of the figures. Such light diminishes three-dimensional form—eliminating cast shadows because there is no specific light source—and reduces objects to flat, two-dimensional configurations. Thus, both the ground and the sky are flat shapes, the same tone from front to back, with no value changes to indicate depth. The woodcut is by the Japanese master, Koryusai.

Dust and Wind ▽
A late afternoon wind sweeps dust and sand over the parched ground. The weather is hot and dry, without rain. A shore bird waits for the air to settle before flying off to seek food. Compare the dense, dusty atmosphere just above the ground with the lighter, uneven tone higher up. The wayward branches and twigs respond to the random thrusts of the winds. The sweeps of tone in the sky convey the raw look of tumult and turbulence.

◁ Rain

Late in the day, the pelting rain has interrupted all activity and everyone runs for shelter except the hapless wayfarers silhouetted in the distance, who apparently have no choice but to continue their plodding way. The Japanese master of the color woodcut, Hiroshige, gives us a rain-soaked, overcast landscape with two distinct aspects of flat light. First, despite the rain, the flat light leaves the rainy foreground transparent so we can see every detail: the tree, figures, baskets, straw mats, thatched roof, and so on. In the background, however, all detail is lost. The dense, rainy air reduces the plodding travelers and the tree at the center to gray silhouettes. The mass of trees at the far horizon is nothing more than a contour line that encloses a lighter gray. The rain streaks are all the same thickness, but Hiroshige leaves just a bit more space between the streaks in the foreground.

Fading Daylight

Late in the day, the arid, craggy peaks begin to sink into the gloom of the receding daylight. The air is cooling rapidly and a swift wind sweeps clouds over the mountains. In the distance, the peaks break through a tenuous sea of mist. In the foreground, the mist has not yet obscured the fading light; we can still see creeping shadows on the steep-walled valleys and depressions in the slopes. The light seems to come from three sources: from the right, intermittent, oblique sun comes through the cloud rifts; on the left, a more delicate light feeds into the edges of the forms; and from above and to the rear, the wind-driven mists and clouds seem to glow with diffused light.

Icy Atmosphere

Among these Antarctic icebergs, full summer daylight is past and the season is slowly changing. The forms are struck horizontally from the right by the low, brilliant sun before it sinks below the horizon. The clear air and unimpeded light create sharp contrasts between the illuminated icy surfaces and the correspondingly deep shadows. In the uneven foreground, the surface ice reflects the light and also shows dark patches of open sea. A cold light permeates the low horizon. High above, the transparent but deepening sky shows a vague, spectral, crystalline light.

Twilight

Reflecting on the shimmering river at the end of a summer day, the setting sun sifts through the spidery network of the bridge. The sky is ablaze with serrated lights, which are mirrored on the water.

Storm

As dusk comes on, the mountains and foothills are beset by a sudden storm of rain and wind, swept in with the massive clouds. The landscape is enveloped with darkness, while an uncertain, flickering light hovers over the brows of the mountainous shapes. The origin of the light lies far beyond the shapes at the horizon, but the rolling mass of clouds and vaporous air reflects the light in every direction, producing an unearthly display of illumination on the landscape.

Snow and Rain

On a winter evening, darkness has fallen early, as wet snow, laced with cold rain, builds up on every surface. People huddle under a shelter, facing a city street and a construction site, and wait for a bus. The snow is drawn in small, rough strokes, so that it looks grainy. The snow mingles with dull, whitish reflections and light halations on all the structures beyond the foreground. A sense of deep space is created by the contrast between the dark foreground silhouettes and the snowy area beyond. The streaks of falling rain and snow are put in with a single-edge razor blade, stroked diagonally upward against the grain of the drawing paper.

Nightfall at Sea
At nightfall, the rising wave is lashed by a stiff wind that brings gusts of heavy rain streaking across the dark. Spume and spray tear loose from the crests of the waves. Icy sleet bears down at a steep angle into the water. The foam and the aerated, churning water create trails of light on the pyramidal wave forms and on the wind-driven swells.

Calm, Moonlit Sea

The silver moon reflects on the calm waters of the sparkling, tropical sea. It is a balmy night of velvet blackness. Large areas of dark are set against lesser areas of light. There is just enough light to show the sailboat, the gently lapping waves, and the limitless, beckoning horizon. The design of curves against horizontals reinforces a sense of rest, relaxation, and sleep.

Underwater Light

As the scuba diver moves through the coral colonies and exotic marine life, a burst of light opens a cavernous space in the darkness. The light comes from above the surface of the water, gradually fading into the mysterious darkness as tiny, ghostlike fish follow the strange silhouette of the diver through the deep, with his trailing, silvery plume.

Light in Outer Space

Illustrator Jerry Robinson contributed this drawing of space vehicles in the unbounded void of eternal night. Light falls on the near vehicles from the sun. The moon wears a circular halo of backlight, no doubt from the sun as well. The dark sky is dotted with the light of the stars. The sky itself contains no light, no gravity, no movement, no atmosphere—only timeless darkness.

CHAPTER 11
TEXTURAL LIGHT

**Textural Light
Reveals Surfaces**
Just as sculptural light reveals three-dimensional form, textural light reveals the surface qualities of these forms. Textural light suggests direct physical contact, as though the eye were a tactile organ—scanning, testing, and probing surface phenomena like a fingertip. But because the eye can explore more of the environment than a fingertip can reach, we can perceive the effects of textural light both close up and at a great distance. That is, we can examine the texture of a small object within arm's reach, and we can also see the texture of a distant landscape.

Western Landscape
Illustrator H. M. Stoops lets the hard, bright sun reveal the massive textural detail of the striated cliffs. Here, the textural light creates strong contrasts between light and shadow—with the detail in the shadows. This is equally true of the great upthrust cliffs of shelved sandstone and the rocky debris below, whose texture is revealed by tiny touches of strong shadow.

Rough Bark
The bark of this desert tree branch shows serried striations that appear to move, twist, and writhe like some strange creature. The texture is quite varied: the bark is hard, rough, and dry; the branches are sharp; and the springy end-growths look like the bushy tails of small animals. The light emphasizes the texture by catching all the high points of the form, while all the low points—even the tiniest crack—sink into shadow.

Parched Ground
The dry, gritty surface of the ground exposes sparse, granular topsoil, coarse sand, and gravel interspersed with stones and layered rocks. The shadows are rendered as clusters of tiny, dark flecks that allow other flecks of light to shine through—as if the picture consisted of granules of light and shadow. Thus, the light and the drawing technique convey a tactile feeling, as if your fingertip were exploring the grainy surface of the land.

Lunar Landscape
In the airless environment of the moon, the brilliant sun burns the dusty, gritty landscape to produce strong contrasts between the foreground light and shadow. In this illustration for the book *Moon Trip,* Jerry Robinson creates texture with light in two ways: he renders the land with small, precise touches that suggest a granular texture, and he also sprinkles sand and grit into the paint. The granular texture of the paint *literally* casts tiny flecks of shadow that convey the tactile qualities of the subject.

Hillside
The varied textures here include: thick groves of evergreens, rocks cushioned in cool grass, scrubby undergrowth, moss, dead leaves, and forest litter. In the valley below, the melted snow forms crystal rivulets and streams. The entire landscape is drawn with crystalline clarity and fine detail in the sharp focus typical of textural light. This sharp, clear light dramatizes every surface irregularity, throwing details into bold relief by drawing attention to the most minute shadows and points of light.

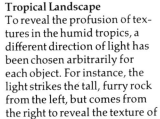

Tropical Landscape
To reveal the profusion of textures in the humid tropics, a different direction of light has been chosen arbitrarily for each object. For instance, the light strikes the tall, furry rock from the left, but comes from the right to reveal the texture of the fallen trees in the foreground. As long as the total effect looks convincing, you are free to choose the most effective light direction for each object.

113

Landscape with Figure and Animals

This page from the author's *Jungle Tales of Tarzan* surveys not only the intricate textures of the tropical growth, but also the smooth skin of the figure, his furry loin cover, the short-haired fur of the monkey, the feathers of the owl and the singing bird, and the slick curves of the lizard and the eggs. The rough, furry, and feathery textures are rendered with lines that seek out and follow the surface irregularities, so that the touches of the pen become linear shadows. However, on the smooth surfaces, the lines simply follow the direction of the form, curving around the muscles of Tarzan and the convex surfaces of the lizard and eggs. The right line must be found for each subject. Thus, simple lines follow the movement of the water in the foreground to convey the impression of a wet surface.

Shiny Object

A shiny, metallic object presents a smooth, highly polished, mirrorlike surface with high reflectance. Such a surface produces bright highlights. In this hose and pipe connection device, the connector is bright metal, while the hose is smooth, dark plastic. Thus, the hose is mostly dark, with limited highlights and edge-light reflections while the metallic connector, on the other hand, shows more light because it has more bright, open areas. The shiny metal has a *dual* highlight system: you can see two rows of light reflections on the upper and lower surfaces, with fine, illuminated curves and rings. The brightness of the metallic highlight is a direct reflection of the brightness of the light source. (Unlike the metal and plastic, the fingers are easily identified as soft, dull, unpolished, and satiny textures. Their mottled tones produce the effect of being *in* the light, but not *reflecting* the light.)

Ripples in Water

When a stone is dropped in water, the pattern of light on high points and troughs can be seen clearly in the concentric ripples on the water's surface. The undulating, up-and-down surface shows the sequence of highlights, dark shadows, and secondary reflected lights within the troughs. As you have already learned, the bright light on the form appears next to the deepest dark. Notice how the sequence of tones moves diagonally, from lower right to upper left, across the major axis of the wave pattern. You will find that similar highlight effects appear on other wet surfaces, from the human eye to the wet *look* of shiny paint, glass, or chrome.

Shiny Cloth

Polished metal is not the only material capable of producing reflected highlights. A similar effect appears on this young sailor's rubberized slicker, with its hard-edged folds, angular corners, deep depressions, and sharp crests—like squeezed tinfoil or finished leather. There are bright highlights on the topmost forms of the wrinkles, particularly on the sleeve, and deep shadows in the troughs. A special characteristic of such shiny material is the presence of secondary, reflected lights within the deep clefts of the wrinkles. Once again, the distinctive quality of textural light is in its precise definition of the crisp lights and shadows on an object—as well as in the sharply drawn reflected lights in this example.

Reflections in Glass and Metal

On the polished glass and painted metal of this car on a bridge, the light is mirrored to create the tactile sensation of smoothness. The characteristic ripple appearance on the windshield and hood is not the result of surface irregularity, but the mirrored image of the trees and sky. The chrome on the lights, grille, and bumper also produces brilliant light and dark reflections like the water in the previous illustration. Around the car, the textural light reveals the intricate pattern of tiny lights and shadows that conveys the surface qualities of abrasive bark, weathered wooden beams and planks, chipped fieldstone, and clumps of leaves.

Varied Landscape Textures

The water, rocks, and trees in this landscape set up a sequence of tactile experiences, all communicated by the textural light—the dense, terraced stone; the splashing, cascading stream; and the intricate foliage. All are revealed and *heightened* by the strong contrasts of light and shadow that are typical of textural light. Thus, the tops of the rocks are brilliantly lit from a high source, which creates tiny pits of shadow that convey texture. The shadows themselves are strong and dark, but are rich in textural detail because they contain a great deal of secondary, reflected light. In the same way, clearly defined lights, shadows, and reflected lights bring the textural details of the trees and foliage into sharp relief.

Silk and Satin

At first glance, a silky or satiny material has a surface that seems similar to the high gloss of metal or glass. However, there is a difference. A polished surface is slick and undisturbed; thus, it is highly reflective. But the woven surface of satin or silk, no matter how fine the mesh, has an airy or dusty look, and is less reflective. Therefore, this woman's dress inherently lacks the brilliant shine of the smoother, "wet-looking" surfaces in the previous four illustrations. Instead, flowing in the direction of the curves and thrusts of the body, the wrinkles of the dress express the tactile qualities of softness and flexibility. To render the textural light on these voluptuous surfaces, the shadows are modeled with lines that follow the contours of the sensual folds and wrinkles of the dress.

CHAPTER 12

TRANSPARENT LIGHT

Transparent and Translucent Light

Transparent surfaces and objects actually transmit light. These light-penetrating or light-permeating qualities are inherent in the structure of such solid matter as glass, crystal, gems, and ice; in captured liquids like water or wine; and even in captured gases, such as bubbles. Translucent substances permit light penetration, but tend to absorb light, interfere with the light, or diffuse the light, thus introducing a degree of opacity that reduces the clarity of the image. This translucent effect is familiar in gauzy fabrics, liquids, the flat surface of ice, and frosted glass.

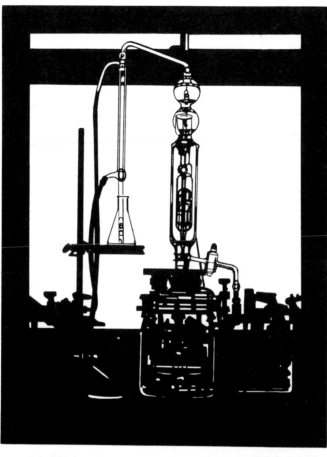

Clear Glass

The clear, transparent glass of laboratory vessels, seen against a window in broad daylight, presents an effect of outlines with no suggestion of solid form or solid matter. Each light-permeable object seems to be made of contours only— looking like a wire construction. Below the window sill, glass jars are set against the shadowy frame. Here, their contours catch occasional light: bright outlines contrast with the dark outlines of the forms above.

Refracted Light

A clear glass bowl—with varied diameters—displays a sequence of see-through elliptical shapes. The light is refracted by the thickness of the glass. Arc-shaped reflections follow the *convex* shapes of the bowl, while the eye-shaped reflections appear within the *concave* curves. The effect of the transparent light is particularly complex and fascinating because you are seeing the inner and outer surface at the same time, since the inner and outer reflections shine through one another.

Glass, Fluid, and Metal

The rounded, frontal surface of the snifter glass is defined by a series of curved, *up-and-down strokes*, with intermittent slashes of highlights. Curving *horizontal strokes* define the concave inner surface beneath the lip at the rear. Curving, *circular strokes* delineate the liquor in the glass; note that the fluid is seen both from the side and from above. Within the fluid, arcs of light define the stem attachment, showing through the liquor. Beneath the glass, these arcs are repeated on the stem and base of the glass. The irregular reflections on the base suggest the imprecise finish of the glass. Through the back wall of the snifter, a fairly sharp image of the silver candle base is seen. But where the candle base is seen through two layers of glass—the front and back walls of the snifter, one wall concave and the other convex—the image is distorted and less bright.

One Glass Behind Another

The two wine glasses contain a colored, translucent fluid. Sharp highlights follow the outer curves of the glasses. On the surfaces of the liquid, elliptical lights vibrate gently. Where the glasses almost touch, we see the dual image of the left glass behind the right. The stems gleam with light from a small pattern—brightest on the higher surfaces. The disk-shaped bases show curved reflections. The lights on the surfaces of the glass are distinctly brighter than the soft, inner light of the wine within.

Ice and Bubbles

The translucent tumbler contains layered, melting ice that floats in carbonated water. Bubbles seep upward, leaving trickling paths as they move toward the surface of the water, from which the random shape of the chipped ice projects. Above the rim of the glass, minute bubbles pop as they escape into the air. The tumbler is clear against the dark background. Only the horizontal strokes on the lower surface of the glass suggest reflected light and affirm the solid structure of the vessel. Note the wet, wavy reflection on the surface beneath the glass.

Ice Cubes

The irregular facets of ice cubes present an intriguing problem because there is no explicit image that you can see through the ice and no reflection of a specific image on the surface. Yet there *is* light penetration and refraction, and there *are* highlights and reflections from sources that may not be apparent—like the dark facets that come through from the dark background. The only way to draw these phenomena is to observe the seemingly random patterns and record them faithfully. If you do so, a convincing effect of transparent light, and a solid sense of form, will emerge by themselves.

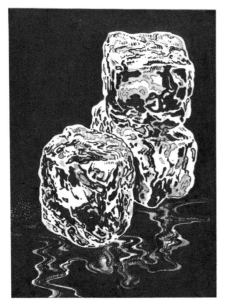

Crystal Form

This symmetrical polyhedron presents brilliant light on some facets, diminished light on others, varied reflections, and reduced transparency where one facet interrupts or overlaps another. The surface light changes with every directional turn of the geometric form, yet each facet is polished and precise as a prism.

Cut Glass

The sparkling highlights on the raised, prismatic pattern of cut glass tend to disguise the transparency of the dark liquid within the glass. But the see-through color of the fluid glows through the upper part of the wine glass. The light shines *through* the stem, revealing the form by the effects of light on the intricate pattern. In contrast, the light shines *on* the base, and its form is revealed by the circular reflections on the surface.

Gem

The prismatic, crystalline quality of the light that emanates from a gem is a kind of transparent light that is *not* seen in glass or any comparable material. The light that strikes the stone is turned *into* the stone instead of passing through, and then reflects outward in a display of spectral colors of great brilliance that gives these minerals their strange and wonderful "fire." Once again, the secret of drawing this type of transparent light is to observe the abstract pattern and record it faithfully, no matter how erratic that pattern may seem. The light has its own secret logic, inherent in the structure of the crystal.

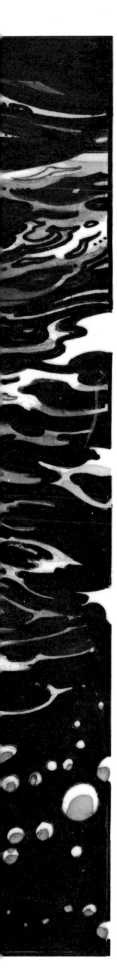

Moving Water

The transparency of water is affected by a variety of factors. Thus, we can see the forms of the figure that are just below the surface, while the rest of the figure is quickly obscured by the density of the water and the increasing darkness below. The form is also obscured and distorted by the motion of the water and the refraction of the light. Finally, the water is really *translucent* rather than transparent, letting only *some* light through and partly obscuring the image beneath the surface. Such ambiguity and obscurity are frequent occurrences in translucent light.

Two Kinds of Translucency

There are two different kinds of translucent effects in this drawing of a car. Although the windshield glass is absolutely transparent, the interior detail of the car is somewhat obscure and pale because of the light that enters the car from the side. The effect is similar to the translucency of air laden with fog, mist, or dust. The other translucent effect in this drawing is seen in the frosted glass of the headlights: the striated surface pattern diffuses the light penetration of such a surface and blurs any image seen through the glass.

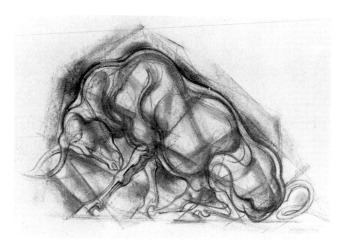

Expressive Transparency

With the advent of Cubism, a form of expressive transparency entered the art style of our time. Images now are made of split, fractionated elements that merge, overlap, and disengage, both with themselves and with the background. As in this drawing of a bull, the effect is a kind of prismatic transparency. Interlaced, see-through lines and segmented parts suggest geometric elements, shot through with light and gleaming like a stained glass window. Such expressive transparency is not an objective view of nature, of course, but a subjective product of the artist's imagination.

Kaleidoscopic Transparency

This image of a *Man of Labor* is set forth in a kaleidoscopic pattern of prismatic forms. Their transparent, geometric structure suggests the life of a man who has been intimately involved in construction. The man tends to merge with the prismatic structure of the crystalline light, which scintillates as if it shines through the facets of a gem. Here is a particularly dramatic example of the expressive quality of transparent light.

Translucent Cloth
Certain kinds of cloth—such as loosely woven cotton, lightweight knit, or fine silk—allow the light to penetrate and thus reveal an unclear image, usually a silhouette. Here, the canvas sail catches low, late afternoon light. Clouds rise in the warm updraft. The boys are illuminated by the hot afternoon sun. The sun is still bright enough to shine through the sail, which transmits the silhouettes of the clouds and the figure of one boy.

CHAPTER 13

FRAGMENTATION LIGHT

Light Disrupting Form

Fragmentation light is an instantaneous or momentary effect of reflected light that suggests disrupted or dispersed form. This is not the changeable light of the Impressionist painters, but a transient light phenomenon of disintegrated form—such as splashing water, flying snow, or an explosion. Such light suggests *motion* happening in a very brief time. Fragmentation light is immediate, passing, and often tumultuous.

Rain

Water run-off in rain produces a distorted reflection of an auto wheel on a wet street at night. The streaming water creates an uneven mirrored surface that imparts a trembling shimmer to the reflected form of the wheel. All the well-ordered elements of the car take on a fractured, corrugated quality as they are reflected on the half-lit, oil-slicked, gleaming street, while the streaks of rain create a sporadic, angular pattern of light over all the forms.

Twilight on the Sea

In the murky twilight of an overcast tropical sky—the moment before a storm erupts—the heaving swells catch the last glimmer of the light. A pattern of alternating crests and troughs gleams brightly, but we see the pattern of the light rather than the actual shapes of the waves. The sea gleams with whorls and eddies in the foreground, changing swiftly as we watch.

Surf

As a surfer plunges shore-ward—impelled by a booming wave—the foam, spume, and spray explode outward in glistening beams and motes of light. The volatile, kinetic display of the surf releases boundless energy, dispersing the light and fracturing the forms seen through the fragmented light.

Explosion in Water

High explosive charges, dropped on a submarine, send radiating geysers and plumes of water in all directions. At the core of the blast is a massive eruption of aerated spume and spray that reflect the brilliant, fragmented light. The rocking of the ship produces a sequence of lateral waves, while the rubble cast out from the vessel creates splash patterns in choppy rosette forms. Against the dark water, the light gleams on these fragmented shapes.

127

Fire
Aboard an aircraft carrier during a battle,
a plane returns disabled and on fire. The
fragmented light appears not only in the
flames and smoke that flare to the rear, but
also in the streaks that fly from the skid-
ding wheels, and in the sheen of the polished propeller blades.

Powdered Snow
The downhill racer moves at a "breakneck" pace through a shower of snow powder and ice. The light disturbance is caused by the shower of snow that explodes skyward, augmented by a heavy updraft of wind from below. The look of speed—which is frequently identified with fragmentation light—is emphasized by the angular strokes of the grainy background, without any identifiable detail.

Sand
A sand buggy plunges downward in a shower of sand, grit, and pebbles. While the front wheels throw up waves of dirt, the back wheels kick up a storm of debris and dust in all directions. The dust-filled air creates a fragmentation pattern that obscures everything around the racing automobile.

Golfer in Action
As the golfer delivers the ball out of a sand trap, the impact of the stroke creates an upheaval of fine and coarse sand—like a miniature explosion in a radiating flare pattern. The fragmentation light dissolves all adjacent forms and details.

Racing Car
This racing automobile creates a variety of light disturbance patterns. First, of course, there is the airflow and slip-stream speed pattern created by the tremendous velocity of the machine. Next, the effluent gas spirals far behind the auto as the exhaust is caught in the air turbulence produced by the vehicle. Third, a chattering pattern of light appears close to the ground as the wheels hit the cobbled road with thunderous force. Finally, the uneven density of the moving air is expressed in spasms of cloudy light-and-dark passages that spread sideward from the speeding car.

Horses in Motion
Racehorses, converging shoulder-to-shoulder toward a dead-heat finish, send up an eruption of track debris that obscures even the galloping hooves. The light is dispersed by the flying granular matter, which cancels out all specific details of the moving legs of the animals.

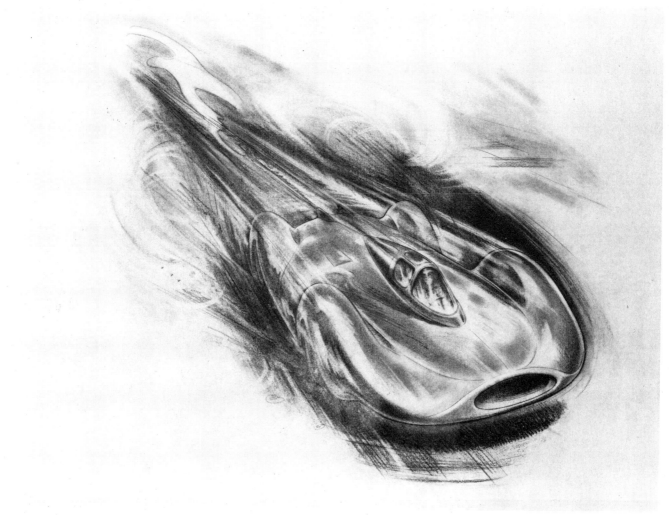

Avalanche
Fragmentation light of another order appears in an earth convulsion when rocks, snow, and ice cascade down a mountainside. Great masses of rock and ice, in riotous collision, explode like bombs and send bursts of rocky rubble and crystalline ice and snow toward the sky. Earth, snow, and debris spread everywhere, rifted with mist, fog, and curls of drifting glitter, all dissolved into pale, cloudy vapor.

Volcanic Eruption
The most spectacular manifestation of form-disintegrating light is the boundless violence of a volcanic eruption. Great, belching coils of smoke and dust spew out in a monstrous flare pattern, cut through with geysers of flame, molten debris, and shattered rock, all flung skyward. An unearthly light bursts through the sky and flaming embers plummet all around the four survivors in their fragile craft.

Light in Motion
A lesser mode of fragmentation light—what might be called *kinetic light*—is shown in this drawing of violent movement, shock, and disturbance. The lines of kinetic light suggest speed and thrust as the knife is driven with great force into the reptile's skull. The frozen image printed on the page does, indeed, *seem* to move; the arm swings and the snake recoils.

Light Conveys Intense Feeling
Kinetic light—or action light—expresses speed and urgency in this drawing of a clash between a jungle man and armed pursuers. A powerful blow—drawn as an explosive burst of light—sends one enemy flying heels-over-head. Curved speed lines convey the action of the blow, while similar lines of kinetic light intensify the frenzy of the hurtling figure. The expressive use of action light conveys a quality of feeling so intense and immediate that one is surprised that artists except for cartoonists, have used it so sparingly.

CHAPTER 14

RADIANT LIGHT

Intense Light

Radiant light is an intensive emanation of
light—natural or artificial—far more powerful than direct, single-source light. Such
light is an assault on the eye because unlike translucent light, radiant light is never
screened, nor is it reflected from a secondary surface. In single-source light, we
see the bounce effect of a strong light on
an object. But in radiant light, the eye is in
direct contact with the light source itself.
The viewer is powerfully aware of temperature and energy. By definition, the
primary and pervasive example of radiant
light is our universal energy source, the
sun. In degree of intensity, radiant light
ranges from the comparatively low illumination of a candle, to the intermediate
range of a lamp or flashlight (or even a
searchlight), to the high levels of radiance
produced by a fire or an explosion.

Glare

Radiant sunlight produces the perceptual
phenomenon of glare—the spill-over of
light rays, striking the eye with so much
intensity that the viewer is dazzled and
discomfited, finding it difficult to perceive
the shape of the light source because of its
overwhelming luminosity. (We have all
experienced the reflex of narrowing our
eyelids so that the eye becomes a thin slit.)
Glare is produced not only by the sun, but
by any "hot" light source that strikes the
eye directly, such as an auto headlight, a
propane flame, an arc light, or vivid firelight. These effects are best seen against
dark backgrounds.

Sun

Breaking through a bank of
clouds, the sun emits a sudden,
unobstructed blaze of dazzling
brilliance. The contour of the
solar disk cannot be seen because of the glare—the spill-
over of radiant light. But, here
and there, flashing rays shoot
through the clouds, sending
beams across the afternoon
sky.

Candlelight

In contrast with the pervasive,
immense power of the sun, we
now see the lambent shine of a
candle flame. Note the soft,
warm illumination of this low-
level light—equivalent to match
light. Its dim luster bathes the
woman's face with a subdued
glow and suffuses the background with a pale half light
that fades gradually into shade.

Firelight

This male head is illuminated by flamelight from logs in a fireplace or, possibly, an open-air campfire. Compared with the soft candlelight in the previous drawing, the planes of this head are sharply defined by the hot blaze. Subtle half-lights have no place here. Bright lights are placed against equivalent, pitch dark shadows that merge with the tenebrous background.

Flamelight

The flame of a cut glass, tallow oil lamp sends scintillant light through the prismatic surface of the glass. The concentrated light is brighter than a candle flame. Thus, the lamp emits sparkling rays, producing marked contrasts of light and shadow on the figure.

Lamplight Outdoors

In Kaethe Kollwitz's great etching, *Schlachtfeld*, a woman carries a low-power lamp as she searches for a loved one on a battlefield. An eerie, feeble, yet intimate light glows on the features of a fallen soldier. The cool light—probably from a carbide flame—is just above a glimmer, and flickers in the damp wind as the fragile gleam threatens to die away in the night.

Flamelight Outdoors

In this color woodcut, the Japanese master Hiroshige gives us flamelight that issues from peat fires, whose bright columns of flame rise almost vertically in the still, cool air of the darkened landscape. The light is not as untamed or dramatic as that of the torch in the previous drawing. Here, the radiant embers and the hot gases rising into the sky have an inviting warmth. Note the small paper lantern that is suspended from the horse's right side; the simple candlelight contrasts with the large peat fires.

Torchlight in Wind

An oil-soaked taper or torch
flares unpredictably in the
wind, acting like a flaming
mare's tail. The light is not
even or constant, but is fitful or
blazing bright. The torn flame
creates uneven lights and shadows that leap and play, looking
both benign and menacing at
the same time.

Flashlight

The strong, concentrated beam
of a flashlight cuts a swath
through the darkened interior.
If we look directly into its glar-
ing beam, we will instinctively
shield our eyes. This battery-
powered light is essentially
cooler than the thermal energy
of a peat or log fire. But the
flashlight is *more intense*. This is
an important distinction: the
peat or log fire is hotter, but not
brighter.

Auto Headlight

Like the flashlight, the automobile light is artificial and therefore "cool." But it is "hot" to the eyes. As we look straight into the bright beam, we see an spill-over of light that spreads fanwise in all directions. We cannot see the contour of the circular headlamp from which the rays originate. We see only a burst of high-intensity glare.

Searchlight

On a far larger scale than the automobile headlight, the battleship's searchlight stabs through the moonless overcast with a beam that can illuminate an area hundreds of yards away. Seen here in a side view, the far-reaching shaft of light pierces the darkness with a knifelike, luminous thrust that can penetrate gloom, mist, and darkness to an enormous depth. Viewing such a powerful light head-on—with the naked eye—one would suffer unbearable pain and extreme optical damage.

Explosion
A conflagration in an exploding ammunition dump looses a series of fires and radiant light effects. Great tongues of flame lick the sky as convoluted volumes of smoke billow upward. Innumerable small fires spread across the ground while the dark sky is rent with a pyrotechnical display of bursting shells, flares, and tracers. It is a garish scene of multicolored radiance, fearful and awesome, yet perversely fascinating.

Fiery Lava
Looking closely at the aftermath of the volcanic explosion, we see the radiant light of the glowing, molten rock, flowing down the sides of the mountain, shooting out sparks and flames, and exuding gaseous smoke. It is an awesome scene, like the open bowels of hell itself.

Volcanic Eruption
Here is another display of light
and energy on a grand scale. As
molten lava pours onto the
flanks of the mountain in fiery
rivers, columns of dust, smoke,
gaseous flames, and sulfurous
debris obscure the sun. The
light is as dim as moonlight,
and flashes of lightning strike
across the gloom. There are
many aspects of radiant light in
this drawing, from the pale
glow of the sun to the fiery explosion below. Each effect de-
serves close examination.

Radiant Light in Space
The jet nozzles of a space
rocket emit hot gases in an incandescent stream of radiant
light, similar to the bright tail
of a comet. As the jet craft
moves at enormous speed,
without gravity or friction, we
see multitudes of distant,
gleaming stars, like radiant
pinpoints everywhere in the
velvety, infinite dark.

CHAPTER 15

EXPRESSIVE LIGHT

Subjective Light
Until now, we have dealt mainly with actual light conditions—objective light that we can see in nature. Now we turn to nonvisual, subjective light—various kinds of light that are invented by the artist to deal with internal, subjective, emotive qualities of mood and introspection. Among these are mystic light that emanates from the human form like a halation to suggest spiritual energy or divine power; light that reveals an emotion or a state of mind, such as emotional stress, alienation, loneliness, or pain; suggestive light, in which a minimal use of tone conveys an emotional message; and light as design, which means organizing the lights and darks to create a pictorial structure that will direct the eye along a specific track.

Spiritual Light and Earthly Light
Albrecht Dürer's woodcut of the *Madonna on the Crescent* shows two kinds of light: spiritual and earthly. The spiritual light of the Virgin and Child radiates glory into the universe, while the sickle moon sends golden rays outward into the cosmos, and the bright stars gather and dance in a halo of divine light above the Virgin's head. In contrast to this subjective, nonvisual light, the forms of the figures are shown in earthly, sculptural light that is not governed by the transcendent heavenly glow.

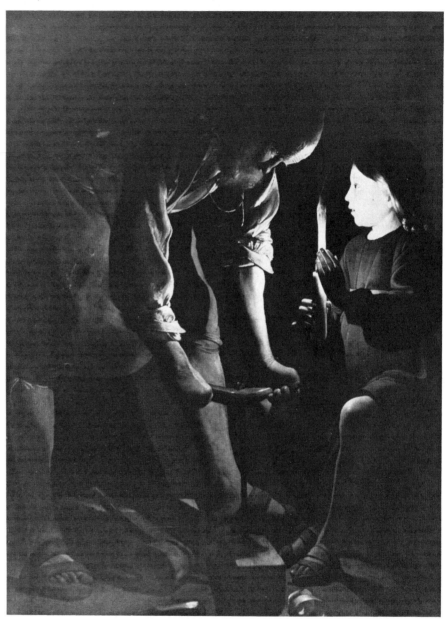

Symbolic Light
Georges de La Tour's *Saint Joseph the Carpenter* seems, at first glance, to exhibit the radiant light described in the previous chapter. Naturalistic light appears to come from an objective source: the burning candle held by a young boy who helps his father with his work. But the man is Joseph the Carpenter, husband of the Virgin Mary, and the boy is none other than the youthful Jesus. Thus, the carefully shielded candle flame is a symbol of the light of God, which falls full on Jesus' face, lights up Joseph at his "goodly works," and is the metaphor for the light that now illuminates the dark void of the world.

Mystic Light
In the Christian tradition, a holy person is illuminated by the *chiaroscuro* that is typical of Baroque art. Deep pools of shadow underscore the lines and forms of this face that has known travail and sorrow. But a faint light is seen above his head, appearing like a crown with rays that fan outward into the world. It is important to note that this subtle halo is *not* the same naturalistic light that illuminates the face of the saint. The halo is an unearthly, mystical light that issues from within the person, expressing his state of grace.

145

Light as Revelation

In a tale told by Edgar Rice Burroughs, "The God of Tarzan," the Jungle Man discovers his personal God of the Universe. Here, in a moment of insight, he faces the light and hails the source of the mystery with upraised arms and hands open in benediction. At the same moment, a white bird with upraised wings—divinely inspired—is about to alight. The glow of the sky magically illuminates the tranquil scene. The man wordlessly greets the miracle as the branches unite their flowery growths to form candelabras that send shoots skyward like living, holy flames.

Charismatic Light

Mystic light is not always cast in a religious mode. Illustrator Don Punchatz conveys both physical and mystical power in this vision of a strong man who wears athletic briefs like a comic book Captain America, flexes his muscles, and displays a radiant heart of strength on his chest. The clenched teeth and gripped hands signalize—with the heart that glows like an incandescent lightbulb—the hero's power to prevail over the influences and temptations that surround him.

Metaphoric Light

A multitude of twinkling, ephemeral lights occur throughout this painting, *Icon of Homage to the Moon Queen*. She is the Great Mother, a fertility symbol as well as a seductive Broadway queen of the night. She is surrounded by lights that refer to the symbolism of ancient cultures—Egyptian, Greek, Buddhist, Christian—as well as contemporary society. The Egyptian Eye of Divine Perception, *Sia*, is in the upper left. The totemic bird halo—vulture, eagle, and crow—is above the head. At the right, you see the glimmering Tree of Fertility and the Lotus Flower. And throughout the painting, flashes of light suggest the glitter and gaudiness of Broadway after dark.

Phosphorescent Light

A luminous halation appears around the head and body of this figure in a painting titled *My Brother Abel*. The arbitrary, phosphorescent light—distinct from the objective light on the figure itself—suggests energy that radiates from the body, symbolizing life, vitality, and resistance to pain and suffering.

Softened Edges

In this reflective, sober drawing of *The Scholar*, the light sits high on the head, obliterating the contour. The shadows descend in characteristic Baroque chiaroscuro, the forms becoming lower in value as they fall away from the light. The most important darks are the pools of shade that obscure the eyes. The drawing avoids hard-edged forms, thus producing a warm mood of profound calm.

Evocative Light
The uncertain, diffused light is charged with mood and feeling. The vague, subjective light and shade communicates the wan, pallid woman's intimations of death, her sense of life ebbing away.

Fragmentary Light
The uncertainty and decrepitude of old age are conveyed by the fragmentary pattern of the light and shade. The shadows are gloomy and the forms washed out, spare, and dehydrated.

Irregular Light
The broken, irregular pattern of light and shade—with the thick, blotchy shadows—expresses the mood of a prize fighter who has seen his best days slip away into an unending series of fights. The head is like a battlefield, a physiognomic record of defeat.

Fluid Light and Shadow
The fluid handling of ink wash and line captures the distorted pattern of the light and shade on the head of Jake the "wino." This pattern communicates the texture of a life steeped in discord, a life wrenched and warped, dissolved in the need to drink. The ragged light reveals a human discard.

Planes of Shadow
The handling of the light and shade was inspired by Stanton's famous comment on the Great Emancipator's death: "Now he belongs to the ages." The brooding image appears to be carved from stone in firm-edged planes. To create this feeling, the shadows are laid in with a single-edged razor blade, troweling tones of tempera. The entire effect depends upon using the tool to render the pattern of light and shade as simply as possible.

Spasmodic Light
This portrait of Stravinsky uses light and shade to suggest the character of the composer's music—often harsh, dissonant, bold, and unpredictable in its rhythms, and with sporadic changes of key. Thus, the tones are loose and fluid, with dislocated accents, frequent darks, and sudden lights.

Multiple Tonalities

In this painting, *A Recollection of Lascaux*, there is no special source of light, but there are multiple light effects that act in counterpoint, like separate musical lines. The figure of the bull is the pivotal form in the painting, partially laid in with deep form shadows and partly with emphatic linear contours—to recall the feeling of line, form, and texture in a prehistoric cave painting on a stone wall. The background values are uneven and oscillating lights and darks that create a dense, yet cloudlike effect. Here and there, disembodied elements appear: the bony hand print of a dead hunter in the upper left; the wasted face of modern man, the hunter, with a radiant, atomic eye, in the lower left. Each component of the painting has its own kind of light.

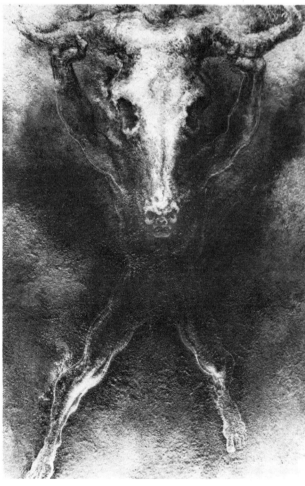

Light and Texture

The figure in *Totem Dance* hovers in the superheated, poisoned atmosphere of a nuclear explosion. The allegorical death's head speaks of the oncoming nightmare. The drama is played in two kinds of light, one from above and the other from below. (In the painting, the upper light is blue-green and the lower light is yellow-orange.) The oppressive drama of the light is accentuated by the palpable, gritty texture of the painting surface. A granular material was mixed with the paint to make the gloomy atmosphere more ominous, the flickering light more lurid and uncertain. Imagine how bland this would look if the surface were flattened and spread thin.

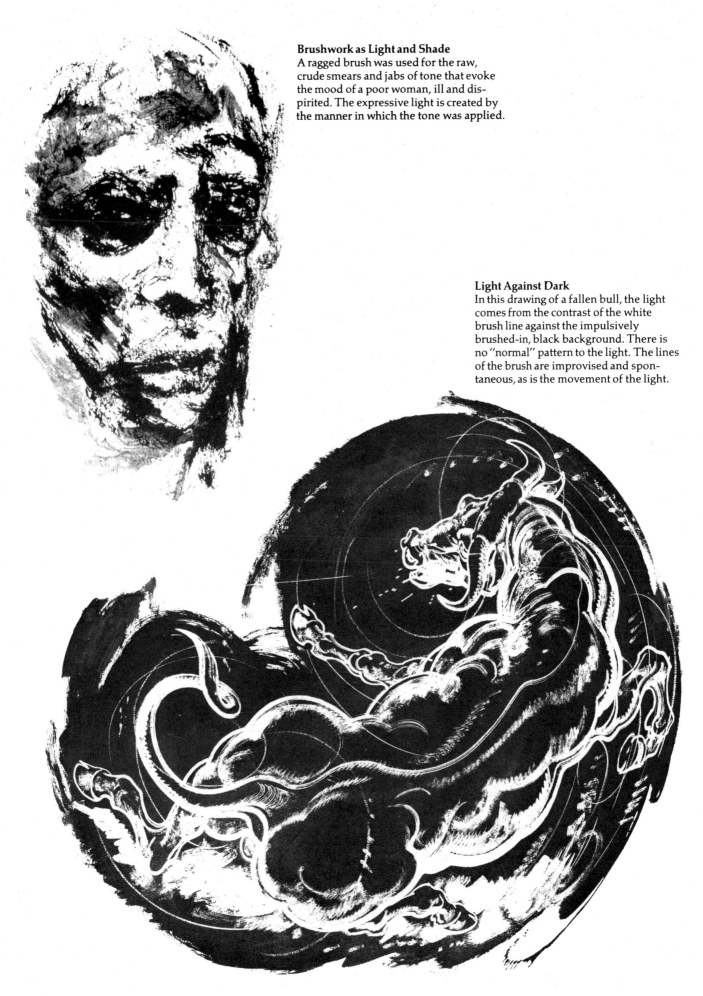

Brushwork as Light and Shade
A ragged brush was used for the raw, crude smears and jabs of tone that evoke the mood of a poor woman, ill and dispirited. The expressive light is created by the manner in which the tone was applied.

Light Against Dark
In this drawing of a fallen bull, the light comes from the contrast of the white brush line against the impulsively brushed-in, black background. There is no "normal" pattern to the light. The lines of the brush are improvised and spontaneous, as is the movement of the light.

151

Hallucinatory Light

The feverish jungle lord sees a hallucinatory demon, whose coiled form is represented by light, rendered with halations and linear strokes. The small, glittering suns represent glare spots before the man's feverish eyes. And the movement of the lurching body is indicated with speed strokes that are like lines of light.

Inferential Light

The jungle man is afflicted with a nightmare brought on by a raging fever, symbolized by the flames that issue from the body and through the enlarged, feverish head with its contracted pupils. The light expresses the body heat.

Decorative Light
In this romantic evocation of an Italian Renaissance prince, the decorative pattern of light and dark conveys elegance, extravagance, and ostentatious wealth. Everything sparkles with jeweled detail, decorative emblazonment, precise chasing, delicate needlework and beadwork, lavish filigree and embossing. The decorative pattern of the drawing infers a crisp, clear light that lets us see every detail close at hand.

153

Light as Pictorial Design

Here the organization of lights and darks
controls the design flow of the picture.
The pattern of light and shadow follows a
curving track like a reverse letter C that
curves around from the top left, to the
right, and then swings left again at the bottom of the picture. As shown here, such a
track should be simple and direct.

Light and Dark Create Visual Flow
The lights and darks in this drawing create
a visual flow pattern like a spiral nebula.
The motif begins with the crossed arms of
the central figure—the top arm moving left
and the bottom arm thrusting right. From
here, the direction of the lights and darks
becomes a sweeping, counterclockwise,
circular flow pattern.

EPILOGUE

I began *Dynamic Light and Shade* with confidence that I would easily cover the material at hand. But as time went on, the territory broadened, and new possibilities emerged that became more varied and complex. I found that the subject of light and shade could involve the entire gamut of art, for whenever form is revealed, it must be defined by some kind of light. Hence, this book barely scratches the surface of this fascinating phenomenon.

I hope you will regard *Dynamic Light and Shade* as a beginning—a preliminary glimpse of a vast, unexplored continent—and that you will be inspired to probe deeper into your own work, finding new insights that will open the boundaries to new solutions of these intriguing problems.

**Geometric Light
and Shade Pattern**
The design pattern of the lights and darks is a very large triangular motif that is built into the elephant's body, and dominates the entire picture. Follow the dark elements, beginning with the head and moving down the outstretched legs. Like the previous two designs, the concept is bold and simple.

SUGGESTED READING

Austen, John. *Shakespeare's Hamlet*. London: Selwyn and Blount, Ltd. (no date).

Ayensu, Edward S., Editor. *Jungles*. New York/Washington, D.C.: Crown Publishers, Inc. and Smithsonian Institution, 1980.

Bayros, Marquis Von. *The Amorous Drawings of The Marquis Von Bayros*. New York: The Cythera Press, 1968.

Bertieri, Claudio. *Graphicar*. Milan, Italy: Fiat, 1976.

Bindman, David. *European Sculpture from Bernini to Rodin*. London: Studio Vista Limited and New York: E.P. Dutton and Co., 1970.

Bittner, Herbert. *Kaethe Kollwitz Drawing*. New York and London: Thomas Yoseloff, Publisher, 1963.

Blaustein, John, and Edward Abbey. *The Hidden Canyon*. New York: Penguin Books, 1977.

Boatner, Charles K., director. *Man . . . An Endangered Species?* Conservation Yearbook No. 4. Washington, D.C.: Department of the Interior, 1968.

Bouma, P. J. *Physical Aspects of Color*. Eindhoven, Netherlands: N. V. Philips Gloeilampen Farbriken, 1947.

Brander, Bruce. *The River Nile*. Washington, D.C.: National Geographic Society, 1966.

Breeden, Robert L., ed. *Nomads of the World*. Washington, D.C.: National Geographic Society, 1971.

Brown, Dale, and editors of Time-Life Books. *The World of Velasquez*. New York: Time-Life Books, 1969.

Campbell, Gordon, and Jim Ivey. *Roy Crane's Wash Tubbs*. New York: Luna Press, 1974.

Cook, Olive, and Edwin Smith. *English Cottages and Farmhouses*. New York: The Studio Publications, Inc., with Thomas Y. Crowell Company, 1955.

Doré, Gustave. *The Doré Bible Gallery*. Philadelphia: Herny Altemus (no date).

Driskell, David C. *Two Centuries of Black American Art*. New York: Alfred A. Knopf and the Los Angeles County Museum of Art, 1976.

Dunham, Barrows. *The Artist in Society*. New York: Marzani and Munsell, Inc., 1960.

Eliot, Alexander. *Three Hundred Years of American Paintings*. New York: Time Inc., 1957.

Feininger, Andreas. *Trees*. Penguin Books, 1968.

Ferris, Hugh. *The Metropolis of Tomorrow*. New York: Ives Washburn, 1929.

Flexner, James Thomas. *American Painting*. New York: Pocket Books, Inc., 1950.

Forrestal, James, Introduction. *U.S. Navy War Photographs*. Washington, D.C.: Department of the Navy, 1945.

Fowles, John. *Islands*. Boston/Toronto: Little Brown and Co., 1978.

Frenzel, Prof. H. K., ed. *Ludwig Hohlwein*. Berlin: Phoenix Illustrationsdruck und Verlag, GMBH., 1926.

Friedlaender, Max J. *On Art and Connoisseurship*. Boston, Beacon Press, 1960.

Gallant, Roy A. *Our Universe*. Washington, D.C.: National Geographic Society, 1980.

Goethe, Johann Wolfgang von. *Theory of Colors*. Cambridge, Massachusetts: M.I.T. Press, 1970.

Grosser, Maurice. *The Painter's Eye*. New York: Mentor Books, 1956.

Guptill, Arthur L. *Drawing with Pen and Ink*. New York: The Pencil Points Press, Inc., 1928.

Haftmann, Werner. *Painting in the Twentieth Century*. New York: Frederick A. Praeger, 1961.

Hawthorne, Charles W. *Hawthorne on Painting*. New York: Dover Publications, Inc., 1938.

Henri, Robert. *The Art Spirit*. Philadelphia: J.B. Lippincott Company, 1960.

Hess, Thomas B., and John Ashbery, ed. *Avant Garde Art*. London: Collier-Macmillan, Ltd., 1967.

Himmel, Paul, and Terry, Watler. *Ballet in Aciton*. New York: G.P. Putnam's Sons, 1954.

Hirsh, Diana, and editors of Time-Life Books. *The World of Turner*. New York: Time-Life Books, 1969.

Holme, Charles, ed. *Sketching Grounds*. London/Paris/New York: The Studio, 1909.

Horswell, Jane. *Bronze Sculpture of "Les Animaliers."* Suffolk, England: The Antique Collectors Club/Baron Publishing, 1971.

Jaques, Florence Page and Francis Lee. *Snowshoe Country*. Minneapolis: University of Minnesota Press, 1944.

Koningsberger, Hans, and editors of

Time-Life Books. *The World of Vermeer*. New York: Time-Life Books, 1967.

Kostelantetz, Richard, ed. *The New American Arts*. New York: Collier Books, 1965.

Krenkel, Roy G. *Cities and Scenes from the Ancient World*. Philadelphia: Owlswick Press, 1974.

Langui, Emile (Introduction). *50 Years of Modern Art*. New York: Frederick A. Praeger, 1959.

Latouche, John, and Andre Cauvin. *Congo*. U.S.A.: Willow, White and Co., 1945.

Levey, Michael. *A Concise History of Painting*. New York: Frederick A. Praeger, Publishers, 1962.

Lorentz, Pare. *The River*. New York: Stackpole Sons, 1938.

Lucie-Smith, Edward, and Celestine Dars. *Work and Struggle: The Painters as Witness*. New York/London: Paddington Press, Ltd., 1977.

Luckiesh, M. *Color and Its Applications*. New York: D. Van Nostrand Company, 1915.

———*Visual Illusions*. New York: Dover Publications, Inc., 1965.

Lundh, Gunnar. *Midsummer in Sweden*. Sweden: LTs Forlag, 1963.

Marshall, Gen. George C., Introduction. *Our Army at War*. New York: Harper and Brothers, 1944.

Mathey, François. *The Impressionists*. New York: Frederick A. Praeger, 1961.

Minnaert, M. *Light and Colour*. New York: Dover Publications, Inc., 1954.

Mitchell, Carleton. *Isles of the Caribbees*. Washington, D.C.: National Geographic Society, 1966.

Muller, Joseph-Emile. *Klee Magic Squares*. New York: Tudor Publishing Co., 1957.

———. *Modern Painting: Expressionists to Surrealists*. New York: Tudor Publishing Co., 1965.

Neumeyer, Alfred. *The Search for Meaning in Modern Art*. Englewood Cliffs, N.J.: Prentice-Hall, Inc., 1964.

Novak, Barbara. "The Meteorlogical Vision: Clouds," *Art in America*, No. 2, February, 1980.

Pivar, Stuart, *The Barye Bronzes*. Suffolk, England: Baron Publishing, 1974.

Pitz, Henry, C. *Pen, Brush and Ink*. New York: Watson-Guptill Publications, 1949.

Poe, Edgar Allen, and Harry Clarke. *Tales*

INDEX

of Mystery and Imagination. New York; Tudor Publishing Co., 1939.

Prideaux, Tom, and editors of Time-Life Books. The World of Delacroix. New York: Time-Life Books, 1966.

Richardson, E.P. A Short History of Painting in America. New York: Thomas Y. Crowell Company, 1963.

Ritchie, Andrew Carnduff. Masters of British Painting, 1800–1950. New York: The Museum of Modern Art, 1956.

Robert, Ainslie, and Charles P. Mountford. The Dreamtime Book. Englewood Cliffs, N.J.: Prentice-Hall, Inc., 1973.

Rudd, Clayton, ed. "Canyonland," Naturalist, vol. 21, no. 2, Special Issue. Minneapolis: Natural History Society, 1970.

Schreider, Helen and Frank Schreider. Exploring the Amazon. Washington, D.C.: National Geographic Society, 1970.

Schultz, Guenther. Under Sail Round Cape Horn. New York: Dodd, Mead and Company, 1954.

Simon, Howard. 500 Years of Art in Illustration. New York: Garden City Publishing Co., Inc., 1949.

Symons, Arthur. The Art of Aubrey Beardsley. New York: Boni and Liveright, Inc., 1918.

Sypher, Wylie, ed. Art History: An Anthology of Modern Criticism. New York: Vintage Books, 1963.

Thiessing, Frank C., ed. Ernie. St. Gall, Switzerland: Zollikofer and Co., 1948.

Traeger, Jorg. Caspar David Friedrich. Munich: F. Bruckmann KG Verlag, 1976.

U.S. Department of the Interior. Our Living Land, vol. 7, Conservation Yearbook Series, 1971.

Wallace, Robert, and editors of Time-Life Books. The World of Rembrandt. New York: Time-Life Books, 1968.

Walker, Jearl, Introduction. The Physics of Everyday Phenomena. San Francisco: W.H. Freeman and Co., 1979.

Wertenbaker, Lael, and editors of Time-Life Books. The World of Picasso. New York: Time-Life Books, 1967.

Wolf, Thomas H. The Magic of Color. New York: Odyssey Press, 1964.

CHOREOGRAPHY

A Basic Approach Using Improvisation

SECOND EDITION

Sandra Cerny Minton, PhD

University of Northern Colorado, Greeley

Human Kinetics

Library of Congress Cataloging-in-Publication Data

Minton, Sandra Cerny, 1943-
    Choreography : a basic approach using improvisation / Sandra Cerny
Minton. -- 2nd ed.
      p. cm.
    Includes bibliographical references (p.) and index.
    ISBN 0-88011-529-7
    1. Choreography.   I. Title.
    GV1782.5.M56   1997
    792.8'2--dc21   96-48348
                                        CIP

ISBN: 0-88011-529-7

Figures 1.5, 1.6, and 4.5 are from Dance Collection, The New York Public Library for the Performing Arts, Astor, Lenox and Tilden Foundations. **Figure 2.4** is adapted, by permission, from S.C. Minton, 1991, *Modern dance: Body and mind,* Englewood, CO: Morton Publishing, 104. **Figure 2.18** is by James Klosty. Dance Collection, The New York Public Library for the Performing Arts, Astor, Lenox and Tilden Foundations. **Figure 2.19** is by Stephen Petegorsky. Dance Collection, The New York Public Library for the Performing Arts, Astor, Lenox and Tilden Foundations. **Figure 2.20** is by Monica Moseley. Dance Collection, The New York Public Library for the Performing Arts, Astor, Lenox and Tilden Foundations. **Figure 3.1** is adapted, by permission, from L.A. Blom & L.T. Chaplin, 1982, *The intimate act of choreography*. Pittsburgh: University of Pittsburgh Press. **Figure 3.2** is adapted, by permission, from illustrations in Doris Humphrey, 1987, *The Art of Making Dances,* Pennington, NJ: Princeton Book Co. **Figures 3.3 and 3.4** are by Arnold Eagle. Dance Collection, The New York Public Library for the Performing Arts, Astor, Lenox and Tilden Foundations.

Acquisitions Editor: Judy Patterson Wright, PhD; **Developmental Editors**: Dawn Cassady and Julia Anderson; **Assistant Editors**: Jacqueline Blakley and Andrew Smith; **Editorial Assistant**: Coree Schutter; **Copyeditor**: Regina Wells; **Proofreader**: Jacqueline Seebaum; **Indexer**: Theresa Schaefer; **Graphic Designer**: Stuart Cartwright; **Graphic Artist**: Sandra Meier; **Cover Designer**: Jack Davis; **Photographer (cover and interior)**: Joe Clithero of B & J Creative Photography, unless otherwise indicated; **Illustrators**: Ilene Van Gossen and Jennifer Delmotte; **Printer**: United Graphics

Human Kinetics books are available at special discounts for bulk purchase. Special editions or book excerpts can also be created to specification. For details, contact the Special Sales Manager at Human Kinetics.

Printed in the United States of America   10 9 8

Human Kinetics
Web site: www.HumanKinetics.com

United States: Human Kinetics, P.O. Box 5076, Champaign, IL 61825-5076
800-747-4457
e-mail: humank@hkusa.com

Canada: Human Kinetics, 475 Devonshire Road, Unit 100, Windsor, ON N8Y 2L5
800-465-7301 (in Canada only)
e-mail: orders@hkcanada.com

Europe: Human Kinetics, 107 Bradford Road, Stanningley
Leeds LS28 6AT, United Kingdom
+44 (0) 113 255 5665
e-mail: hk@hkeurope.com

Australia: Human Kinetics, 57A Price Avenue, Lower Mitcham, South Australia 5062
08 8277 1555
e-mail: liahka@senet.com.au

New Zealand: Human Kinetics, P.O. Box 105-231, Auckland Central
09-523-3462
e-mail: hkp@ihug.co.nz

To my parents, who made me aware
of the value of an education and of having perseverance;
to all the teachers who encouraged my creative projects and ideas;
and to my husband, Clarence Colburn,
who had infinite patience during the completion of this book.

Contents

Preface

This book invites choreography students to share the joys of creating in movement by discovering the infinite variety that can be found within the dance art form. Movement is thus viewed as a medium for artistic expression. At the same time, I hope the information here will help you to become more aware of the subtleties found in the movements of daily life so you can use these new perceptions to enhance creativity in composing dances. The basic ideas and suggestions provided are adaptable to creative work in different dance forms, and many of the dance concepts can be used for modern, jazz, ballet, or tap dance choreography.

I based this text on my many years of experience in teaching and directing dance. Throughout, I've used my experiences to help you become comfortable with the creative process of forming movement into dances. The book uses a basic approach and is arranged so that you begin creating by using a discovery process. Whereas the first edition of *Choreography* began with a discussion of form and addressed movement discovery later, here the order of materials has been changed to help you create with a sense of freedom and without concern for immediately shaping movement into a form.

Improvisation—the key to the choreographic process—is the focus of chapter 1. Improvisation is the ability to explore spontaneously and conceive dance movements that are representative of an *idea*, a concept, or a dance style. Many motivations are suggested for movement discovery, along with exercises to help you use these motivations. You'll also find solutions to common problems for beginning choreographers, including the ability to focus, to work through creative blocks, and to learn to remember movement. I hope you can use the information provided to avoid some of the difficulties typically experienced by beginners during the initial stages of creating.

Chapter 2 explains the use of the craft of choreography in designing and shaping the dance. You'll learn how to make more out of less by manipulating and varying the movements discovered through improvisation. The material has been expanded in this edition to include more information on how to use nontraditional choreographic methods. Use of stage space is also discussed.

In chapter 3 you are given an idea of what to strive for in shaping and forming a dance, as well as descriptions of dance forms commonly used by choreographers. Finally, in chapter 4, you are introduced to the steps involved in putting your dance onstage.

You'll find that the chapters are organized similarly. Exercises entitled "Developing Your Skills" allow you to apply the knowledge you've learned from the text. Exercises are arranged from simple to more complex, with personal and feeling-oriented experiences introduced later, so that you can gradually gain confidence with creative work. These exercises have been created to appeal to people with different learning styles—*visual, auditory, kinesthetic* (emphasizing movement), and even *tactile* (emphasizing sense of touch). You'll note that some of the exercises are intended for one person, while others are for groups. If you lead a group through these exercises, remember to choose your words carefully so that your descriptions are precise and movement-oriented. For example, if you want your dancers to twist or rotate the arm at the shoulder, instruct them to turn the arm with the palm up and then down, rather than telling them to make circles with their arms. Chapters 3 and 4 include exercises entitled "Experience in Action," which guide you step by step through the process of observing a finished dance by focusing on specific aspects of the choreographic craft. Each chapter ends with a list of questions, designed to help you organize your own ideas as they relate to the materials presented.

The two appendices at the end of the book are also new to this edition. Appendix A contains information about sources for dance videotapes, music copyright, dance floors, and lighting equipment. In appendix B you will find forms to help you

assess your finished dance and plan a performance. One of the forms, the Choreographic Assessment Sheet, can be used to discuss and compare works created by different choreographers. A glossary is also included. To help you identify glossary terms, each is italicized when it is first used in the text.

While a book, by its nature, is organized in a linear manner, the creative process itself can best be described as circular. As you choreograph, you will probably find that discovery of movement materials occurs along with forming those materials into a dance. You'll also likely find that dance making involves a cyclic process in which you will repeatedly use the materials presented in the first three chapters of this book. Movements you discover through the creative process will be molded by your knowledge of craft and form, so that you gradually refine your raw materials with increased insight to produce a finished dance. This process should become easier with practice and through observing the choreography of others. Many of the exercises you'll encounter here encourage you to observe finished dances, and to keep a journal of your observations. It is also recommended that you keep a journal of all your choreographic ideas and movement materials throughout the dance making process. According to Lavender (1996), writing is an important part of learning to choreograph, because it causes you to reflect and thus encourages greater perspective and clarity of thought than simply engaging in an impromptu discussion.

Another goal of this second edition is to increase your understanding of the recently published National Dance Content Standards. These seven standards deal with both the technical and creative aspects of dance, outlining what students should know and be able to do as related to each of the standards. The seven National Dance Content Standards (National Dance Association 1994, pp. 28-31) are:

1. Identifying and demonstrating movement elements and skills in performing dance.

2. Understanding choreographic principles, processes, and structures.

3. Understanding dance as a way to create and communicate meaning.

4. Applying and demonstrating critical and creative thinking skills in dance.

5. Demonstrating and understanding dance in various cultures and historical periods.

6. Making connections between dance and healthful living.

7. Making connections between dance and other disciplines.

The National Dance Content Standards are accompanied by a detailed list of achievement standards that are divided into three age-appropriate groups: those for grades K-4, 5-8, and 9-12. The publication also contains an appendix of glossary terms and a second appendix of sequential learning experiences for each standard. (You can order your own copy of *National Standards for Dance Education: What Every Young American Should Know and Be Able to Do in Dance* from either the Princeton Book Company at 800-220-7149 or the American Alliance for Health, Physical Education, Recreation and Dance at 800-321-0789.)

Each of the seven standards describes a specific area of dance knowledge or movement skills, but it will be your responsibility, if you become a dance teacher, to bring these standards to life. You can use the achievement standards to design classroom experiences appropriate for the age level, needs, and experiences of your own students. By using the standards as a guide, you should be able to provide quality and meaningful learning experiences in a well-rounded dance learning environment. Thus, you can use the information in this book in two ways: to improve your present choreographic abilities, and as a resource for the future when you might be responsible for teaching the information outlined in the standards.

The materials presented in this text relate specifically to Dance Content Standards 2, 3, and 4. Use information from the text to increase your understanding of these standards, and then put them into practice by using the exercises outlined in the chapters.

Acknowledgments

I would like to thank Dan Guyette and Charles Houghton, University of Northern Colorado faculty, and Brian Garrett and Tim Sutherland, former students, for their advice in preparing the lighting information in chapter 4. I would also like to thank the four students, Tamara BeVier, Laurence Curry, Jacob Mora, and Kaci Wilson, who posed for the studio photographs; and Cheryl Schneider, who typed and retyped this manuscript.

Exploring and Improvising Movement

have always found the creative process to be a wonderful, yet mystifying experience. It's wonderful because the *dance*, the end product, is an entity that can entertain, communicate, and inspire. It's mystifying because through the creative process the *choreographer* is able to energize a previously empty space and make it come alive. Discovering the right movement through improvisation is an important part of this choreographic process. I've noticed that when I felt strongly about improvised movement—when it felt "right"—others felt it was "right" too. Often people would later remark about the section of the dance containing such movements as being appropriate or beautiful, or as having meaning.

Chapter 1 explores the goals of the third *Dance Content Standard*—to be able to create and communicate meaning through dance (National Dance Association, 1994). This standard is aimed toward the initial stages of the choreographic process in which you discover movements that fit a motivating idea or that express specific meanings. In the beginning, choreographing involves divergent thinking, in which the creative process is important for discovering many possible movement solutions. This chapter begins with an analysis of the creative process and how its stages parallel the steps used to make dances. Suggestions to facilitate creating, such as relaxation and concentration, are also included. Following that discussion are analyses of exploration and improvisation, methods you can use to discover movement, and detailed examples of exploration and improvisation sequences. The chapter concludes with sections on how to meet challenges during the improvisation process, fit movement materials together, and find appropriate music for your dance.

The Creative Process

Choreography is a creative process that requires practice as well as some knowledge of how the process functions. It was once a popular notion that creative work occurred through divine intervention and that only certain individuals had the capacity to create. Fortunately, today we recognize that although people differ in their innate capacity to do creative work, anyone can benefit from and enjoy being creative. The task is not easy, but having a knowledge of creative problem-solving strategies should enable you to work through blocks that surface during your choreographic efforts.

Experts on the subject of creative problem solving recognize distinct stages to the process. Weisberg (1986), for instance, suggests that creative problem solving usually includes *preparation*, *incubation*, *illumination*, and *verification*. Amabile (1989) takes a similar but more defined approach, noting a five-stage process of problem presentation, preparation, incubation, *validation*, and *outcome assessment*. These five stages of creating can easily be applied to the process of choreography. In dance terms, one could say that the choreographer needs to (a) decide on a basic choreographic problem to be solved; (b) have the right kind of preparation; (c) allow enough time and work for the discovery of appropriate movement; (d) *experiment* with the use of the different movement solutions discovered in stage three; and (e) decide whether the dance needs further work or if it is complete. The stages of the creative process as they relate to the subjects covered will also be discussed in chapters 2 and 3.

The Beginning

Before you begin to choreograph, it's essential to decide on the intent or motivating factors that will guide you throughout the dance making process. This is when you as choreographer set the creative task or tasks and decide on the scope or *framework* of the problem to be solved. This first step in the choreographic process is synonymous with the first step of the creative process, and at this point you are free to select one of many directions. For example, if you decide to choreograph to a specific piece of music, the creative problem to be solved would be to find movements that correctly interpret the various qualities and dynamics of the musical score, while a choreography based on human gesture would involve exploring and then varying these gestures. Likewise, a dance growing from an emotional base would involve investigating the subtleties and nuances of these feelings.

While the choreographer can alter or change the scope or nature of a dance at a later stage, you must have a place or *motivation* from which to begin.

The second step in the creative process is preparation, which generally involves gathering your resources together so that you may begin. To a choreographer, preparation means several things. First, the process of creating a dance means developing a sensitivity to and awareness of your body so that you are able to connect with and act on *impulses* for movement. These movement impulses are closely connected with the motivation for your creative work. Keep in mind that the ability to tune in to bodily movements is not the same as having a high level of dance *technique*. It has more to do with being aware of the kinesthetic feelings or the *visual imagery* associated with each movement or movement *phrase*. Dancers who possess a heightened body awareness have a command and versatility of movement—an ability different from having advanced technique. Technique in and of itself can get in the way of creating, because it can cause the choreographer to think in terms of steps, rather than discovering movement from a fresh viewpoint.

Choreographic preparation also involves learning about the *craft* of choreography. Craft includes such elements as:

- Understanding use of *stage space*.
- Working with the relationship between dancers.
- Using movement variation and *manipulation*.

Choreographic craft is explained in chapters 2 and 3. The important point is to use your understanding of the choreographic craft so that craft does not get in the way of creating. If you rely solely on the craft, you will have problems discovering new and inventive ways of using movement.

Research is another aspect of preparing to choreograph a dance. Choreographic research can take many forms, including:

- Analyzing your accompaniment for an in-depth knowledge of musical form, development, and feeling qualities.
- Gaining an understanding of your dancers' movement styles and capabilities.

- Studying background information on the *subject matter* of your dance.
- Learning about the philosophy of a historical period.
- Comparing elements of *design* as used in movements in the arts such as *realism, cubism,* and *expressionism.*

Through research, the choreographer finds a nucleus from which creating can begin, and from which it can continue to develop.

Developing Your Skills
Choreographic Research

1. If your choreographic inspiration is a piece of music, try to gain an in-depth understanding of your accompaniment. Listen to your music many times before you begin the movement discovery process. Gain an understanding of the metric structure, and notice where one section of the music ends and another begins. Pay specific attention to how the composer has developed the score. For example, does the music build to a high point and then come to an abrupt conclusion, or does it build and then end gradually? Be aware of changes in the feelings evoked by the music as well.

2. Determine whether the music is suitable for the *style* of your proposed choreography.

3. Many dances include specific characters or a progression of events. Listen to the music to determine if the musical form and development fit the visualized development of your dance.

4. Take time to watch your dancers move in class or in an improvisation session. Observe such elements as the dancers' preferred movement style and the specific movements in which each is particularly skilled.

5. After analyzing your dancers, visualize the point in your choreography where specific dancers might best be included, or which dancers should perform a particular role.

6. Decide if you can showcase specific dancers' abilities in one or more parts of your dance. You might even want to make a portion of the dance an elaboration of a dancer's talents.

7. Be sure to keep a journal or written record of the metric organization and dynamic changes of your accompaniment, the possible relationship between musical progression and the visualized development of your dance, and the movement strengths of your dancers. In some instances you might prefer to use drawings or diagrams to help you remember movements, relationships among dancers, and other moments of inspiration. Keeping a record of your ideas will help you recall them at later choreographic sessions.

8. Another form of choreographic preparation or research is to review background material on the subject matter of your choreography. These materials might include:

   • Historical events or episodes

   • Information about well-known personalities

   • Stories or myths associated with a specific cultural group

   • Descriptions of important artistic trends or movements such as the blues in music, impressionism in the visual arts, or the dance forms of the ancient Greeks

9. When researching background materials, take detailed notes. Later you can review them to determine which elements can be adapted most easily to a movement format. You'll find it very helpful to condense your notes and group together the elements and ideas that relate to the same character or event.

The Creative Act

The third stage in the creative process, the focus of the rest of this chapter, is the one with which most people relate original or artistic work. In choreography, the creative act is the discovery of movement for your dance. It is in this step that you generate ideas and possibilities. This stage can also involve a period or periods of incubation when the work being created is put aside for a while to allow you to test and perhaps gain some insight into aspects of the work being created. Later you can shape movement into a *composition* using your knowledge of the choreographic craft.

Appropriate movement is usually discovered through *improvisation*. During improvisation, the choreographer moves spontaneously while concentrating on the intent of the work. In some situations, the dancers improvise using suggestions made by the choreographer, and the choreographer then decides which movements or phrases will be included in the dance.

Before moving on to discussions of exploration and improvisation, you should be familiar with the benefits of concentration and relaxation as a part of the creative process.

Concentration and Relaxation

As a beginning choreographer, you can do many things to perfect your creativity. The first of these is to strengthen the connection between your mind and body by developing your ability to concentrate. Through better concentration, you will be able to identify and recall movements that come to you during the improvisational process because you will learn to dance and create from the inside. Taylor and Taylor (1995) recommend focusing on performance-relevant aspects of the attentional field in order to develop and maintain good concentration—learn to be aware of everything inside and outside of yourself that can aid your performance of dance movements. In the improvisational setting, this means that you should learn to focus on the kinesthetic feeling of each movement and any accompanying visual *images* that arise, while still being aware of your surroundings and of other dancers sharing your space.

Concentration is enhanced by the ability to relax and be more receptive to *movement ideas* and images as they come forth. Richard Suinn, a psychologist at Colorado State University who is

engaged in improving the performance of athletes, uses the imagery of a mental rehearsal of a successful performance to help bring out the best execution of movement skills in each competitor. The individual's concentration on mental imagery is preceded by exercises in deep relaxation. Suinn believes the key to tuning in to your mental imagery is having this ability to relax (Bry, 1978).

Authorities on creative work also discuss a state of mind that tends to be compatible with successful creative problem-solving. This state is partway between the conscious and the unconscious, one in which daydreaming and reveries take place. In his book *Imagination*, Rugg (1963) notes that creating requires one to find the threshold level of a mental state in which the mind is off guard, relaxed, and receiving messages or ideas related to the creative work at hand. In other words, you need to arrive at a mind/body condition in which your mind hovers between conscious and unconscious states and in which your body is fairly relaxed. Total and complete relaxation, however, is not appropriate, since creative work requires a sufficient amount of tension or anxiety to keep the creative act moving forward.

Many popular courses in stress reduction employ relaxation techniques. Jacobson (1976), for example, created a system called Progressive Relaxation, which enables a person to identify points of tension in the body by distinguishing them from relaxation in the same part. The reasoning is that people who have little or no sensitivity to body tension allow these tensions to accumulate, and over time they accommodate to the tensions, unaware of their building intensity. In Jacobson's method, the individual bends a joint such as the wrist in order to learn to distinguish tense or contracted muscles. Once the individual can identify a contracted muscle, the method suggests releasing the tension by permitting the body part to fall back to a neutral position.

Another good relaxation technique is to concentrate on your breathing. Learn to focus on the bodily feeling of inhaling and exhaling with each breath you take. Follow this heightened awareness of breath by deepening your breathing and by breathing into different parts of your body (Dowd, 1981). You can deepen your breathing by imagining inhaling all the way to the pelvic floor; to breathe into a body part, imagine your breath flowing into a particular body area (e.g., an arm or leg).

Mental images that suggest relaxing scenes are also helpful for releasing tension. Rossman and Bresler (1983) devised a system under which they coach their clients in various exercises that improve their ability to focus on their mental imagery for the purpose of taking better care of themselves. Rossman, a medical doctor, and Bresler, a psychologist, who have done considerable work with mental imagery, call their technique "guided imagery." In this system, imagery can be used to aid relaxation, to create a heightened self-awareness, and to influence the outcome of an illness.

Dancers can improve concentration and the *mind-body connection* by learning to pay attention to bodily sensations. You can begin to develop your ability to concentrate during *technique classes*. While you are in these classes, do not allow your mind to wander; if you find this happening, pull your mind back to the body level. At the same time, try to remain as relaxed as possible while still maintaining your concentration.

Developing Your Skills
Concentration and Relaxation

1. To learn to distinguish muscular tension, lie on the floor in a comfortable position with your legs straight and your arms at your sides. (You may want to cushion your body by lying on a mat.) Focus your attention on one arm, making it as tight and as tense as possible. Your arm should feel tense, and your hand should make a fist. Now, beginning with your fingers, relax your hand so that the sensation of relaxation flows inward toward the center of your body. Distinguish tension from relaxation by tuning in to the different kinesthetic feelings associated with the two different states. Try tensing and relaxing other body parts. Finally, tense the whole body, and then initiate relaxation by beginning at the periphery of the body.

2. Relaxed breathing can be practiced in almost any body position. For this exploration, however, again assume a position in which you are lying on the floor with your legs straight and your arms at your sides. Begin by taking several deep breaths. Imagine that your lungs are two balloons or sacks, and *visualize* these two sacks filling as you inhale and emptying completely as you exhale (Minton, 1989).

3. Another relaxation exercise consists of breathing into different parts of your body. Focus your breathing in your center, and then as you continue to breathe, see your breath extend into other parts of your body as it flows outward. Make a special effort to direct your breath into tense places in your body.

4. Try breathing in different directions as well, so that your breath flows horizontally and vertically through your body.

5. Attempt to breathe all the way down to your pelvic floor and up through the top of your head.

6. Many mental images encourage relaxation. For example, imagine that you are lying on a featherbed or on a beach on a warm day, or see your body floating or hovering above the ground. Create some of your own images. Begin by selecting a relaxing image, focus on it, and see it in your mind. (You can improve your *focus* by closing your eyes.)

7. Samuels and Bennett (1973) describe the following exercise that combines breathing with use of imagery. Take several slow and deep breaths from the abdomen. With each exhalation imagine that you are taking energy from the universe to become more relaxed; see the inside of your body growing brighter and more radiant from the center outward. This exercise is designed to produce relaxation and increased energy.

8. You can use time in technique class to learn how to focus on sensations that arise from your body. Begin by identifying the kinesthetic sensations that accompany specific technical exercises. For example, feel the widening and narrowing of the plié; the abrupt flatness of the flexed foot; the roundness of second position arms; or the spreading of the toes when the foot is flat on the floor. Also, you'll find technique class becomes more interesting if you can concentrate on such kinesthetic sensations.

Discovering Movement Through Exploration

One way to develop competence in dance improvisation is to begin with movement *exploration*. Like improvisation, movement exploration is spontaneous, and the movements that come forth are unplanned. The process of exploration, however, is guided largely by suggestions that produce fairly brief movements, while improvisation is a much longer and more involved process. Exploration is usually guided very closely by your teacher's or your own use of more superficial *stimuli*, such as suggestions for movement. Improvisation, on the other hand, begins with a motivation, but it continues because the creator is stimulated by more personal and internally oriented *cues* (Hawkins, 1988). During the improvisational process, the motivation serves mainly as a point from which you begin moving. You continue to improvise by drawing on your own inner cues and images. (See table 1.1 for examples of movement explorations and improvisations.)

You can begin exploration experiences with motivations based on the body's movement possibilities or other simple movement ideas. Novice dancers find that such motivations are concrete and easy to use. Following are some specific examples of movement exploration experiences. You may want to try some of these exercises with your eyes closed to heighten your ability to concentrate; when possible, focus on both the visual and kinesthetic aspects associated with each suggestion. As you begin to move, see an image in your mind while you concentrate on the resulting kinesthetic sensations in your body.

Table 1.1 Examples of Exploration and Improvisation

Motivation	Exploration	Improvisation
Direction	Move one arm in front, behind, to the side, and in diagonal directions in relation to your body.	Begin by moving one arm in different directions. As you move your arm, let your body follow in that direction. Try moving other body parts, letting your body follow these parts as well.
Shapes	Move one arm in a geometric shape such as a circle. Trace this same shape with other parts of your body.	Begin by moving one arm in a circle. Try circling in other parts of your body. Change the size of the circles, and then move through space as you continue to trace circles with different parts of your body.
Gravity	Lift one arm to the side of your body. As gravity pulls down on your arm, let it get heavy and move downward in response. Do this exercise slowly.	Begin by lifting one arm and lowering it in response to the pull of gravity. Try lifting and lowering other parts of your body. Continue to concentrate on the heavy feeling created by gravity. Slowly lower and lift your entire body. Practice lifting and lowering different parts of your body while you move through space.
Mirroring	Stand and face your partner. The leader begins to move by exploring the potential for movement at different joints. The other person mirrors the movements of the leader. Do this exercise slowly.	Stand and face your partner. The leader does a short movement and stops. This movement should be motivated by a specific idea, image, or feeling. When the leader stops, the other dancer moves in reaction to the leader's movement.

Developing Your Skills
Movement Explorations

Seated Explorations

All of the following explorations take place in a seated position. Use the tailor position with the legs crossed, unless it is uncomfortable.

1. Focus on your right shoulder. Lift your shoulder up toward your ear. Lower your shoulder to a centered position and immediately press it to the back. Return your shoulder to the center, and then lower it. Finally, after return-ing your shoulder to the center, press it forward and then return it to the center. Use the shoulder to connect each of these *directions*—up, back, down, and forward—with a continuous circle. Try circling your shoulder in both forward and backward directions (Minton, 1989).

2. Use the same type of exploration in the upper body that you did for the shoulder, so that you take the upper body forward, to the side, back, and to the other side. End this exploration by circling the upper body from the waist.

3. Explore the possible movements in the different joints of your arm. Notice that the shoulder, for example, has a greater *potential* for movement than the elbow. See how many different ways each arm joint moves.

4. Concentrate on your right arm, and allow it to begin to move in space. Try moving your arm in different directions and at different *levels* in relation to your body.

5. Lift your arm to the side of your body and trace a shape such as a circle. Use your arm to trace other shapes such as triangles or zigzag lines.

6. Concentrate on connecting the *flow* of *energy* from your torso with the energy in your arm. Hawkins (1988) suggests that there is a tensional relationship between the extremities and the center of the body. You can feel this relationship kinesthetically by allowing energy to flow back and forth between the center and periphery of your body. See the ebb and flow of energy in your mind while you feel the energy expand and shrink in your body. Then let the energy flow move your arm in space. Try this same exercise with other body parts.

Standing Explorations

1. Hawkins (1988) points out that dancers must contend with gravity at all times. You can use the pull of gravity to motivate an exploration. Start from a position in which you are sitting on the floor and are relatively relaxed. Allow your body to begin lifting very slowly off the floor, and concentrate on the feeling of heaviness as gravity pulls down on all parts of your body. Feel gravity's pull and heaviness as you rise. Sense your body growing taller as you lift off the floor. When you are reaching as tall as you can, descend slowly back to the floor. Be aware of body tension and the pull of gravity throughout the whole standing and sitting process.

2. As a variation, remain standing and lift one part of your body away from the floor,

focusing on gravity as it pulls down on that body part. As the body part grows heavier, allow it to give in to gravity.

3. As you stand, allow yourself to slump forward from the waist, and then slowly uncurl the body to a tall standing position. Try this slumping and uncurling action at a fast, medium, and slow tempo. Perform the same action intermittently rather than continuously so that the movement proceeds in a stop-start manner. Explore other torso movements, such as stretching up, reaching diagonally, or twisting, but continue to concentrate on the kinesthetic feeling of each of these actions.

4. Concentrate on your right arm, and allow an impulse of energy to move it. Try applying different amounts of energy to your arm, and notice where and how far your arm travels in space. Be sensitive to tensions and muscular feelings associated with a varied use of energy. Do this same exploration in another part of your body.

5. Pick a simple movement such as reaching, and try it with one arm. Make this movement as large as possible, and then see how small you can make the same movement. Finally, choose a *size* for your reach that falls between large and small. See if you can change the size of this movement without stopping. Try this same exploration with other body parts and with other movements.

6. Rest quietly in a well-aligned stance. Be aware of the swaying of your body as you maintain a normal standing position. Increase the swaying of your body to see how much you can sway before you go off balance.

7. Throw your hips to one side so that they extend beyond your base. Experiment by shifting your hips forward, backward, to the side, and in diagonal directions. Determine how far you can shift your hips before you fall. According to Hawkins (1988), balance is maintained by shifting your hips in one direction and your upper body in another.

Play with being on and off balance. Then allow yourself to shift so much that you must take some steps in order to realign and center your body. Experiment with losing and recovering your balance as you move across the dance space.

8. Move slowly around the dance space, and be aware of how your total *alignment* tilts forward as you move. You'll find that maintaining good posture is more difficult while you're moving. Practice changing the degree of tilt in your whole body as you move, and then shift a single part of your body out of line while you're moving and see what happens. Change the speed of your locomotion from slow to fast and back to slow again to see how this affects your alignment and ability to travel across space.

9. In another exploration, you can experiment with different uses of space or time. This exercise begins by moving on a basic *pulse* or beat. The pulse could be supplied by playing recorded music or by beating on a drum. Try changing the level or direction of your movements every eight *counts*, every four counts, and then every two counts. Next, try making changes in the *tempo* of your movements at similar intervals, or hold a position for a certain number of counts before continuing with your movement.

Partner Explorations

For the next set of explorations, *following* and *mirroring*, you need a partner or partners. Following and mirroring allow you to enjoy exploration experiences while developing your ability to perceive the movement of another person (see figures 1.1 and 1.2). Throughout these explorations remember that the dancer who is the leader initiates the movement, and the follower must see these movements and duplicate them. Leaders can easily find movements by exploring the *movement potential* of different parts of the body. Keep your movements slow, short, and simple in both following and mirroring exercises. If you are following, do not try to

Figure 1.1 The dancers closer to the camera are following the movements of the dancer who is farther away.

Figure 1.2 Mirroring in which one dancer is facing the other.

anticipate the leader's actions, but rather experience movement as it happens (Minton, 1989).

1. Stand behind another dancer, and attempt to follow and replicate the lead dancer's actions. Be aware of the *shape*, flow, and direction of your leader's movements. If you are the leader you may be most comfortable by beginning to move a single body part. Later, let your movement extend into other parts of your body. Attempt to connect one body shape to the next by being sensitive to energy flow and impulses.

2. Mirroring is done while *facing* another person. In mirroring, one person is again designated as the leader and the other person attempts to mirror the leader's movements. When the leader moves on the right side, the person following does the same action on the left. It is also necessary for the leader to remain facing the partner while moving, since turning back to back destroys concentration. To begin with, the leader can again explore the movement potential of different joints.

3. The next exercise is for a group of four. Begin by standing in the shape of a square. (Each dancer stands on one corner of a square, and all face the same direction, with the leader positioned in front of other group members, as shown in figure 1.3.) As the leader begins to move, the other dancers in the square follow the movements. At some point, the leader gives his or her role to another dancer by turning toward or extending the gestures toward that group member. The second dancer then assumes the leadership role without allowing a pause or break in group momentum.

4. Mirror the movements of another dancer after he or she has done each movement. (The leader's movement sequences need to be short so that the person following can remember all the actions and thus move after, rather than simultaneously with, the leader.) Continue by mirroring the leader's movements each time the leader stops.

Figure 1.3 The dancers are doing an exercise in which three of those involved follow the movements of the dancer located at the front point of the square.

5. Stand facing your partner. After the leader has done a short movement, attempt to move in a direction opposite to the direction of the leader's action. Continue moving by choosing actions that are opposite to the direction of the leader's movements, but try not to change any other aspects of the leader's actions.

Discovering Movement Through Improvisation

Appropriate movement is usually discovered through improvisation. During improvisation, the choreographer moves spontaneously while concentrating on the intent of the work. In Hawkins's (1988) view, the choreographer is guided in improvisation by the initial motivation selected for composing a dance. In some situations, the dancers improvise using suggestions made by the choreographer, and then the choreographer decides which movements or phrases will be included in the dance. Improvisation is a more complete and internally motivated experience than exploration. In improvisation, the creator has a hand in selecting the

motivation for movement, or at least part of the motivation, because it's necessary to relate to the motivation by using memories and past experiences as a stimulus for continued action. Improvisation also provides more opportunities to vary movement and get involved in the process of feeling and forming. While you improvise, be aware of how your movements connect and develop, and notice the beginning, middle, and end of your actions. When you have discovered many possibilities, find a *closure* for your movement by letting the ending develop naturally. Hawkins also contends that a successful improvisation should leave the individual with a feeling of unity, satisfaction, and fulfillment.

Going With the Flow

Once you begin improvising, allow your body to go with the flow of energy that comes forth. Dance is a nonverbal experience, and excessive thinking blocks the body's energy flow. This ability to go with the flow can be compared to being able to turn off your conscious mind and come to a mental state that is more global and less detailed. Rugg (1963) describes this state as being poised between the *conscious* and *subconscious*—receptive to images and messages from within, but in control from without. In other words, you should be sensitive to the inner motivation for movements, yet able to visualize and remember movements as they come forth. Continued practice in improvisation will help you to identify and summon this receptive state, although it may take many sessions before you're able to readily connect with the condition of mind and body that allows movement to develop freely.

Proper mental imagery or visualization is very important in many but not all improvisations. For example, you can react to the movements of other dancers rather than being guided by imagery. As you are improvising, sensitize yourself to mental pictures that may appear in your mind. These pictures usually evolve from the motivation with which you're working. Learn to focus on the images so that you can recall a picture that was particularly interesting or important to you. Taylor and Taylor

(1995) suggest that the most vivid and useful images are drawn from your most familiar memories and experiences. Practice moving while you concentrate on your mental images to see what kind of movements come forth.

Developing Your Skills
Going With the Flow

As you practice each of the following exercises, try not to think too hard or to anticipate actions as they develop; just let movement happen. It helps to be still at first in order to concentrate on inner movement impulses. Always avoid forcing this process.

Hawkins (1988) recommends closing the eyes to increase concentration when you first begin doing improvisations. For many people, moving with the eyes closed eliminates external distractions and heightens receptivity to internal and personal images. Once you have learned to concentrate, open your eyes and continue to move, but attempt to maintain your *inward focus*.

1. Lie on the floor in a comfortable position. (Use of some padding or a mat may help you feel more relaxed.) Take several deep breaths to bring your focus to your body. Begin to allow your body to follow some of the small movements that develop.

2. As a follow-up to the previous exercise, let some of these movements become larger, or let them lead you into new and extended actions.

3. Try the preceding exercises while soft, soothing music is playing.

4. Lie on the floor and visualize a setting in which you feel comfortable and relaxed. Slowly allow your body to begin to move by relating to the qualities or feelings that you experience in this visualized setting.

5. Perform the previous exercise, but gradually begin to change the image or images on which you are focusing. At the same time, allow your movement to change or develop along with the new imagery.

Stimuli and Motivations

Improvisations can be initiated by a number of different motivations or stimuli. These stimuli can be visual, auditory, tactile, or kinesthetic. Various types of *props* and imagery can also be used to facilitate improvisational experiences. Examples of each type of movement stimulus or motivation follow.

1. Visual

   - Pictures from magazines and books.

   - Colored paper cut into different shapes.

   - Various kinds of line patterns such as scallops, zigzags, spirals, or a combination of these.

   - Interesting natural objects, including shells, pinecones, leaves, or starfish.

2. Auditory

   - Recorded music, particularly modern or *electronic music.*

   - Music played live in the dance studio on drums, cymbals, bells, tambourines, or any other instrument.

   - Body sounds such as slapping, clapping, snapping the fingers, or stamping the feet.

   - *Rhythmic patterns* made with the body by slapping, clapping, and so on.

   - Vocal sounds such as hissing, clacking the tongue, or whistling.

   - Nonsense syllables, words, or even poetry or prose phrases.

   - Words with kinesthetic qualities such as ooze, melt, soar, collapse, or dart (Ellfeldt, 1967).

3. Tactile

   - Objects having interesting qualities to the touch such as furry, slimy, slippery, sharp, or soft.

   - Natural objects with interesting tactile qualities.

   - Objects providing for tactile and spatial explorations such as a chair, the inside of a large box, or a corner of the dance studio.

4. Kinesthetic

   - Pedestrian movements from daily life, including walking, running, lifting, or falling.

   - Waving, saluting, shaking hands, and other gestures from life experiences.

   - Movements from technique class such as leaping, skipping, or turning.

   - *Combinations* of movements from dance technique classes.

   - *Pathways* traced on the floor or in the space around the body.

   - Writing words or names in space or as a *floor pattern.*

5. Props

   - Various pieces of clothing pulled from the costume closet or brought from home, including capes and skirts of different lengths and fullness.

   - Pieces of material draped on the body in a variety of ways.

   - Hoops of varying colors.

   - Scooters used in children's physical education classes.

   - Sticks and poles of varying lengths and thicknesses (see figure 1.4).

   - Elastic bands that stretch in many directions (see figure 1.5). (The elastic bands need to be about 2 inches wide and long enough to form a loop to surround a dancer's body.)

   - Elasticized sacks covering the body (see figure 1.6). (Such sacks can be pulled into a variety of shapes.)

   - Scarves and streamers of different lengths to create designs in space as a dancer moves.

6. Imagery

   - Beautiful scenery, such as mountains, lakes, or plains.

- Body feelings, which can include the feeling of lying on a warm, comfortable mattress or of having your feet on a hot sidewalk.

- Dramatic situations such as pretending that you are being chased by someone or that you are finding your way across a darkened room.

- Unusual *environments* such as the inside of a block of Swiss cheese or the inside of a piano (Hanstein, 1980).

Imagery depends on memories and past experiences, and dancers are able to use various images as motivation by relating the image to their memories. Thus, imagery used for improvisation should be meaningful for those involved in the improvisation. If you have spent very little time in the mountains or at the beach, for example, it would be

Figure 1.4 The dancers are using a scooter and sticks as props.

Figure 1.5 Use of elasticized bands to create designs in space. Nikolais Dance Theatre performing *Tensile Involvement.*

Figure 1.6 An example of a sack-like costume that can be pulled and stretched in many directions. Nikolais Dance Theatre in Group Dance from *Sanctum*.

difficult to relate to these images. Instead, choose those that come from your own experiences.

Images can also be quite varied. Select motivating images that are easy to use and that suit the way in which you learn. For example, use visual images if you like pictures or diagrams, and *kinesthetic images* if you find it easy to tune in to bodily feelings. Keep in mind that visual and kinesthetic are only two kinds of imagery; table 1.2 provides a more detailed explanation of the different forms imagery can take.

Structuring Improvisational Experiences

Finding and maintaining the right mental state is important for successful improvisation to occur. As discussed earlier, the right mental state is one in which you are concentrating yet relaxed. Sufficient concentration is needed so that mind and body are synchronized and the mind is open to the impulses and flow of movement ideas from the body. Excessive concentration and effort can create tension, blocking the creative pathway between mind and body.

Creating Atmosphere

You can do several things to create conditions that facilitate the kind of mind-body connection desired in an involved improvisation session. First find an environment or place in which you can move comfortably and in which you feel content and "tuned in" to yourself. Consider size, shape, color, temperature, floor surface, and other factors in selecting an appropriate space for your creative work. Experiment with different spaces before deciding on one. The time of day you choose to work is another important and personal consideration in creating the right conditions for improvising. Think about your progression through each day and note when you feel "up"—these "up" times are likely to be your most productive. Try to do your improvising during these periods, because it's difficult to create when you feel dull, bored, or sleepy. When you must work in spaces that are less than ideal, or at times when your energy is low, you'll need to discipline yourself to stay focused. If you're improvising in a dance studio, you may also improve your focus by turning away from the mirrors.

Consider the following additional points to help create an atmosphere conducive to creative work. The physical environment—the room in which you

Table 1.2 Types of Imagery

Type of imagery	Definition	Example
Visual[a]	A picture in the mind.	Visualize your body as a star.
Kinesthetic[a]	Body feelings. What the body should feel.	Imagine the feeling of your feet on a hot sidewalk.
Direct[b]	Similar to mental rehearsal or seeing specific movements in your mind.	Visualize yourself performing a leap.
Indirect[c]	A metaphor for the movement. Exists outside your body.	Move like a dry leaf as it floats to the ground.
Specific[d]	An image directed to a particular part of the body.	Lift one arm and focus on the feeling of heaviness in that arm.
Global[d]	General images that include the entire body.	Imagine your whole body as transparent.

[a]Paivio, 1971
[b]Overby, 1990
[c]Studd, 1983
[d]Hanrahan & Salmela, 1990

choose to improvise—must be large enough to allow freedom of movement and some sense of privacy, particularly if you share the space with other dancers. In addition, you have to allow yourself enough time to get involved in the process of movement discovery. Improvisation also works best in a psychological environment of "openness." Try to maintain an attitude of daring and experimentation without worrying about how your movements will be evaluated. Schneer (1994) advises that when improvising you should use your own judgment and not feel that you need to explain your improvisation to anyone. In other words, focus on internal motivation, not on external evaluation; remain positive, and have fun during the improvisation process. The ability to get involved in creative activities is largely dependent on having the right feeling. Emotional safety, Schneer adds, is most important here because in such an environment you will feel free to be yourself. A final recommendation is to observe others who are more experienced in improvisation to determine how they create an environment that encourages the right frame of mind.

Choosing Appropriate Motivations

The types of stimuli used in an improvisation are also relevant. First of all, select motivations for improvisation that suggest movement. Consider that a noun such as "rock" or a verb such as "sit" has little potential to inspire movement. How can you move while trying to create the impression of being a rock? Waves or a river, on the other hand, have a much greater potential to stimulate movement. Second, in order to be more involved, choose motivations that relate to your world and what you know. Such intrinsic motivations, coming from your own experiences, will be more interesting and enjoyable. Third, choose motivations that are structured within a framework. The framework allows some openness and gives you the freedom to make choices and work in your own way, while limiting your movement choices to a manageable number. For example, improvisations based on body sounds are limited to exploring these sounds; motivations that deal with tactile sensations allow for improvisations within the tactile sphere. Both examples

contain a movement-related framework within which you can improvise, as opposed to having the entire scope of human movement open to you as a creative possibility.

Finally, consider how different movement stimuli relate to the different *modes of sensing* and *perceiving*. In this book, the motivations for improvisation have been divided into groups, many of which relate to specific sensory modalities. Movement stimuli, for example, which are kinesthetic, auditory, visual, or even tactile, have already been described. Be sure to practice improvising using stimuli that draw from all these senses. Initially, you may find that some of these motivations are easier to work with than others. Visually and spatially oriented individuals, for instance, find visual stimuli more appealing, while those who have musical talent may be more creative when using auditory stimuli. The key is to learn to choreograph using motivations that appeal to a variety of *learning styles* in order to expand your abilities.

Sequencing Experiences

The sequence, or *order,* of the motivations for your improvisational experiences is another concern. According to Hawkins (1988), you should begin a sequence of improvisations with those that are more concrete or structured. Examples include an improvisation dealing with auditory stimuli, or one using a prop. Hawkins recommends that later improvisations should involve feeling reactions to an imaginary situation; these are less concrete and allow you more freedom for individual responses at a time when you should be ready for such responses. It might be worthwhile to repeat feeling-oriented improvisations, because you may need more practice to get involved and relate spontaneously to these stimuli. The most important point is to have a focus or goal while improvising.

Developing Your Skills
Improvisations

Examples of improvisations are provided in the following list. Compare these experiences with those suggested for explorations earlier in the chapter, and notice here that the creator has more freedom to supply his or her own ideas. Also, in improvisation you are allowed to continue for a longer period of time in order to give your own sense of development to the movements. Notice, for example, that Standing Exploration number 5 (in "Developing Your Skills—Movement Explorations"on page 8) began with a specific movement, reaching. Improvisation number 3 in the list that follows also begins with a specific movement, or gesture, but is more open-ended than the exploration, since you are encouraged to select several gestures from a vast repertoire of human gestures and then vary them. In addition, in the succeeding improvisation, you are encouraged to create a story using these gestures. The exploration, on the other hand, tells you to reach with your arm and to limit variations of the reach to changes in the size of this movement.

As you read each of the following improvisations, pay attention to how the experience progresses. In some improvisations you are encouraged to explore freely, make some movement selections, and then vary, refine, and develop the selected actions. In other experiences you begin with a limited number of movement responses that are then developed, varied, and expanded.

1. Improvisations based on auditory stimuli are fun and also provide accompaniment. Move throughout the room trying out different body sounds, such as slapping, clapping, and snapping the fingers. Pick two or three of the body sounds that you like best, and perform these sounds together with appropriate movements. Allow your movements to vary in direction, size, level, and tempo. Vary the order of these sounds and movements, selecting an order that you like. Continue experimenting with the sequence until it fits a specific *pattern* that you can repeat. Practice the sounds and pattern as you move around the dance space, and also notice the patterns being performed by other dancers. See if you can copy these other patterns, then return to your own pattern.

Develop one of these patterns into a longer movement sequence.

2. Select an object that has a variety of tactile qualities. Touch this object and explore all its parts. For example, a hand drum is smooth on top of the head, more textured underneath, and angular along the rim; the fasteners that hold the rim to the head are smooth and sometimes cold. Focus on each of the tactile qualities present in the object, and begin to move. (One way to move smoothly is to glide, while a possible response to angular shapes is a jagged movement.) Select some of the movements you have discovered and produce your own variations.

3. Pick several of the gestures listed earlier for kinesthetic movement stimuli under "Stimuli and Motivations" on page 12, and decide how you can change each gesture. Try changing gesture size, direction, tempo, or use of energy (see the movement manipulation section in chapter 2 for some suggestions).

4. Connect the gestures used in the preceding exercise by means of a short story. Integrate each gesture into the story, and then try doing each in the different ways suggested.

5. Props can help you develop many interesting movements. Begin this improvisation by discovering how your prop moves, and then experiment with varying uses of space, time, and energy. Allow your body to travel in different directions and at different levels as you continue to move your prop. Take note of the ways in which the prop changes or extends the movement of your body (refer back to figures 1.4 through 1.6).

6. Imagine that you are in a cool, quiet forest. Feel and sense this situation. Think about the spongy pine needles beneath your feet, the sunlight filtering through the trees, small animals scampering out of your path, and the closeness of the foliage and vegetation. Begin to move while you focus on how you feel about this imagined situation.

7. Improvisations can also be created using your reactions to a beautiful natural object such as a seashell. Begin by picking up the shell and examining it carefully. Sense all of its qualities, including its color, *texture*, shape, *line*, and visual patterns. Experience both the visual and the tactile qualities of the shell, exploring its qualities inside and out. Put the shell down, and move off to your own space in the dance studio. Concentrate on your sensations of and feelings about the seashell. Be quiet initially; focus on your body and your imagery. After you have improvised for a while, find an appropriate conclusion for your movement. An improvisation that develops from sensory reactions to a shell or other natural object is an example of *abstraction*, which will be discussed further in chapter 3.

Solving Improvisational Challenges

A *study* is a short dance, and as such it should have attributes of an effective choreography (as described in chapter 3). You'll have many opportunities to do studies in your dance composition classes. The first step in creating a dance study is to discover appropriate movement through improvisation. Here again it is important to know your intent or motivation and to concentrate on that motivation when finding movement.

Most of the improvisational motivations described earlier can be molded into a dance study or a completed dance, although you might use some of the ideas suggested for exploration to develop a dance or study as well. Early studies are usually based on simple *themes*, and as you progress, you will be expected to create studies that are more complex and expressive.

Mental Blocks

As you learn to choreograph you will find that at times, your work in improvisation flows easily, and

at other times, improvising is much more difficult, and you feel "blocked." When this happens you need to be patient with yourself, since you cannot expect your mind and body always to be equally receptive. Finding ways to work through improvisational problems is part of the process of learning to choreograph (see "Developing Your Skills—Solving Improvisational Challenges," below).

Remembering New Movements

Many students have trouble remembering movements discovered during an improvisation session, but this problem can be solved through practice. Remembering improvised movement is important because later these movements will be molded and formed into a study or piece of choreography. You will find that the ability to remember movement is comparable to standing outside yourself and watching as you improvise.

Fitting It All Together

You'll also discover that movement ideas do not always come forth in a logical manner. For example, the end of a study or dance may come to you during improvisation before the middle is completed. It requires patience to learn how all the parts fit together; the ability to give form to your choreography takes time. Hawkins (1988) states that each individual needs the proper environment and enough practice and encouragement; no two people can be expected to pass through the levels of creative development in the same manner or at the same rate of speed. The goal is for the dance to fit together with a sense of wholeness, and to grow from a natural or *organic* development of movements and phrases.

Developing Your Skills
Solving Improvisational Challenges

1. A dance takes shape in stages, so allow yourself enough time for your creative urges to incubate and emerge.

2. It may help to put your improvisational work aside and come back to it at a later date.

3. You may want to try some *brainstorming* techniques to solve improvisation problems. To brainstorm, come up with all the movement materials that could be used in your choreography without judging any of them. (It may help to write these movement ideas down in a journal.)

4. Next, make a list of all the possible associations that can be attributed to your choreography. Then continue to improvise to see if you can discover new and better movements or phrases.

5. Try breaking your choreographic problem into smaller and more manageable parts, and improvise within a *section* of your dance or within restricted measures of music. When you have found suitable movement, go on to the next section of your choreography.

6. Movement memory can be improved through *repetition*. When you find a movement phrase that feels "right," go back and perform it again. You may need to repeat movements until they fit your imagery or motivation. As you repeat movements, you should find that these actions begin to be defined and clarified.

7. Movement memory can also be improved by improvising while you concentrate on how your movement might look to the audience. This requires making a part of you an external and somewhat uninvolved observer, a skill that comes with practice.

8. One method of fitting the parts of a dance together is to be aware of the evolving shape of your choreography and its development from beginning to end.

9. As you improvise, avoid forcing a composition into a specific form; let form develop naturally in relation to your motivating ideas. Gradually you should come to know how various movement materials fit together as the dance takes form.

10. If a piece seems to be taking shape in a certain direction, explore this direction even though it differs from your original conception of your work. The creative process requires that you be open to the possibilities as they occur.

Finding the Right Music

Many different kinds of music can provide appropriate accompaniment for dance. The goal in selecting music is to find accompaniment that fits the motivation or intent of your choreography. Humphrey (1987) advises that a dance should not mimic or parrot musical structure, but that the music should be a sympathetic mate, not a master, of the dance. After you gain confidence with the use of accompaniment, you might like to experiment with music that has a feeling different from the motivation behind your dance. You could create a comical effect, for example, by such a mismatch, or you might like to simply use your music as background rather than relating to it in any specific way.

Other criteria should be considered as well when selecting accompaniment. Instrumental music, for instance, usually provides better accompaniment than vocal because it allows a greater freedom for choreographic interpretation. If you use vocal music, try to avoid movements that pantomime the words; instead, draw from your internal responses. Music with variety in structure, rhythmic patterning, and *quality* also provides better accompaniment, as dancers usually create repetitious movement when working with music that has little variety. Try to avoid music performed by large instrumental groups such as a symphony orchestra, since an entire orchestra can overpower the movement of a small number of dancers. Such accompaniment requires a large number of dance performers to complement its volume and intensity. Small musical groups such as a trio or quartet usually provide excellent accompaniment for dance. Another suggestion is to avoid popular music for your dance compositions. This music does not leave freedom for choreographic interpretation because your audience will have heard these pieces many times and may have preconceived ideas about the choreography.

The foregoing recommendations refer primarily to accompaniment for *modern dance* and *modern ballet*. In the case of a *classical ballet*, such as *Giselle* or *Coppélia*, accompaniment is determined by historical tradition. Another exception is *jazz* choreography, which is best accompanied by jazz music, although it is preferable to select a jazz accompaniment that fits many of the criteria already described. The music used in musical theater productions, on the other hand, is set when a musical is first produced and should not be changed.

Investigate a variety of sources when searching for appropriate accompaniment. Local tape or compact disk stores and libraries can be good sources, particularly if they carry a selection of classical, semiclassical, jazz, and modern or electronic tapes or disks. Look for appropriate music in a number of sections of these stores or libraries; try checking under the categories of new age, meditation, folk, ethnic, historical, contemporary, and jazz music. The music of a flute, harp, or percussion ensemble can also be inspiring. Your radio can be another source of musical ideas; listen carefully, and learn to keep notes on the title, composer, and label of selections that appeal to you. Later you can order them at a store or find them in a library. Music collections owned by friends can offer some ideas as well. It's even possible to compose your own music or have someone compose it for you. Such accompaniment could be traditional or modern in sound, or be developed from words and nonsense syllables.

A Word About Copyright

Once you have selected the accompaniment, be sure to check to determine if your music is still under copyright. Scores written after 1850 and any recorded music may be protected by copyright (Schlaich and Dupont, 1988). Remember to get permission to use copyrighted music in a public performance; you will waste a lot of time if

permission is denied after your dance is completed. Your dance teacher should be able to give you some advice concerning regulations governing use of recorded music. In addition, you could talk to professionals who provide legal advice to your group or institution. Some organizations such as Broadcast Music Incorporated and the American Society of Composers, Authors and Publishers can help you with information about copyrighted music, and they may also know if your music has been used by other choreographers (see appendix A for a listing of some of these organizations). Topaz (1995) suggests contacting the music publisher so that a company representative can talk to the composer concerning permission. It is usually customary for choreographers associated with educational institutions to pay a small royalty. Make sure that you receive all permission agreements—including the amount of the royalty—in writing, and keep them on file.

Most composers, particularly those who are young and just getting established, are usually pleased to have you use their music. Many composers are also pleased at the prospect of having a different audience hear their work when it is performed or played at a dance *concert*. Remember to give proper credit in the printed program, and, if possible, invite the composer to the concert. You could also send the composer and/or the music publisher a videotape of the completed choreography, but make sure to include all credits on the tape. Royalty payments are required for the production of musicals and must be negotiated with the owner of these rights.

Working With Your Accompaniment

Before you begin to choreograph, you must know the structure of your music. Listen to your accompaniment carefully and be familiar with its musical *phrasing*, rhythmic patterning, and *tone* or feeling. Teck (1994) also suggests that you understand the dynamics, pitch, texture, style, and methods of development used in your music: *Dynamics* refers to the degree of loudness, *pitch* to choice of scale and range, texture to the density or sparseness, style to the era or cultural context, and development to the materials and methods used to create

the score. If you are using metrically organized music, know how many counts are included in each measure. Most pieces are written in 2/4, 3/4, 4/4, or 6/8 *meter*. Music written in *mixed meter* has a varied number of counts included in each bar or grouping (see figure 1.7). Modern electronic music can have more freedom in terms of metric structure so that you are free to choreograph without having to count the music. However, you still have to be aware of the changing sounds and feelings found throughout such accompaniment, because the composer has followed certain patterns in developing the score, and it is the choreographer's job to discover these patterns. The performers must also become familiar with specific sounds in the score and use them as movement cues.

Begin choreographing by listening to your music. Try to maintain a relaxed, yet concentrated state.

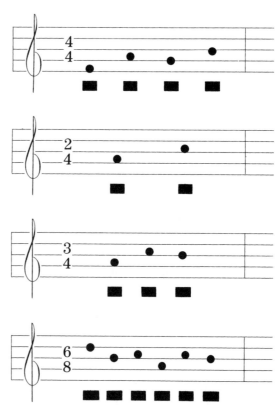

Figure 1.7 It is important for a choreographer to understand how a piece of music is organized. The dashes indicate the underlying beats in each measure for different time signatures.

You'll discover that the music brings basic ideas or feelings to mind. Continue to concentrate as you begin improvising; you'll see that certain movements and movement phrases come forth. Remember these movements, and if necessary, write them down. Later you can vary and manipulate movements to form the entire composition.

Turn the music off for a while, but continue to concentrate and improvise. This technique should help you clarify your movements. Later return to your accompaniment, performing the movement with the music. You may find yourself repeating this process of concentrating and improvising many times throughout the development of your choreography.

A dance and its accompaniment should fit together. The dance and music should:

- Exist in a complementary relationship without one component being dominant; each should have a form of its own.

- Have similar styles and evoke similar feelings in the observer without having the dance mirror or repeat musical structure.

- Relate and synthesize at certain points throughout the choreography so that the two coexist in a mutually supportive relationship.

Developing Your Skills
Working With Your Accompaniment

1. If you do not understand musical structure, you might want to refer to a basic music text before beginning this set of exercises. Select a metrically organized piece of music, and listen to it to analyze its structure. Write down a description of this structure that includes the underlying beat or pulse, the meter or groupings of pulse beats, and rhythmic patterns that occur in relation to the pulse. Note changes in dynamics, pitch, and texture as well. (Do not use music written in mixed meter.)

2. Clap the underlying pulse in the music you selected in the preceding exercise, then begin to move with this beat. Allow your body to move on every pulse beat at certain times and over the beat at other times.

3. Listen to this same piece of music to determine how the dynamics, pitch, and texture of the melody change throughout the selection. Improvise movements that fit with these changes. You should find that the music stimulates kinesthetic responses that are high, low, expansive, calm, bold, or frenzied, and so forth, as you hear different musical qualities.

4. Play the same piece of music, and move in a way that produces a simultaneous response to pulse and quality. (Remember that the pulse is the ongoing or underlying beat.)

5. Choose a piece of nonmetric music and improvise with this selection as well. Again notice changes in tone or quality and how these changes affect the quality of your movements.

Review Questions

What is the beginning of the choreographic process, and why is it important to begin choreographing with this idea in mind? How is the first step in choreography similar to the first stage of the creative process?

◆

What is the second stage of the creative process? What types of choreographic activities are synonymous with the second stage of the creative process? Describe some of these second-stage choreographic activities in greater detail.

◆

Beginning choreographers must learn how to concentrate yet relax. What does this statement mean? Describe what you could do to help create such a focused, yet relaxed state. How does this state aid creating?

◆

What is movement exploration? What is improvisation? What is the difference between them? Give specific examples of each. How do these two

activities relate to the various stages of the creative process?

♦

Why do movement exploration and improvisation aid dance making? Which process should be used when you are first learning to choreograph? Why?

♦

Select one of the suggestions for movement exploration described in this chapter and explain how you would use this technique to find movement materials.

♦

Describe how you would use one of the improvisational stimuli to discover movement. What kinds of cues or suggestions could you use to keep the improvisation going for a longer period of time? How could you relate the improvisation to your own background and experiences?

♦

Why is it important to practice improvising using motivations that draw from different *sensory modes*? In other words, what advantage is there in using kinesthetic, visual, and tactile motivations?

♦

What is imagery, and how can it stimulate improvising? Describe at least two different forms of imagery that can be used to motivate improvisation.

♦

What physical factors could you consider to create an environment that encourages creative work? Describe the psychological aspects of an environment conducive to creating.

♦

Motivations for improvisation are usually sequenced. Make some suggestions concerning how you would order several motivations in a sequence to facilitate your creative process.

♦

Explain the concept of a framework and how it relates to improvisation. How does using a framework facilitate the improvisational process?

♦

Make two suggestions to help with blocks to creativity during improvisation. How can you develop your memory of movements discovered during improvisation?

♦

Explain the following statement: Movement materials discovered during improvisation may not appear to you in the same order in which they are to be used in your dance. How might you solve this problem?

♦

What are some of the criteria suggested for selecting accompaniment? Why are these musical criteria important to the development of your dance?

♦

Describe what you could do to help you begin to improvise to a piece of music. What is the nature of this improvisational process when working with a nonmetric score?

♦

Ideally, what relationship should you try to achieve between your dance and the accompaniment? Why is this important?

Designing and Shaping the Dance

have often used the process of *movement manipulation* as a teaching tool in choreography classes. Manipulating and varying "known" movement allows creativity to take place within a solid framework so that the creative "unknown" is digested in very small bites. One former student, whose dance experience consisted of ballet technique and performance, was able to begin experimenting with movement using the manipulation approach. By the end of the choreography class, she had gained enough confidence to create a dance using *percussive* movement. She had taken a big step, since her choreography was considerably different from the style of the dance form she had studied up to that point. Manipulation, a rather concrete process, allowed this student to experiment with movement and extend her vocabulary beyond her comfort zone of beautiful, graceful movement.

Choreographers use exploration and improvisation to find movement materials, but it is craft that enables them to shape these movement materials into a dance—a process of finding possibilities and then putting the pieces of the puzzle together. This chapter relates to the fourth Dance Standard, which addresses how to apply creative and critical thinking skills to dance making (National Dance Association, 1994). You'll learn how to manipulate *space, time,* energy, and shape by experimenting with the many suggestions provided for ways in which movement can be varied using these *elements.* Choreography has the power to communicate, but the success of this communication depends on the final form of the work. You will also learn to use stage space, *unison, sequence, opposition,* and groups of dancers in relation to the intent of your dance. An analysis of some of the techniques discovered by the post-modern dancers follows, and you're encouraged to explore these techniques to make dances as well.

Once you have found movement and movement phrases through improvisation, you can begin to mold your dance. This is the point at which the craft of choreography becomes important.

Choreographic craft is the ability of the choreographer to give form to movement so that the dance has a sense of wholeness. A knowledge of craft also involves the process of movement manipulation—the varying and extending of movement. Through manipulation, movements remain compelling in repetition because their appearance has been changed and varied. Finally, by using craft, the choreographer knows where to place the dancers in the stage space to achieve maximum effect. With appropriate placement of dancers on the stage, you can heighten projection of movement and create meaningful relationships between performers.

The materials presented in chapters 2 and 3 move the choreographer into stages four and five of the creative process: validation and outcome assessment. Through the tools of craft the choreographer can check out the possibilities and see what works by using aesthetic judgment. The final form and organization of a dance can be determined by experimenting with different solutions.

Manipulating Movement

Through manipulation, the choreographer varies movements based on an understanding of the elements space, time, energy, and shape. Each of these, in turn, is an important aspect of all human actions. Movement occurs in space, takes time, is propelled by energy, and goes through a series of specific shapes as it is executed by performers.

Choreographers can use manipulation to create movement *variety* in any dance form. You can change the use of space, timing, energy, or body shape of any action, or have dancers perform the same actions on different pathways with a different use of focus or arm movements. Such variations are fun to learn and frequently test coordination at the same time.

Space

The movement element of space refers to the area occupied by a dancer or dancers, and to how dancers move in and around this area. The concept also includes how the choreographer chooses to mold and design the aspects of space. Space can be divided into aspects of direction, size, level, and focus.

A movement can go forward, to either side, and backwards. Human movement can also travel in a variety of diagonal directions, including the two diagonals in front and the two diagonals in back of the body (see figure 2.1). Dancers can move the body in all eight directions, or may simply *face* the body in any of the eight directions. (The concept of eight basic directions is used here as a point of orientation, although in reality the dancer can also move or face directions that fall between the eight.) In addition, dancers can trace many different floor patterns by moving and continually changing direction.

Choreographers can play with the possibilities in size by making an action larger or smaller. They can also change the level—high, medium, or low—and alter a dancer's use of focus, since dancers can focus in many different directions while still performing the same movement series (see figures 2.2a, 2.2b, and 2.2c). All of these changes make the same movement look different and allow the choreographer to use movements more than once in a dance. You can learn to manipulate and vary the spatial element through the skill development exercises provided.

Developing Your Skills

Space

The following exercises deal with direction, an aspect of space.

Direction

1. Stand in one spot and perform a simple *axial* movement such as bending, twisting, reaching, or stretching. Observe yourself in a mirror while you do this movement, and then try doing the same movement while you face your body in different directions.

2. Walk across the space using a variety of directions, such as forward, backward, sideways, or any of the four diagonals.

3. Use a basic walk to move around the space, and as you walk, begin to change direction on specific counts. Practice changing direction on every eighth, fourth, and second count. Then see what it feels like to change direction on every count or pulse beat.

4. Walk for 16 counts, but change direction on specific counts of your own choosing. Try several variations of this exercise by altering the direction of your walk on different counts.

5. Perform exercises 2-4 using other *locomotor* actions such as run, hop, jump, slide, skip, leap, or gallop.

6. Design a movement sequence of 24 counts in length. Use three different axial movements and two different locomotor movements to create this pattern. Create a variation of this 24-count sequence by changing the direction of some of the movements.

Size

The following exercises deal with the spatial aspect of size.

Figure 2.1 Facing dancers in different directions creates a varied effect for the audience. The dancer facing the back lacks the feeling and expression projected by the other three dancers.

Figure 2.2 (a) The three dancers demonstrate a gradually widening, or larger, movement from right to left. (b) There are three basic levels of movement—high, middle, and low. (c) Changing focus from normal or middle level to high level alters the appearance of a body shape or movement.

1. Select a common human gesture such as waving. Experiment with this gesture to see how small it can become.

2. Perform the previous gesture repeatedly, but allow it to become increasingly larger in size until it can become no larger. Notice the difference in the kinesthetic feeling when the movement is performed large, smaller, or in a medium size.

3. Try varying the size of a locomotor movement such as walking. Again, notice how it feels to vary the size of this movement. You

may also notice that there is a normal, or comfortable, size in which to perform most actions.

4. Create a 30-count sequence by using several typical human gestures combined with locomotor movement. You could base the development of this pattern on a story. Then change this sequence by changing the size of some of the movements. Decide how these changes affect the appearance of this pattern.

Level

The following exercises deal with the spatial aspect of level.

1. Walk around the space while changing the level of your walking from middle, to high, to low. Be sensitive to the different bodily feelings associated with these level changes.

2. Try altering the level of some of the other locomotor movements.

3. Walk and change level every eighth, fourth, and second count. Then try changing level on every count as you walk.

4. On separate sheets of paper, list 10 common everyday actions such as pushing, sitting down, or picking up an object. Select five of these sheets and combine the movements listed into a sequence or pattern. Then decide how many times you will perform each movement and the order in which these actions will be performed. (You may need to provide *transitional* movements between the actions.) Finally, create a variation of your sequence by making several changes in the level at which the movements are performed.

Focus and Floor Pattern

The following exercises deal with the spatial aspects focus and floor pattern.

1. Walk around your dance space, and change your focus or the direction of your face as you walk. Notice the different feeling that accompanies walking while looking down, up, or to the side.

2. As you walk, focus first in the direction of your movement, and then away from your movement direction. Repeat this altered use of focus several times.

3. Using walking steps, trace a simple geometric pattern such as a circle, square, or triangle on the floor. This geometric shape is your floor pattern.

4. As a continuation to exercise 3, alter the direction of your focus as you continue to walk in the same geometric floor pattern.

5. Choreograph the changes of focus in the preceding exercise by performing them at set intervals, but continue to move through the same floor pattern.

6. Draw a new floor pattern on a piece of paper. This pattern should carry you across and around the entire dance space. See if you can use both curved and straight pathways in this floor pattern. Move through your pattern using walking steps to trace it on the floor. You should notice that, as you move through the pattern, changes in direction are already taking place. Trace your pathway again on the floor, and this time try changing your focus. You can create other variations by adding *silences* and by changing the size or level of some of the movements.

7. You can create another interesting spatial variation by adding arm movements to the floor pattern you created. You will discover that the arms can trace many different shapes in space while the feet and legs continue to follow the same pathway using the same locomotor steps. Try moving the arms in a circular and then in a sharp or angular manner.

8. Change the position of the body while tracing the same floor pattern as in the preceding exercise. Try curving the body forward

Figure 2.3 Different ways of placing the arms and body also change the way movement looks.

from the waist, arching the upper back, or even tilting the torso to the side as you move through the pattern (see figure 2.3).

9. Perform this same pattern or combination of movements backwards, starting at the end and progressing to the beginning.

10. You can also make floor patterns by tracing your name on the floor or by using randomly selected letters and numbers placed in a sequence.

Time

Choreographers can play with variations in *timing*. You'll find that manipulation of tempo or time is easier if you move with a basic underlying sound or pulse beat. Once the pulse is established, you can try changing timing by moving faster or more slowly than the beat. Understanding how to use the element time includes working with changes in *accent* and *rhythm* as well. Accents can be created by making a movement stronger or larger to produce a point of emphasis within a sequence. Rhythms or rhythmic patterns are generated when a dancer moves at a varying tempo within a movement sequence or within a specific number of pulse beats (see figure 2.4). Adding silences or places where you hold a pose or body shape also contributes to rhythmic patterning.

Developing Your Skills

Time

1. Pick a simple movement such as an arm circle. Gradually increase the tempo of this action, and then slow it down.

2. Try increasing and decreasing the tempo of a locomotor step as well. You will find that some movements can be done faster, while others cannot be performed skillfully at a more rapid speed. Actions in elevation, for example, can't be slowed to any great degree. Try to take this exercise as far as you can by experimenting with extreme changes of tempo.

3. Choose one of the floor patterns you developed while experimenting with the use of space, and make some changes in the timing of some of the movements. Try to vary the tempo of the pattern at several points. Compare the different variations.

4. Insert some silences into one of the floor patterns you developed in the previous section.

5. You can also vary timing by introducing points of emphasis or accents. Walk around the dance space and perform a movement with one arm to indicate points of accent in your walk. Try performing these accents on specific pulse beats. For example, in 4/4 meter, accent counts one and three; then try putting the emphasis on counts two and four. Putting the accents on counts two and four creates a pulling feeling known as *syncopation*. Experiment with the use of accents in 2/4, 3/4, and 6/8 meters as well.

6. Do the previous exercise using other parts of your body to produce the movement accents.

7. Move around the dance space while taking one step on each beat of your music. Then

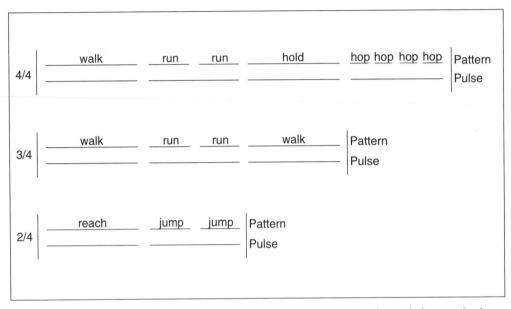

Figure 2.4 The upper row of dashes indicates a rhythmic pattern over the underlying pulse beat, shown in the lower row of dashes. *Adapted from Minton 1991.*

create rhythms by altering the tempo of your movement. In other words, you will move faster, slower, or on the musical pulse at various times.

8. Create a single rhythmic pattern that is eight counts long. This exercise may be easier to understand if you make a diagram of the rhythmic pattern first (refer again to figure 2.4). First, try clapping the pattern, and finally create this same pattern with movement. See if you can perform the pattern more than once without altering it.

9. Create a longer rhythmic pattern that includes some silences.

10. Create a third rhythmic pattern, and practice this pattern using sound. Teck (1994) suggests using body sounds such as slaps, swipes, rubbing, scratching, fist to chest, and finger snapping to provide a range of dynamics and pitch. Try to repeat the pattern with movement alone.

You will find new movement patterns taking shape as you experiment with changes of tempo or with the addition of accents and silences. Compare the rhythm of the new patterns with those in the original.

Dance Energies

Energy, or *force*, propels movement. While it initiates movement, sometimes energy or force is also needed to stop action. Energy in dance can be channeled in six basic ways, known as qualities—sustained, percussive, vibratory, swinging, suspended, and collapsing.

- In *sustained* movement, the dancer moves smoothly, continuously, and with flow and control. Sustained movement can be stopped easily at any point during the action. It lacks accents and an obvious beginning and ending.

- In contrast to sustained movement, percussive movements are explosive or sharp. They are accented with jabs of energy and have an obvious start and stop.

- *Vibratory* movement, as the term suggests, consists of trembling or shaking. It produces a jittering effect that is really a faster version of percussive actions.

- *Swinging* movement traces an arc or curved line in space. When you perform swinging movement, allow your body to relax and give in to gravity on the downward part of the motion, followed by an upward application of energy. The length of the swinging body part and the nature of the joint determine the speed and rhythm of the swing. A swing is also very repetitive.

- Dancers performing *suspended* actions hover in space, creating the illusion of defying gravity. Ellfeldt cites the feeling of hovering at the highest point of a leap as an example of suspended action, which is marvelous to observe (Ellfeldt, 1967).

- The sixth energy quality is a release of tension, or *collapsing*. A collapse can be performed at a slow or fast tempo. A dancer using a slow collapse gradually gives in to gravity, making a slow descent to the floor. A slow collapse could be described as a melting or oozing action in a downward direction, whereas with a fast collapse, the dancer drops suddenly to the floor.

A varied use of energy eliminates the monotony of performing all movements with the same quality. Choreographers should also use the six qualities to complement changes in the tone of the accompaniment or in relation to the meaning(s) to be communicated in the dance.

Developing Your Skills
Dance Energies

1. Kinesthetic understanding of energy quality can be enhanced through vocalization. In this exercise, you will sing and perform the different energy qualities. For example, a continuous blowing or whistling sound could be used with sustained movement, a harsh shout or a grunt with percussive actions, and sounds made with vibratory movement could be intermittent, like the sound made by flapping the tongue rapidly across the upper lip. After you discover sounds to fit each of the six energy qualities, try moving and making sounds at the same time to provide a kind of self-accompaniment. The movements should, of course, be performed in the same quality as the accompanying vocal sounds.

2. Select a single movement such as pushing, and perform this action using each of the six qualities. Focus on the different kinesthetic feeling each energy quality produces in your body, and notice how changes in quality produce changes in the use of space and time as well.

3. Think of a long word with multiple syllables. Decide how many times you wish to say each syllable and then say the separate syllables with a different vocal quality. Create movements to complement each of the vocal qualities you used throughout the word.

4. Choose a series of movements or movement phrases learned in dance technique class. Practice this pattern, and then change the quality in several places. Experiment with a number of different uses of energy throughout this movement combination.

5. Create your own movement combination by linking a series of axial and locomotor actions together. Determine the number and order of the axial and locomotor movements in your pattern, and then practice this pattern several times. Finally, vary this movement combination by making several changes in your use of energy.

Shapes

Shape, as used in this section, refers to the configuration of body parts, or how the entire body is molded in space. The body can be rounded, angular, or a combination of these two. Dancers can take on and discover many shapes as they move,

and choreographers can use these changing body shapes to vary movement.

Developing Your Skills

Shapes

1. Let your body assume a shape, and concentrate on the kinesthetic feeling of this shape. For instance, you might explore the different kinesthetic feelings of expansive and then narrow shapes. Try another body shape, and be aware of the kinesthetic feeling or feelings that accompany it.

2. Use a full-length mirror to study the different shapes you can make with your body. Experiment with many variations, such as high, low, wide, narrow, rounded, or angular.

3. Practice moving around the dance space, stopping suddenly in an interesting shape. (You can use a cue to stop your actions, by having someone clap or beat a drum. Then assume a shape when the sound stops.)

4. Put some of the shapes you have discovered into a series. Practice moving from one shape to another. Vary the way in which you move between the body shapes by altering how you use space, time, or energy during the transitions. For example, you could move very slowly or really fast between body shapes; you might change shape by using a straight pathway, or one that's curved; or you could change the quality of energy used to make transitional movements.

5. Choose a prop and begin to move. Be aware of the many shapes that can be created with the prop. Use a mirror to observe how shapes made with the prop can be combined with those made by your body.

6. Assume a body shape, and relate that shape to the shape made by another dancer. Move with this individual, allowing the shapes formed by both of your bodies to intertwine in space. Move over, under, around, and

Figure 2.5 The dancers are moving and relating one body shape to another.

through the shapes made by your partner. Be aware of how you both move from shape to shape. Try to remember the sequence of shapes and transitions that you created so that you and your partner are able to do them again. Create some variations of this sequence by changing aspects of space, time, and energy as indicated in the preceding sections (see figure 2.5).

You may have discovered that in the foregoing exercises it was easier for you to perform certain aspects of the elements in a specific way. For example, you may prefer a large use of space, fast movements, sustained energy, or rounded body shapes. Movements that are easier to perform, or that feel more comfortable, probably fit with your innate movement preferences. Keep in mind, however, that you should try to expand your use of space, time, energy, and body shape in order to increase your movement vocabulary. A varied use of these elements will also enable you to create dances that are more varied and stimulating for the audience.

Arranging Movement for Effective Communication

Communication through movement is sometimes the aim in choreography. At other times, choreographers design compositions emphasizing movement alone. In the latter type of dance, one of the goals is to experiment with variations by manipulating the movements in terms of space, time, energy, and shape.

In either case, the movements have a message for audience members, as the potential for communication is difficult to avoid. From the early years, children learn to recognize certain gestures, and each gesture has a message based on life experiences. Waving, for instance, is a friendly gesture, whereas a slapping or striking action is interpreted as aggressive or threatening. Humphrey (1987) says that no movement would be made at all without its being initiated by some type of motivation.

Hawkins (1988) believes that movements transmit feelings because of the way in which the elements are used in these movements. While essentially all people have learned to recognize this varied use of the elements, the recognition usually is subconscious. An expansive use of space, for example, is usually recognized as being bold; a small use of space could be timid or tentative. Likewise, viewers can see upward focus as uplifting, and downward focus as sad. Dancers who perform quick, darting movement can portray urgency or perhaps anger, and those who move slowly usually appear tired or calm. A low energy level suggests weakness, while many find energetic movement to be strong.

When out in public, learn to observe the movements of others—it can be a fascinating experience. Be aware of the way people carry their bodies and how their posture is organized. Many individuals have a postural orientation that causes a forward tilt as they walk. Others lean backward as they move, or poke their chins out in front of their bodies (see figure 2.6). Also watch the gestures people use while communicating with each other. Relate your observations to the use of space, time,

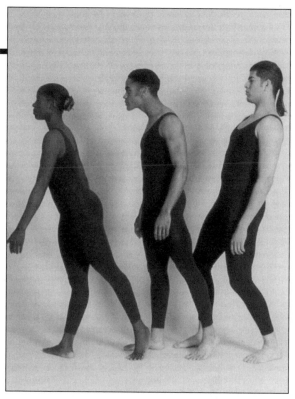

Figure 2.6 Various uses of posture project different feelings to the viewer.

energy, and shape involved, and keep a notebook or journal of the different actions you see (see figure 2.7). As you observe, keep in mind that many human gestures are specific to a culture.

Creating a Total Picture

As you view your choreography, imagine it as a painting or series of paintings enclosed in a frame. Onstage, the picture frame is already in place in the shape of the *proscenium* arch that surrounds the stage, and your dancers are the colors, lines, and figures in your painting (see figure 2.8). Decide whether everything fits together to comprise a total picture; be aware of the space between and around your dancers, since this space is also part of the total vision you create. You may notice that the space between dancers will appear to be moving as if it had a life of its own. This is true because this space becomes part of the dance as well.

Many dance critics have tried to analyze why this empty space becomes part of the choreography. Before a dance is performed, the audience sees an empty stage as a vast expanse of open space. Hawkins (1988) says that it is the choreographer's job to design movement that brings this space to

life, because an empty stage is dead until a dancer moves through and around the space. Many feel that the energized nature of this space is an illusion created by the performers' ability to throw energy outward. Langer (1957), a well-known philosopher, has described the illusion created in a dance as a *virtual entity*—one that is different from the actual physical components of bodies in motion. The virtual entity of the dance is real because we see it, but it lacks the concrete nature of our physical world. In other words, the choreographer creates a magical entity for the audience—an entity that consists of many separate movements, shapes, and energies but that, in a successful piece of choreography, forms a whole from beginning to end. The more successful the choreography, the less the actual physical components of a dance will be noticed. It is essential to think of your choreography in terms of a whole, and to keep this entity in mind when working on any part of the entire dance.

Figure 2.7 We have learned to interpret the meaning of gestures such as reaching, waving, or punching. Such interpretations are based on how space, time, energy, and shape are used in the gestures.

Figure 2.8 The proscenium arch surrounds the stage like a picture frame.

Creating a Total Picture

1. Watch a dancer move straight across the space in front of you. (You should notice how this corridor of space becomes energized or alive.)

2. Continuing from exercise 1, watch while this same dancer moves throughout the entire space. (You should notice a growing visual awareness of the whole studio.)

3. Have this same person stand in one spot and move his or her arms and legs in different directions. (You should see the sphere or area surrounding the dancer's body come alive.)

4. Repeat exercise 3 with more than one dancer, and then compare this effect to the one created previously.

5. Experiment with the location of each dancer in exercise 4. Does this change in location affect your awareness of the entire space?

Staging the Dance

A choreographer usually stages a dance following the work in movement discovery and manipulation already described. Staging a composition involves several steps, the first of which is to decide on an order for the selected actions. Then the choreographer determines which actions each dancer is to perform, and how these dancers are placed and moved around the stage space. During this process, the choreographer may move each dancer singly or arrange them in interesting groupings to create well-proportioned pictures. Beginning choreographers should consider the following ideas to help stage their choreography.

- Dancers can move in many directions, including toward the audience, or *downstage*, and away from the audience, or *upstage*. Movement to the side is to *stage right* or *stage left* according to the performer's orientation.

- The stage is also divided into a number of *areas* that differ in relative importance, so that movements performed in each of these stage areas can have a varying impact. According to Humphrey (1987), dancers positioned center stage attract the most attention, and a solo or lead dancer should perform center stage. On the other hand, she warns that the center should not be emphasized continuously, because its power is easily weakened through overuse. Upstage dancers appear remote or mysterious, whereas downstage action is more intimate and is often reserved for comedy. The areas at the side, to stage right or left, are weak (see figure 2.9).

- Various pathways onstage differ in terms of importance. Dancers who execute movement in straight lines appear strong and direct. It is very powerful, for example, to advance from

Figure 2.9 The dancer in the center attracts the most attention. The downstage dancer projects intimacy, while the two upstage dancers to the right and left are more remote from the audience.

an upstage position directly downstage toward the audience, because the dancer becomes visually larger while traveling on this path (see figure 2.10). Movement done on the diagonal pathway from an upstage to a downstage corner is powerful as well. Curved pathways lack the strength of movement performed in straight lines; when an individual follows a curved pathway, the facing changes constantly, and the visual impression is less forceful.

- Choreographers block, or arrange the movement sequences, in a dance by being aware of how the dancers move in relation to each other. When you work with groups of several dancers, do not place the downstage performers directly in front of those who are upstage. An overlapping arrangement of dancers can be very effective, but there is no reason to place an individual upstage if the

Figure 2.10 The dancer closest to the audience has moved downstage and appears visually larger and more powerful.

downstage performer completely blocks that dancer (see figures 2.11 a-c). On the other hand, choreographers should not position dancers in extreme stage right and left positions when these dancers are part of one group. This placement of performers divides audience attention, making it impossible to focus on either dancer for any length of time (see figure 2.12). However, do use a divided focus if there is a reason for having each dancer or group of dancers viewed separately.

- The direction dancers face is equally important. Choreographers should instruct dancers to face in a way that allows action to be viewed to the greatest advantage, and not in a direction in which part of the movement is hidden. Arm or leg movements executed in front of the body, for example, cannot be seen when the dancer is facing upstage. Similarly, the audience cannot see an *arabesque* when it's performed with the body facing directly toward the audience; a diagonal or side facing should be used for an arabesque instead. In addition, diagonal facings are often a much more pleasing way to view a dancer's body (see figures 2.13a and 2.13b). Take care and use discretion when placing dancers in ways that could be offensive to the audience. For example, positions that expose female breasts or the crotch could be objectionable to some individuals.

- The performer's *facial expression* may have bearing on the intent of a choreography. Choreographers should consider the dancers' faces when positioning them in the stage space, since facial expressions can enhance the appeal of a work. Remember that the impassive face is most appropriate for choreography that is devoid of feelings or messages.

Occasionally, there is a need to choreograph a *dance in the round*. Dance in the round presents numerous possibilities, but the choreographer's job is more complex because the performers are viewed from all directions. When choreographing in the round consider *blocking*, facing, and direction from all perspectives.

Figure 2.11 (a) An example of poor blocking. (b) The appearance of a group of dancers is improved with better spacing. (c) An interesting effect can be achieved by placing one dancer directly in front of another dancer.

Figure 2.12   The audience sees these two dancers separately rather than as a part of one group.

a

b

Figure 2.13   (a) An example of poor use of facing, hiding the overall shape of the movement. (b) Improved facing.

Staging the Dance

1. Have a group of dancers stand in various positions in the studio, and notice where your eye is drawn. The dancer at center should attract more attention. Assess the relative impact of the dancers who are standing in other areas of the studio. Experiment by placing the center or solo dancer at different points in the space. You may decide that you prefer to position this dancer somewhere else.

2. Watch a single dancer use straight and then curved pathways to move around the space. Decide whether straight or curved paths have a more powerful effect.

3. Watch while one dancer walks slowly and in a straight line from upstage center to downstage center. Notice how much larger and more powerful the dancer appears in the downstage position. Watch this same dancer walk slowly from an upstage to a downstage corner.

4. Arrange three dancers at points that are far apart in the studio space. Gradually move these three dancers closer together and decide at what point the dancers can be viewed as one group, rather than as separate dancers.

5. Following from exercise 4, group the three dancers so that their bodies overlap. Arrange and rearrange them so that their bodies overlap to a greater or lesser degree. Decide which effect you like the best. Finally, try grouping the dancers so that the bodies of the upstage dancers are hidden, and then have all the dancers move their arms and legs.

6. Select a body shape, and have a dancer assume this shape. Ask the dancer to face in different directions, and then decide which facing is most complementary. Notice how some of the facings hide parts of the dancer's body.

7. Have a dancer repeat a movement sequence using different facial expressions. Decide what effect, if any, the changed expressions have on movement projection or communication.

Arranging Dancers in Space and Time

Dancers move through many different singular shapes and group shapes as they perform a piece of choreography. The choreographer creates these shapes by designing groupings, and by arranging dancers in ways that are balanced or unbalanced to the eye. When the body shape of a single dancer is balanced, or *symmetrical*, the right side of the body mirrors the left side, while *asymmetrical* shapes are unbalanced from the right to the left side of the body, and tend to be off-center and more exciting to watch (Humphrey, 1987). You can use the concepts of symmetrical and asymmetrical to help you arrange groupings of dancers as well. Here the group of dancers should be viewed together as a total picture or arrangement within a picture frame. A symmetrical grouping is one in which the shapes made by the dancers on one side of the group mirror the shapes on the other side of the arrangement. In an asymmetrical grouping, the use of body shapes is unbalanced, and one side of the arrangement does not match the other (see figures 2.14a, 2.14b, and 2.14c). When arranging such groupings, see the total visual picture created by the dancers, and notice the *focal point* of the visual design. It is also necessary that choreographers see such groupings as dynamic, rather than static. The essence of dance is motion, not a stagnant positioning of performers. If dancers do hold a grouping, make the grouping interesting and have the individuals retain a sense of energy so that the group shape remains alive.

a

b

c

Figure 2.14 (a) The downstage dancer is in an asymmetrical body shape, while the upstage dancer is positioned symmetrically. (b) A symmetrical grouping of three dancers. (c) An asymmetrical grouping.

Developing Your Skills
Shapes and Groupings

1. Find several symmetrical shapes and several asymmetrical shapes with your own body. Look at each of these body shapes in the mirror and decide why each type looks different to you. Which type of body shape looks more exciting?

2. Practice grouping dancers by forming several symmetrical groupings. Then position dancers in several groupings that are asymmetrical. If performers are well placed, your eye travels comfortably around the whole arrangement. See if you can find the focal point for each grouping, and look at the kind of lines that the performers create in space with their arms and legs. Try groupings in which all of the dancers make straight lines with the parts of their bodies. Next experiment with groupings in which all body lines are curved. Finally, mix straight and curved body lines in the same grouping.

3. Try adding movement to your groupings by having the dancers move around the space while retaining a group shape. Then have them move through a grouping rather than stopping and holding the shape. Next have your dancers make transitional movements from one grouping to another. These transitions can consist of movement pathways that take them directly from one grouping to another, *direct pathways*, or they can be longer, *indirect pathways*.

4. Try building a group shape. Begin by having one dancer assume a shape, then have the other dancers connect to the first dancer to gradually form the whole group. You can continue to build new arrangements by moving the first dancer to a new location to begin a new group shape. (This exploration is easier if all dancers are given a number to indicate when they move to a new location.)

Negative spaces are another aspect of both individual and group shapes. The term refers to the

Figure 2.15 The spaces between parts of the dancers' bodies and between the dancers are negative spaces. A focal point for the whole design is located at the waistline of the middle dancer.

spaces between parts of a dancer's body, as well as to spaces between individual dancers (see figure 2.15).

Developing Your Skills
Negative Spaces

1. Look again at some of the shapes you can make with your own body. As you look at these shapes in the mirror, notice how the spaces between parts of your body are also part of the overall shape.

2. Practice moving in various shapes, and watch the changes in the size and shape of the negative spaces.

3. Arrange several dancers in a group shape, and notice the size and shape of the negative spaces.

4. Following on exercise 3, have the dancers move in the group shape, and again focus on the changes in the negative spaces.

5. Choreograph a series of group shapes that emphasize the spaces between the dancers and the spaces between the parts of their bodies.

Dancers relate in both space and time throughout a single piece of choreography. Unison movement, or having all the dancers do the same movement simultaneously, is one way choreographers can arrange dancers with respect to timing. While unison movement can be strong and powerful, it is boring when used repeatedly in a composition, or weak when not performed with precision by all the dancers in a group. Another technique choreographers use to set timing in a piece is to have the dancers begin the same movement sequence on different counts. Dancer number one, for example, begins moving on count one of a sequence, while the second and third dancers in the *ensemble* start on counts two and three respectively. Hayes (1955) calls such an arrangement *sequential* movement, because it creates an overlapping effect; movements are seen once and are then seen again. Choreographers can create sequential movement by having dancers enter the stage at different times or by stopping the action and having the performers begin again on different counts (see figure 2.16).

A third method for arranging movement, called opposition, involves an understanding of both space and time. Opposition, which means that the dancers move in opposite directions in space, can be developed from unison or sequential actions. In opposition, the performers move from side to side, or can travel diagonally between upstage and downstage corners. Opposition creates an effect in which the negative space between and surrounding the dancers seems to narrow and widen as they move toward or away from one another (see figures 2.17a and 2.17b). Dancers can also achieve the effect of opposition by rotating their bodies in opposite directions.

Unison, sequence, and opposition provide three possible ways in which you can arrange movement. It could also be effective to try other possibilities, or to have all your dancers doing entirely different movements at any point in your choreography.

Developing Your Skills
Unison, Sequence, Opposition

1. Develop a short movement sequence, and teach this sequence to a small group of dancers. Then have all the dancers perform the sequence by beginning their movement on the same count. You'll notice that the dancers must perform unison movement in exactly the same way, since differences in execution are noticeable.

2. Select a single action, such as reaching upward. To produce a sequence of actions, have each dancer begin one or two counts later than the dancer to the right or left. Sequential actions usually produce a wave or domino effect.

3. Vertical opposition can be created by having two dancers stand close together, and while one dancer moves up the other one goes down. You can create side-to-side opposition using a swaying action, and turning opposition can be produced by having the

Figure 2.16   An example of sequential movement design.

Figure 2.17 (a) Use of opposition. Notice the space between the dancers as well as the area surrounding them. (b) Opposition on a diagonal and more vertical direction.

dancers turn in opposite directions. Notice how opposition produces a pulling feeling, and how the negative spaces between the dancers expand and contract.

4. Teach three entirely different movement phrases to three dancers. Have the three dancers simultaneously perform their own sequence, and then experiment with the location of each dancer with the goal of achieving a unified effect.

Choreographic Ideas From Post-Modern Dance

Many professional dancers have experimented with new choreographic forms and ideas during the last 35 years. Some of these innovative dance forms still exist, while others have vanished. In either case, novice choreographers can profit by studying the structure, development, and content used by these innovative artists—sometimes known as post-moderns or post-modern dancers. Kreemer (1987) describes *post-modern dance* as a broad category that includes formal choreographic ele-

ments, mathematical systems, or improvisations used to create unique and original approaches to making dances—particularly those choreographic approaches that came into being during the 1960s and 1970s. The post-moderns introduced changes that were a radical departure from choreographic form and method as it was understood and accepted at the middle of the 20th century. Originally, in the 1960s, this group of experimental artists was known as the Judson Dance Theatre, since they presented their first series of experimental works at Judson Memorial Church in Greenwich Village. According to Banes (1993), the Judson Dance Theatre began a historic process that initiated the post-modern dance movement and changed the nature of dance making forever.

Post-modern choreographers experimented with the basic elements of dance form and rejected the idea that a dance had to communicate a message. They were not interested in creating dances using methods developed by the choreographers who preceded them; like many of the visual artists and composers of their era, they were intent on exploring new ground. Among their accomplishments, these innovative dance artists (a) broadened the range of movement used in their dances; (b) changed the traditional method of choreographic order, sequence, and timing; (c) often worked with dancers

who had various levels and types of training; (d) danced in unique and sometimes unusual environments; (e) incorporated aspects of technical theatre or mixed media into their works; (f) explored the use of different kinds of accompaniment; (g) altered their dancers' relationship with the audience; and (h) changed the traditional dance costume (McDonagh, 1990). *Minimalism*, the use of repetitive movement or movement patterns, was another favorite post-modern theme (Siegel, 1977).

Beginning with the 1980s, a noticeable shift occurred in the nature and style of works produced by post-modern choreographers. Banes (1987) indicates that a younger generation of dancers was growing tired of making meaningless works and, as a consequence, became more interested in content. The '80s saw (a) an interest in virtuosity or a high level of technique resulting in some choreography that was almost acrobatic; (b) use of language and language-like systems such as American Sign Language; (c) a return to the narrative dance structure; (d) use of materials from vernacular dance such as the style of Fred Astaire or the choreography of MTV; (e) an interest in multiple channels of communication through use of multimedia; and (f) a greater interest in accompaniment to produce a new fusion of music and dance (Banes, 1987).

As a novice choreographer, you should learn to create dances following traditional methods of form and development before attempting to experiment with post-modern methods. Once you have a solid understanding of dance form and development as it existed prior to the 1960s, you should find it easier to experiment with some of the ideas and concepts discovered by the post-moderns.

Dance by Chance

One post-modern method of choreography, known as dance by chance, was first used by well-known dancer Merce Cunningham. Dance by chance is a *nontraditional* choreographic method based on the idea that there are no prescribed movement materials or orders for a series of actions. In dances developed by *chance*, the choreographer gives up some control and allows chance methods to deter-

mine the content or organization of the work. Blom and Chaplin (1982) report that sometimes chance methods such as a throw of dice are used to select movements for a dance or to give order to the movements in a piece. You can learn to use chance as part of your creative process by exploring some of the developmental skills suggestions.

You'll notice that in the sections that follow, the exercises are arranged from the simple to the more complex. Suggestions for improvisation are included after those for exploration.

Developing Your Skills
Dance by Chance

1. Have your dancers learn the same movement sequence. Then experiment with use of stage space by having the dancers begin these same movements at different points in the space. Use chance to select the area in which each dancer begins.

2. Accompaniment can also provide an element of chance. Have your dancers perform several movement sequences to different pieces of music. After you experience the effect of different musical selections, choose the one you like best. Cunningham used the chance coupling of movement and accompaniment in the premiere of his *Rainforest* choreography (see figure 2.18).

3. Choreographers also use chance to determine the order of an entire section in a dance. Let each dancer practice the same set of movement sequences, and then arbitrarily designate the individual sequence each dancer is to perform. Have each dancer begin moving at an arbitrary point during this section of the dance. Change the order of the movement sequences. Look at how the dancers relate in the stage space, and select the order or arrangement of sequences that appeals to you for this section.

4. Write the names or descriptions of several movements and body positions on different pieces of paper—for example, walk, hop,

James Klosty

Figure 2.18 Meg Harper and Merce Cunningham in Cunningham's *Rainforest*. Set designed by Andy Warhol.

sit, and stand. Put these pieces of paper into an arbitrary order, and decide how many times you want to perform each movement. Perform this chance sequence by connecting the separate movements with appropriate transitional movements. Next devise variations of this chance sequence by altering the movement elements of space, time, energy, and shape. You could also have your dancers choose the pieces of paper and have them determine the order of the movements and the number of repetitions of each movement or pose in the sequence.

5. Cunningham constructed charts listing various movement combinations, and then selected the order of the patterns to be performed by tossing coins onto the charts (Charlip, 1992). Try experimenting with this method of chance determination.

6. Another chance method is to change the order of a dance using games or signals. Here the choreographer sets up a situation in which the actions of one dancer trigger movement in other dancers, producing an

action-reaction scenario. According to McDonagh (1990), Deborah Hay used the game concept in her dance titled *Ten*. In this piece she had two poles onstage—one vertical and one horizontal. When the group leader used the horizontal pole, the rest of the group was expected to respond by copying the leader's stance. Use of the vertical pole was the signal for the group to form a chain. Practice making up a series of instructions or signals that determine the sequence or order of movements in your dance.

Pedestrian Movement

Pedestrian, or everyday, movement is another device used in some post-modern choreography. Banes (1993) records that in *Proxy*, Steve Paxton created a slow-moving dance in four sections for three dancers. Movements in this piece included walking, carrying, and standing; in addition, the dancers drank a glass of liquid and ate a piece of fruit (see figure 2.19 for an example of Paxton's choreography). Try experimenting with pedestrian movements in the following exercises.

Developing Your Skills
Pedestrian Movement

1. Using chance methods, select a series of pedestrian movements and put them in an arbitrary order. Try as many variations of these movements as you can think of.

2. Broaden your scope of pedestrian actions by thinking about categories of everyday actions. These might include tasks (hammering, sweeping); daily activities (brushing your teeth, eating, sitting); or typical sports actions (a baseball swing, a tennis serve, a basketball throw). See how many ways you can perform each of these movements, and then link these movements together in a sequence.

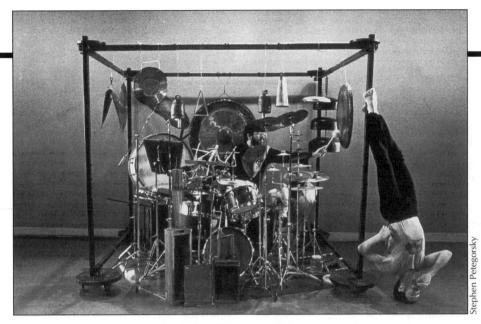

Figure 2.19 Steve Paxton in *Backwater Twosome*, 1978.

Stephen Petegorsky

3. Choreograph several different movement sequences based solely on pedestrian actions. Link these pedestrian actions together with transitional movements such as traditional locomotor steps. Try varying the locomotors used as transitions to see how using different locomotors affects each pattern.

4. Next choreograph a combination of traditional dance movements, and interject some action of a pedestrian nature at intervals.

Time Alteration and Repetition

Time is one of the basic elements of dance movement. Many of the post-modern choreographers altered the normal sense of time or used repetitive actions as a way to discover new dance structures. Laura Dean choreographed many works with this minimalist approach. In *Jumping Dance*, for example, the performers jump in place and say "Ha" on every push-off; this jumping continues until the dancers tire, and then they recover in order to begin more jumping. Siegel (1977) writes that in Dean's *Circle Dance*, the dancers walk in four concentric circles, changing direction in one ring at a time, while the interval between changes of direction gets smaller.

Group Size and Technical Level

The nature and size of a group can do much to affect the dynamics in a dance. The post-modern

dancers often incorporated extremely large groups in their choreographies or used groups that included dancers of varying technical abilities. Deborah Hay and Meredith Monk, for example, worked with large groups, while Rudy Perez used the team concept in some of his works (McDonagh, 1990). These choreographers usually developed such dances from simple rather than complex movement materials, since both trained and untrained dancers performed in them.

Developing Your Skills
Group Size and Technical Level

1. You can experiment with groups of different sizes. Construct a short movement sequence and teach it to one or two dancers. View the movement pattern, and then add more dancers to the group. Continue the addition of dancers to determine the effect produced by small and large groups when they perform the same pattern.

2. The use of dancers of different levels can also set up a unique creative problem. You could try using two different movement vocabularies for the two different groups. The lay dancers would do simple movements and pedestrian actions, while the trained dancers could perform more complex and traditional dance movements. It would also be interesting to have the untrained performers move in place, while the trained dancers travel around them. Experiment with the possibilities by changing the stage area used by each of the two groups, or by altering the point at which each group begins to move.

Unusual Environments

Post-modern choreographers have often danced in unusual environments such as on the altar of a church, in the street, or in an art museum. Meredith Monk also enjoyed doing works that evolved from and were inspired by different environments. At Woodstock, she adapted to the environment by presenting *Blueprint* in two brick buildings that faced each other. McDonagh (1990) tells us that Monk's dancers performed the first part of this composition in a space on the ground floor of one of the buildings. The audience then moved outside and watched the dancers appear in the window of the facing building; a performer concluded the work on the roof. Monk often gave her audience maps so that they could follow the dancers from one choreographic setting to another. Use of different settings can provide another stimulus for dance movement (see figure 2.20).

Developing Your Skills
Unusual Environments

1. Create an experimental environment in the dance studio by placing or suspending props such as hoops, chairs, boxes, and scooters at points around the room. Other props, large enough to hide a dancer or dancers, could include a screen or piano. Have your dancers discover many actions by relating to the objects in different ways and by reacting to each other. Stimulate movement imagination by having your dancers move over, under, around, and through the objects in the dance space (see figure 2.21). After the improvisation has continued for a while, select some of the most effective sequences, and set them in a short dance.

2. Extend the movement possibilities in the preceding exercise by having your dancers copy or relate to the movements of others as they continue to improvise.

3. Check your campus or dance building for other spaces that could provide a new environment for improvisations.

4. You can also discover new dance environments by exploring a bare stage or by using the theatre-in-the-round concept.

5. On a warm day, go outside and improvise. Have your dancers concentrate on the objects in this new setting, and then ask them

Figure 2.20 Meredith Monk, *The House at Goddard College*, 1972.

Figure 2.21 Many different objects can be used to create a changed studio environment for improvisation.

to move over, under, around, and through the objects.

6. Choreographers have also used slides or other kinds of projections to alter the performance setting. Project a slide on a bare wall and watch your dancers move in front of this projection. (Slides of modern art are very effective for this exercise because the projection contains large designs or blocks of color without realistic images.) Notice how the projection changes and takes on a life of its own as the dancers move in front of it.

Accompaniment

Accompaniment has an important effect on the kind of choreography you create. The post-modern dancers used many different and often unusual forms of accompaniment. In some of her early works, Twyla Tharp danced in silence or to the accompaniment of the rhythmic sounds of nature; Yvonne Rainer used the human voice and the amplified sounds of her own body as accompaniment (McDonagh, 1990).

Developing Your Skills
Accompaniment

1. Try improvising to different sounds of nature such as the wind, running water, or cricket sounds. (Before you begin to move, concentrate on the unique quality of these sounds, trying to experience them in terms of the six qualities of movement discussed earlier in the chapter.)

2. Make your own accompaniment by recording words, nonsense syllables, or the sounds of walking on different surfaces. (Walking on gravel, for example, creates an interesting crunching sound.) Try improvising with each new form of accompaniment.

3. Alter the pitch and quality of the sounds in the preceding exercise by changing the speed of your tape recorder, or record these sounds at a different speed so they take on another quality.

4. Have your group of dancers move around the space while making body sounds or rhythmic patterns by clapping, stomping, or slapping their bodies. Encourage the dancers to try different rhythms and to copy the patterns of other dancers from time to time.

5. Select five or six names or words that fit a category. Categories could be colors, flowers, cars, and so forth. Have one of the dancers in your group pick one of the words and say it loudly, in a way that suggests a movement quality such as sustained or percussive. The dancer should also move while saying the word. Immediately encourage the other dancers to respond to the first dancer by saying the same word and moving as well. Try to keep the action going by altering the quality of movement and vocalization. (When movement begins to quiet down, another dancer should be ready to call out a second word from the category to initiate the process again. In this exercise, it's important for the dancers to be aware of each other so that they can respond to and play off of the sounds and actions of others in the group.)

Group Interaction

The proscenium theatre creates a performer-audience relationship in which the two entities—performer and audience—remain separate. The edges of the top and sides of the proscenium arch, and the floor of the theatre, form a picture frame that surrounds the performance area and separates it from the audience. The post-modern choreographers challenged this traditional separation of performer and audience by having dancers perform in the audience area or by having them enter the stage from the *house.* Some of these new choreographers even tried having the dancers pick up sounds or gestures made by audience members.

Developing Your Skills
Group Interaction

1. Have your group begin this improvisation by moving freely around the dance space. Then suggest that the dancers initiate changes by copying the movements and gestures of the observers. These changes could occur at random, or on a signal from someone inside or outside the group. (Accompaniment may help initiate movement.)

2. Variations in movement could be produced by manipulating the movement elements or by reacting to the actions of the other dancers.

3. Begin with an empty dance space. Place your dancers at various points along the periphery of this space, and have the dancers enter and exit the dance space when they feel ready to do so. Keep the action going by encouraging the dancers to relate to each other while they move within the dance area. (The idea here is that there is an exchange between performers and audience, because the same dancer is both an audience member and a performer, but at different times.)

4. Try the previous improvisation using unusual movements during entrances and exits. You might have the dancers roll, crawl, or slide their bodies into the dance space.

Structured Improvisation

The *structured improvisation* is another post-modern idea, similar to the game concept. Here,

the choreographer uses certain criteria to determine where and how the dancers move in the performance space. An example of a structured improvisation is one proposed by Dilley (1981) in which the choreographer instructs the dancers to move only in a circular and counterclockwise pathway, using select movements such as walking, running, crawling, and standing. The dancers are also told to be sensitive to each other by picking up the movement of other dancers when it feels right. Dilley based another structured improvisation on spatial corridors. In this improvisation, the individuals are instructed to move across the room in several selected corridors of the dance space; the kinds of movement to be used are again prescribed. Dancers who cross the entire space must exit and reenter through a different corridor.

Developing Your Skills
Structured Improvisation

1. Limit the movements or poses to be used in this improvisation to four or five possibilities. For example, the dancers' movements could be walk, run, stand, and hop. Have your dancers move counterclockwise in a circle using only the selected movements and moving only in a circular pathway. Let the dancers do these movements in any order, and encourage them to copy the actions of other dancers from time to time.

2. Next decide on how many corridors of space divide the dance studio. Then choose the four or five movements to be used to cross the space. Let your dancers move across the space while staying in the corridor that they entered. Again, encourage them to copy the actions of others from time to time, and when they exit, have them reenter the dance space in a different corridor.

Both of these improvisations should be allowed to continue for three to five minutes. Try to remember the interesting points in each improvisation, and write them down for use in a composition.

Contact Improvisation

Contact improvisation, another creative idea that has emerged, is used in the studio to discover movement and as a performance medium. Contact work is a spontaneous form drawn from functional actions performed while relating to the environment or to a moving partner. Motivation is taken from a dancer's reaction to being in contact with another moving body or bodies, and from learning to take and receive impulses from another. Contact improvisation is very spontaneous, since the point of contact between two bodies or between several bodies is not predetermined, but rather is allowed to evolve and progress naturally. Often the weight of one dancer's body is supported by another. Sessions in contact improvisation should be conducted with care, and participants should employ mechanically efficient movement techniques. Dancers must know how to relax when falling, roll when meeting the floor, bear weight safely, and catch themselves protectively, yet be able to keep the energy going. According to Brown, in contact improvisation, one is able to watch "the ever changing forms of the human body as it falls, supports, jumps, catches, lifts, and follows another body. This quality of functional grace is shared with most sports" (Brown, 1980:7).

Developing Your Skills
Contact Improvisation

1. You can play with contact improvisation. Begin in a position in which your body weight is supported by another dancer, and start to move slowly, being aware of how movement of both participants alters body contact, weight, and body shape. Notice the point at which one body supports the other and how support and contact change as body shapes change.

2. Try the preceding exercise while you and your partner move in space, rather than remaining in one area doing axial movements.

3. As a variation on contact improvisation, stand facing a partner. (You and your partner should be about the same height and weight.) Grasp both of your partner's forearms with a good grip, and pull away so that you and your partner counterbalance one another. Continue counterbalancing, but change body shape by taking one foot off of the floor, or by changing levels. See how many movements you can create while you continue to counterbalance your partner (see figure 2.22).

4. Try contact improvisation in a larger group once you have practiced with one person. Take care to move slowly and cautiously throughout this process.

Figure 2.22　The dancers are counterbalancing.

Review Questions

What is movement manipulation? How does it contribute to the process of choreography?

◆

Explain how you can use the elements space, time, energy, and shape to manipulate movement. Be specific with your answer. For example, being able to manipulate the element space means that you understand how to vary the aspects of this element—direction, level, size, focus, and pathways. Use all aspects of the movement elements time, energy, and shape as well in answering this question.

◆

Movement communicates nonverbally. Explain this statement using examples from daily life. If you are sitting in an airport, for example, what elements of nonverbal communication can you use to learn something about the people you see around you? Can any of these observations be incorporated into a dance?

◆

How do the elements of movement contribute to nonverbal communication? Again, be specific. How can different uses of direction, accent, or focus, for example, change the message of your dance?

◆

The stage space is dead space until a choreographer brings this space to life. What simple technique enables a choreographer to bring this space to life?

◆

A dance can also be viewed as a series of pictures created within the frame of the proscenium of the theatre. How does such a series of pictures bring the stage space to life?

◆

What is a virtual entity? Why is this concept important in choreographing a dance?

◆

In the dance you are staging, you want to emphasize the soloist. How could you design use of movement direction, pathway, area, blocking, facing, and accompanying facial expressions in order to highlight this dancer? What changes would you make in your use of these techniques if you were choreographing for a less important dancer or a weak character?

♦

What are two types of body shapes and groupings, and how are they different? When might it be more appropriate to use one or the other of these types of shapes or groupings?

♦

What are the differences between unison, sequence, and opposition? Should unison movement be used consistently in a choreography? Why or why not? What effect is produced by using sequence and opposition?

♦

What is negative space? Can it become an important part of a choreography? Look around you in your present environment and find the negative spaces.

♦

What is post-modern dance? How does it differ from earlier approaches to choreography?

♦

Name several of the choreographic devices created by the post-moderns, and give some specific examples of each device as it was used by a well-known choreographer.

♦

Explain how you could use one of the post-modernist devices in your own choreography. Answer this question by first describing your basic choreographic idea, and then explain how you would use the device.

Identifying Choreographic Form

hen I first began to study choreography, I was fascinated with many of the dances performed by the professional companies. Each of these works had an innate, special quality, yet they had a kind of magic and aliveness in common. Initially, I thought there was a recipe to be followed that could produce such dances, but later I began to realize that no one formula existed with respect to the choreographic forming process. At best, it is possible to provide some general words and phrases that describe aspects of an effective dance. Eventually, you should come to realize that there are many ways to structure a dance, and that producing a successful work depends on how all parts of the work are organized and how they relate.

In any case, one of the best methods to help you understand dance form is to see as much choreography as possible. Gradually, through observation, you'll begin to discover how to make your own dances, and how to apply the materials presented in this book. One of my former choreography students told me she was very glad I had shown many videotapes in her class, because it gave her some concrete ideas of how to bring the information presented in this text together with her own creative ideas.

I've also found assessment forms helpful. Use of assessments tends to make choreographic discussion and evaluation more concrete and less subjective. Use the Choreographic Assessment Sheet in appendix B to help you look at your own work as it develops.

Any creative work, dance included, exists within a *form* that is shaped from the motivation or *intent* of the work. In this chapter, you will read about choreographic form—as it relates to the second Dance Standard, which states that students should understand choreographic principles, processes, and structures (National Dance Association, 1994). The dance phrase and criteria of effective form are also described, followed by a discussion of how you can use these techniques to shape a dance. Common dance forms are introduced next, along with explanations to help you understand literal, abstraction, and nonliteral choreographic methods, and the concept of style. The chapter concludes with advice on selecting appropriate subjects for your choreography, working through the developmental stages of dance making, and putting finishing touches on your work.

Choreographic Form and Development

An effective piece of choreography has a special quality that makes the observer want to get involved. The observer is lifted from the theatre seat and transported along during the performance.

Many people not trained in the choreographic craft are nevertheless capable of knowing and identifying a successful dance. These individuals intuitively know an effective work when they see it. What they can't do, however, is analyze why a dance is successful, or describe what distinguishes an effective piece of choreography from a lesser work. In these pages we'll consider some of the elements involved in designing a dance—one that creates an illusion of being larger than life and that conveys a sense of magic and wonder.

One of the criteria of an effective dance is that it has a shape or form—a form that progresses through time from the beginning to the end of the choreography. In learning how to choreograph, therefore, you need to develop a sense of how to give overall form to a composition. One description of the development of a dance is that the choreography has a beginning, middle, and conclusion or end. The choreographer learns to shape a dance so that each of these parts is essential and fits together with the others to form a whole. In learning to compose a dance you will develop your ability to choose an appropriate beginning, middle, and end that relate to the form and feeling of the whole choreography.

Later, you can use videotape to help in an analysis of your own dances. Through the use of videotape, the choreographer can stand outside a dance and view form and development with a clinical eye.

As you choreograph, be aware of the total structure of your dance as it evolves, and resist the tendency to get lost or completely involved in any single movement or sequence of movements. In other words, learn to stand outside the work and maintain a mental picture of the *overall development* of the dance.

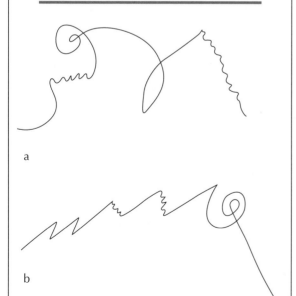

a

b

Figure 3.1 The two drawings represent the overall form of two different dances. *Adapted from Blom and Chaplin 1982.*

The Phrase

Many smaller pieces of movement make up the overall shape or development of a dance composition. These small units of a dance are known as phrases and can be likened to the phrases that make up sentences in a written composition. Blom and Chaplin (1982) describe the phrase as the smallest unit of form in the whole dance. Beginning choreographers need to learn movement phrasing—an ability that can be acquired using both the visual and *kinesthetic sense.*

A phrase must have a sense of development. You need to understand how others have used phrasing, while developing a kinesthetic awareness of the phrasing in your own work. One example of a phrase is a unit of movement marked by an impulse of energy that grows, builds, and finds a conclusion and then flows easily and naturally into the next movement phrase in the dance. A phrase could also have a different form based on other uses of energy, so that the separate movements connect in a more abrupt manner or are developed by arbitrarily linking movements together. When linking movements arbitrarily, however, you will need to give thought to the way the movements are connected. Blom and Chaplin (1982) say that each of the separate movements in a phrase must be related to a common intent. Many phrases make up a section in the choreography, and the sections together form the entire dance.

Movement phrases should be varied in length and shape. When all phrases in a dance are of equal length—eight counts long, say—phrasing becomes very predictable and boring for the audience, and the dance can become monotonous. Likewise, movement phrases that all begin with an impulse of energy and end with a slow decline in that energy would have a similar shape because each would be developed in the same manner.

Dance phrasing is not always easy to understand. You may have difficulty, for instance, if you have learned dance technique or movement skills by learning *steps.* To alleviate this problem, you need to realize how movements connect and where one energy impulse ends and a new impulse begins. Some dancers have learned movement patterns

that have poor transitions or no connecting link at all between the basic movements or steps. As a beginning choreographer, you should develop an awareness of the connectedness of movement and stop thinking about the steps learned in dance technique class.

Experience in Action

1. Watch a videotape of a well-known choreographer's work. Notice where the phrases begin and end. See if you can pick out the movement phrases throughout the work.

2. As you watch the video in exercise 1, notice where the choreographer has used recognizable steps, and try to understand how these steps are integrated into the overall development of the dance.

3. Discuss your analysis of movement phrasing with a classmate to compare your understanding of phrasing to your classmate's ideas.

4. Write down your observations in a journal.

Developing Your Skills

Phrasing

The point of these exercises is both to give you a chance to practice movement phrasing and to increase your understanding of the concept. You will develop phrases by using a number of motivations and then reinforce this understanding by doing exercises using different sensory modes. You may find a visual model such as a drawing or diagram to be a helpful aid in comprehension. A classmate, on the other hand, may respond to auditory cues, such as singing the rhythmic development of each phrase. Approaching phrasing, or any other concept, in various ways should increase your understanding.

Breath Phrasing

The following exploration allows you to practice constructing breath phrases.

1. Practice inhaling and moving a single body part with each breath. Allow your breathing to go into and propel different parts of your body.

2. As you breathe in, allow your breathing to move a single part of your body in any direction you wish. Let this movement continue until you have finished exhaling. On the next breath begin another breath phrase. Make the length and points of emphasis different in each phrase by playing with both a smooth and an interrupted use of breath.

3. Do the preceding exercise while letting your breath move other parts of your body.

4. Finally, let your breathing move your whole body to form phrases that travel across space. Each phrase should continue for one inhalation and exhalation of breath.

Count Phrasing

Another method of developing a sense of phrasing is to use a certain number of counts for each phrase. For example, you could make the first phrase 10 counts long, the second one 16 counts long, and so on. It might help to have another person clap or beat a drum while you are devising these phrases. This person could even count the number of beats to be included in each phrase so that you're free to concentrate on your movement and its development.

1. Start with a movement in one part of your body, and let it grow and build. Find a conclusion for this developing phrase at the end of 10 counts.

2. Build a second phrase that's longer or shorter than the first one.

3. See if you can link two phrases of unequal length so that as one concludes the other begins. Determine the number of counts to be included in each phrase.

Energy Flow Phrasing

Energy flow, a third method of developing phrases, requires that you be kinesthetically

aware of how you are using energy in your body.

1. Begin with an impulse of energy in a single body part, and let it play itself out to an ending. Be sensitive to how you find an ending, or closure, for your movement, and let it develop naturally.

2. Create a series of phrases in this part of the body by using repeated impulses. When one phrase ends, begin another impulse to start a new phrase.

3. Allow your energy impulses to extend into other parts of your body.

4. Begin to let your energy impulses move your body across space.

5. Vary the quality of energy used to develop individual phrases. Use sustained, percussive, vibratory, swinging, suspended, or collapsing qualities to create movement.

Set Movements Phrasing

Set movements can also be used to construct movement phrases.

1. Practice making a phrase by putting three or four set movements together. For example, a phrase could include two walking steps, four running steps, and a lifting of the arms.

2. Go back over the phrase to analyze how the separate movements connect and how each leads into the next. Decide whether there are adequate transitions between movements.

Music Phrasing

The following exercises should help you construct phrases to music.

1. Listen carefully to a piece of music, and then begin to move. Try to move both on and over the musical pulse beat.

2. As you move, begin to notice where your movements end and how another series of actions begins.

3. Analyze your movement phrasing as it relates to the musical phrasing. Make sure you're not constantly copying the phrasing of the accompaniment.

4. Create several additional phrases with your accompaniment, and include some moments where you hold a pose to provide silences within the phrases.

Understanding Phrasing

The following exercises provide a more concrete way to understand phrasing.

1. Try performing each of the phrases in the preceding exercises while chanting or singing its rhythm or development.

2. Clarify this chanting exercise with the use of a visual diagram. In such a diagram the line goes up when the movement or energy goes up, drops down when the movement goes down, becomes shorter for faster movement, and is absent to accompany pauses in the phrase. Create visual diagrams for several of your movement phrases (see figure 3.2).

Dance Characteristics to Watch For

While there is no single approach to creating a dance that has a clear sense of development, certain characteristics are common to many effective pieces of choreography. These qualities include unity, continuity, transition, variety, and repetition.

It is essential that a dance have *unity*. The separate movements in the choreography must fit or flow together, and each must be important to and contribute to the whole; phrases not essential to the intent of a work should be eliminated. An example of a dance that lacks unity is one in which all movements seem at first to have the same *character* or ambience about them, but then suddenly a movement or series of movements appears that is very different in feeling. Such movements do not fit with the feeling of the choreography, but rather stand out as distinct from the *essence* of the piece and interfere with the interconnectedness of the

Figure 3.2 The two drawings represent the development of two different dance phrases. *Adapted from Humphrey 1987.*

dance. In the opinion of Hawkins (1988), it is easier for observers to absorb and get involved in a choreography that maintains unity because it has the capacity to attract and hold audience attention.

Continuity is a second characteristic of an effective piece of choreography. A choreography with continuity develops in a way that leads to a logical conclusion. The emphasis is on the process of happening, and the observer is swept along to the end. The choreographer provides a natural and organized progression of phrases so that one movement phrase leads naturally into the next.

Transitions from one sequence into another are acceptable because each is an integral part of the choreography and contributes to the unity of the dance. On the other hand, if the observer finds progression from one phrase to another noticeable, transitions are probably poor. Poor transitions are distracting to the audience because they interfere with *involvement* in the performance of the dance and draw attention to the structure and design of the

choreography, rather than allowing the audience to focus on the overall feeling or form of the work. Hawkins (1988) notes that transitions should act like a bridge by binding the parts of the dance together.

To maintain audience interest, the choreographer must also provide variety within the development of a dance. The same phrase or movement performed again and again becomes tedious and boring. Contrasts in movement forces and *spatial designs* within the unity of a work add excitement.

Some repetition, however, is important to dance form. Certain phrases need to be repeated in a choreography so that the audience can see these movements again and identify with them. Repetition gives a feeling of closure to a work. Hawkins (1988) observes that repetition allows the audience to take in and absorb momentary movements or phrases in relation to the intent of the work. Successful repetition of movements usually occurs later in the dance after other phrases have been presented in the intervening time period.

You have probably guessed that a choreographer must maintain a delicate balance between variety, or *contrast*, and repetition. A dance consisting of different movement phrases throughout is just as ineffective as a choreography comprised of continuously repeated phrases. In the first situation, the audience can't identify with the unrelated string of movements, while in the latter instance movements become predictable. Too much variety destroys unity. To help balance variety and repetition, remember that variety is essential to good composition, but it must be provided with discrimination.

All the characteristics of an effective choreography—unity, continuity, transition, variety, and repetition—are organized to contribute to the development of a meaningful whole. All phrases in a work should be designed to form the integrated sections of your dance, and all the sections of the dance should be placed in a sequence that moves toward an appropriate conclusion or closure. The development of a work should lead the audience logically from the beginning, to the middle, and on to the ending of the dance. The conclusion is the choreographer's own choice; it could be sudden, or gradual so that the dance fades from view.

Experience in Action

Keep a written record of your discoveries as you go though the following exercises.

1. Watch a videotape of a piece of choreography and decide if the work has a sense of unity and continuity. If you feel the choreographer has used these characteristics effectively, try to point out why you believe this is so.

2. Look at a videotape of the dance in exercise 1 and decide if the work contains enough contrast or variety. Can you point out or describe some of the actions that provide variety in this choreography?

3. Next, view the same videotape with an eye for the way in which the choreographer has included transitions. Does one phrase lead appropriately into the next, or is the sense of

the whole disrupted at certain points with movements that do not fit?

4. Notice how the choreographer connects the separate sections of a dance. You may find that use of lighting or music provides a connecting link between sections, or that a dancer or dancers remain onstage to perform transitional movements to connect parts of the dance.

5. As you continue to view the videotape, be aware of repeated movements and movement phrases. Try to describe how these repeated movements are used through the work. In other words, are these movements repeated in exactly the same way, or has the choreographer changed them? Do you find that some movements or phrases are repeated too many times?

6. Discuss your observations with a classmate who has observed the same videotape. Then write down your observations in a journal.

Developing Your Skills
Variety and Transitions

1. One way to provide variety is to avoid repeating a movement or phrase in the exact way each time it is included in a work. Try changing the direction, use of energy, or timing of a selected movement.

2. Another method of varying movement is to avoid repeating the movement or phrases on both sides of the body. Constant repetition of a movement right-to-left or left-to-right is predictable and uninteresting. Stop and reconsider when you begin to fall into this pattern. Develop a phrase that has one continuous thread of action and that avoids repeating the same movement on the right and then left sides of the body.

3. To practice transitions, find two shapes for your body. Assume the first shape. Move to the second shape by finding a transitional action or actions that carry

you to the second shape. Repeat this process several times.

4. Experiment with a variety of transitions between the two shapes in exercise 3 by using both direct and indirect pathways to get from one shape to the others.

5. Choreograph several short movement sequences. Next, decide in which stage areas these sequences are to be performed. Finally, choreograph movement transitions that take you from one stage area to the next and that provide continuity between the sequences.

Common Choreographic Forms

The overall shape of a piece of choreography can follow many different threads of development. Some of these choreographic forms are unique to dance, but many are based on musical forms developed at an earlier period.

AB

The *AB* is a very simple choreographic form that consists of a beginning section called A, followed by a second section known as B. While sections A and B fit together in terms of the common feeling of a composition, each contains elements that are contrasting in tone or quality. It could be said that sections A and B share some of the same ground but explore it from different points of view. The choreographer must devise a transition to link the two sections of a dance developed in the AB form. The transition could be presented abruptly or could be produced in a more gradual manner (Blom and Chaplin, 1982).

ABA

Another frequently used dance form, the *ABA*, has a sense of development that goes a step further than the AB. The ABA derives from a musical form and has two sections, A and B, followed by an ending A section. In the first part a series of movements, or theme A, is stated and

manipulated. Part B then presents a contrasting theme, and in the final section there is a return to theme A with a different twist. Horst and Russell (1987) comment that a work that follows an ABA format is like life in that it proceeds through the universal pattern of being born, living, and dying. All three sections—A, B, and the return to A—fit together to form a unified whole. There should be contrast between parts, yet they should be similar enough to suit the character of the entire dance. Section A, for example, could include large, broad movements, while part B, although choreographed in the same style, might use less space and energy. Part three, the return to A, would be more expansive, but with aspects somewhat different from the original A. Again, skillful use of transition is needed between each of the three sections.

Suite

A form of music called the *suite* is also used as choreographic form. The most typical suite has a moderate beginning, a slow second part, and a fast, lively third section. Many pieces of music written in suite form are excellent accompaniment for dance.

Rondo

The *rondo* is a fourth common dance form, recognizable by its many different sections following one after the other. It can be described as an ABACADAEAFA development of movement ideas (Horst and Russell, 1987). The rondo form includes an initial section A followed by an alternate or contrasting part B. The third section is a return to A, either in its entirety or with some changes. The return to A is followed by a fourth section, C, and another return to A. The remainder of the choreography includes parts D, E, and F interspersed with variations or restatements of A.

Theme and Variations

Theme and variations is a fifth dance form, developed in a manner similar to the musical form with the same name. Here the choreographer must

select a series of movements, called the theme, which is then changed or varied throughout the development of the entire work. The theme can be a single phrase of movements or several movement phrases put together in a sequence. The theme or original movement series can be changed in a number of ways as the dance progresses, but the timing and movement sequence of the original theme remain. Changes in a theme could include altering its movement direction or level, or giving the movements a different use of quality or dynamics. There should be no repetition of the original form of the whole theme. The theme and variations dance form is helpful to the choreographer because it provides a limited framework within which movement choices must be made (Humphrey, 1987).

Narrative

The *narrative* form of choreography was very popular during the earlier years of modern dance. A narrative composition is sometimes known as a story or *dance drama*. *Dramatic dances* differ in length and can tell a simple story or communicate a tale of psychological relationships between performers. Narratives choreographed for large groups and those that communicate more complex ideas have been as long as an hour or more, while dances choreographed for small groups or for a solo performer may be only minutes long. Humphrey (1987) states that the narrative choreographic form provides a ready-made framework, since movement choices must relate to the development of the dramatic idea.

Collage

The dance form known as *collage* consists of pieces of movement that are often unrelated but that have been brought together to create a whole. The effect created through this form is at times *surrealistic*, incongruous, comic, or even absurd; it lends itself to dances dealing with insanity or dreams. Humphrey (1987) describes a collage as having movement ideas that may seem disconnected, or body parts that may appear disassociated from each other or from actions of the trunk. Blom and Chaplin (1982) suggest that in a

collage it is necessary to have a point of focus in the actions with an overlapping or quick succession of movements.

Other Choreographic Forms

While the following additional methods of choreographing can at times provide a formula for a whole dance, these methods usually provide sufficient movement ideas for only a portion of a composition. These forms include the canon, ground bass, and dances devised by chance.

A *canon* consists of one phrase of movement or a longer movement pattern performed at different times by at least two different dancers, although many more performers could be used. In a canon, each dancer executes the entire phrase but starts a number of counts behind another dancer. Each dancer could also begin the phrase at a different point in the series so that one dancer starts on count two while another starts on count six of that same phrase (Blom and Chaplin, 1982). In either case, an overlapping visual and temporal effect is achieved.

The *ground bass* represents another choreographic technique. Lockhart and Pease (1982) explain that in a ground bass there is a repetition of a movement theme over and over again, as other themes are brought forward in contrast to the repeated theme. Usually the repeated theme is performed by a group, while a soloist or smaller group dances the more complex combination of movements. A ground bass can also be performed in a circle; here the dancers in the circle would be performing the simple, repeated phrase, and more complex and contrasting movements could be executed by a soloist or smaller group in the center. In either type of ground bass, the choreographer exchanges the dancers performing the more complex movements with those in the larger group. This exchange can occur at various times throughout the piece.

Chance, first employed by well-known dancer Merce Cunningham, is another method of manipulating and developing movement. Dance by chance, as was mentioned in the last chapter, is a nontraditional choreographic method based on the idea that there is no prescribed order for a series of actions. In dances developed by chance, the

choreographer gives up some control and allows chance methods to determine the content or organization of the work.

of movement. These new sections should each be several phrases long. Perform section A followed by a new section, a return to section A, another new section, another return to section A, and so on.

4. In the theme and variations form, the choreographer must vary the same series of phrases. These phrases are the theme. Come up with a theme and decide how to vary it. You could, for example, change the direction of the thematic movements. Or try moving backward through the sequence instead of forward, large instead of small, or with a different quality or flavor of the separate movements in a sequence. Try performing each of these variations by connecting them with transitions.

5. A narrative choreography is based on a story. First decide on the characters and a story, but be clear about how each character fits into the story and relates to the other characters. Then begin to develop movement based on this narrative, but avoid using *pantomime*. You might want to think about a dance with a number of sections, each of which deals with a specific character or with the relationship between certain characters.

6. In a collage you can use a common thread or element to link the parts together. This common element could be different colors, varieties of cars, types of flowers, and so on. Using the idea of different colors, come up with movements and phrases that represent each color. Link these phrases together by providing transitions between each.

7. Choreograph a series of movements of at least 16 or 32 counts in length, and have all of your dancers learn the whole sequence. To create a canon, have the dancers perform the whole sequence with each dancer beginning on a different count. The dancers could begin at evenly spaced intervals two or four counts apart, or at unevenly spaced points in the sequence.

8. To create a ground bass, choreograph a simple movement pattern and several more detailed sequences. Have all the dancers learn the simple movement pattern. (It helps if this simple pattern can be repeated from side to side or in a circle. For example, several walking steps plus a turn constitute a simple pattern.) Teach the more detailed sequences to specific dancers, and then begin by having all the dancers perform the simple, repeated pattern. Next have one or two dancers move out in front of the group or into the center of the circle to perform the more complex actions. You will need to supply transitions to move dancers out of and back into the group. These transitions should be choreographed so that dancers can reenter the group and immediately begin performing the repeated pattern of the ground.

Relating Form and Content

Movement materials discovered during improvisation are gradually shaped or formed into a dance during the choreographic process. This form should be based on the nature and intent or purpose of a composition, and should be suitable to the feelings or ideas that you—the choreographer—are trying to present. In the end, you may choose to follow one of the dance forms already described, or you may decide to develop a unique form more appropriate for your choreography. In either case, it is important to perfect your skills so that you have a good sense of development and understand what constitutes a whole dance. Practice in constructing dances based on a prescribed format, such as ABA or theme and variations, is one way to refine your sense of how to shape a dance. When you gain confidence in working with these prescribed forms, you can then dare to experiment with developmental ideas that are more personal and uniquely your own. When you have the ability to identify what works choreographically, you are free to mold a dance as you see fit.

In order to choose an appropriate form for your choreography, you need to identify what it is that you are trying to project or communicate to the audience. Hawkins (1988) writes that making such decisions is extremely important to dance making, because when motivation determines form, the resulting dance has an organic form instead of being an arbitrary arrangement of movements. The following sections describe several methods of analyzing the motivation of a dance.

Literal Choreography

In the early years of modern dance it was traditional to design or choreograph dances that told stories. Dances that contain a message or that communicate a story to the audience are known as *literal choreography* (Turner, 1971). The famous modern dancer Martha Graham created many full-length works that may be described as dance dramas. In these works the performers dance the roles of specific characters and attempt to communicate a story or message to the audience. Two examples of Graham's literal choreographies are *Appalachian Spring* and *Acrobats of God*. The first of these portrays a young bride and her new husband taking possession of their home and beginning life together on the frontier. In the second choreography, Graham's intent was to communicate the problems and feelings encountered by a choreographer and the struggle involved in producing creative works (see figures 3.3 and 3.4).

Nonliteral Choreography

In more recent years the trend has been away from the literal to create dances in which the choreographer has no desire to tell a story. Such dances are based on design and manipulation; the main concern is experimenting with movement rather than relating a story. A dance deriving its intent from movement design is known as a nonliteral work. *Nonliteral choreography* communicates directly to the audience without explanations; its value is determined by its impact on the perceiver. The viewer cannot find traditional meanings, messages, or morals expressed because nonliteral dances exist for their own sake and for the sake of the

movements used in them (Turner, 1971). The chance dances created by Cunningham are a good example of nonliteral works. Cunningham has no interest in conveying meanings, but instead finds his motivation in movement (Blom and Chaplin, 1982).

Choreography Using Abstraction

Some dances, however, are neither literal nor nonliteral. Such works do not tell a specific story, but they do draw inspiration from reality and thus could be considered abstractions from it. Hawkins (1988) observes that these dances draw from life and contain only the essence of the real experience. As an example of a dance that would be an abstraction from life, consider one about the sea or the seashore. In such a choreography, the dancers' movements would suggest the sea or hint at reactions to the seashore, but there would be no movement included that depicted a pantomime of waves or that portrayed activities traditionally done on a visit to the seashore. Instead, movements would suggest something more general with which most people identify when they think of the sea. A dance that is an abstraction brings forth the essence of the original motivation. It contains a *semblance* of reality that we can identify but cannot put into words.

A sense of form is important to all types of choreography whether literal, nonliteral, or an abstraction, and whether or not it follows one of the established dance forms described in this chapter. All movements should relate to the intent or motivation for creating a work regardless of whether that work is traditional or *experimental*. A sense of wholeness is also necessary. A choreography created with an integral synthesis of parts will be immediately recognized, because such a dance has a life of its own.

Blom and Chaplin (1982) state that form is not independent, existing like an external container. Rather, when best used, form grows from content, providing a natural or organic dance structure. Organic form, then, is a method of choreographic development that draws on concepts of form that exist in the many patterns and shapes found in nature.

Arnold Eagle

Figure 3.3 Martha Graham and Bertram Ross in *Appalachian Spring*.

Arnold Eagle

Figure 3.4 Martha Graham and members of the Graham Company performing *Acrobats of God*.

1. Watch a videotape of a choreography and decide if the work fits one of the categories described in the preceding section. Ask yourself whether this piece is literal, nonliteral, or an abstraction.

2. Attempt to describe the form and development of the choreography viewed in exercise 1. Keep a journal of your observations.

3. How would you describe the preceding work if it does not fit into the literal, nonliteral, or abstraction categories?

4. Does the form used in this choreography fit the motivation? Briefly explain your answer.

5. Would you describe this dance as organic or as having organic form?

6. Describe how you might have used a different approach to develop this dance.

Developing Your Skills

Using Literal and Abstraction Models

The following exercises are suggested to clarify the concept of art as literal or as an abstraction from reality. While doing these explorations remember that abstraction does not mean taking the shape of a motivating object or pantomiming the typical movements of an animal or person. More sophisticated work in abstraction grows from in-depth movement responses. Nonliteral choreography can be understood by doing the explorations that deal with movement manipulation and variation included in chapter 2.

Literal Exercises

1. Choose a character in a story you have read, and identify the personality traits of this individual. In other words, did this person seem to be bright, cheerful, sad, depressed, ruthless, gentle, and so forth? Then come up with several movement phrases that you feel express the nature of this character.

2. Think about the preceding story again, and decide how this same character changed throughout the book. There were probably some developments in the plot that caused this individual to react or take on a different attitude. Choreograph several more phrases that express these changes.

3. Connect the movement phrases that you developed in the preceding two exercises so that you have a short dance that expresses the changes in reaction and attitude experienced by this character. Try to make your transitions fit the tone and quality of the phrases you have already created.

4. Choose a story that describes a relationship between two people. Improvise movements that suggest the traits of each character. Then decide how to combine the movements of each to express the relationship between the two. Write down your movement ideas together with a description of the proposed form and development of this piece.

Abstraction Exercises

1. Play a tape of various kinds of sounds that have contrasting qualities. These sounds might include those that are low and calm and others that are high pitched, like screeching. (This exercise works best with simple, distinct sounds, rather than complex music.) As the tape is played, draw on a blank sheet of paper. Drawing should be done without a lot of thinking, and in response to the quality of the different sounds. Relax and use your whole arm to make these drawings. (A felt-tip pen and a fairly large sheet of paper are recommended for this exercise.) If you could compare your drawings to those of another person, you would probably find that a certain kind of sound produced drawings that had similar quality and shape. This is the essence or abstraction of the motivating sound.

2. Listen to each of the preceding sounds again and respond by moving instead of drawing.

Movement responses should be based on the quality and shapes discovered while drawing. Continue to respond to the quality of each sound without thinking about how to move. In this exercise, the drawing and then the movement serve as an abstraction of each sound.

3. Abstraction can be understood by using visual motivations as well. Use construction paper in various colors to motivate your movement responses. Although individual response to specific colors may differ, hot colors such as red usually stimulate quick, excited movements, while cool colors such as green or blue are met with a more calm reaction. You can respond to the element of shape by cutting the colored construction paper into various shapes.

4. It is easy to connect your understanding of abstraction with the real world. Notice the many sounds, colors, shapes, lines, and designs found in your environment, and use them as motivations to create an abstraction in the form of a short dance.

5. Use your own personal objects as a motivation to create abstractions. These objects could include prints, photos, feathers, plants, pottery, and so on. Begin by selecting the colors, lines, patterns, shapes, and textures found on these objects. Then use these characteristics to stimulate movement.

6. Try using realistic magazine photographs as the motivation for abstracted movement as well.

Dance Style

A final motivation or intent for creating a dance is to follow a specific movement style. The form of such a choreography is determined by the style selected as its motivation. Overall development of a dance could follow some of the forms described earlier in this chapter, or the dance form could be of the choreographer's own design. Common dance styles include jazz, lyric, comic, and geometric. Dance style, in particular, relates to the feeling of a piece, to the way energy and rhythm are arranged in a work, and to how the choreographer has used line and shape. It is usually easy to distinguish among various dance styles.

The term "jazz" style is used here to describe traditional jazz dance and its vocabulary of steps as well as original movements and patterns performed in the manner or having the dynamic qualities of traditional jazz. Jazz style dance has a syncopated rhythmic pattern similar to that of jazz music. For a jazz style dance, select movement that is vital, energetic, and alive with a captivating energy and rhythm. Jazz style dancing can be sharp or smooth but frequently involves movements known as *isolations* that are performed with only one part of the body. The rhythms and energy of jazz dance are contagious, and it is difficult to resist the temptation to move yourself when watching such a performance (see figure 3.5a).

In contrast, *lyric* dances are smooth, calm, and controlled. In fact, the movement style in lyric dance is very similar to that of classical ballet, with a rounded use of line and shape. Lyric dancing is traditionally what many individuals imagine when they think about dance (see figure 3.5b).

Creating *comic* style dances requires a special outlook. Comedy does not need to involve the use of complex movement patterns and ideas, but rather can grow from somewhat simple themes. To compose a comic dance, the choreographer must be able to see the humor in everyday happenings; comedy relies on an odd placement or juxtaposing of the elements of dance design (see figure 3.6a).

Finally, a *geometric* style dance is one in which the emphasis is on line and shape. The style of dance described here is sometimes called *abstract*, but the word "geometric" is used in this book to avoid confusion with the word "abstraction," which is a choreography based on the essence of something real—a distillation of reality. The process of creating an abstraction was described in the preceding sections. Geometric dances are nonliteral; the goal is to manipulate or vary movement for its own sake, not to express feeling or intent. When watching a geometric style work, the observer is drawn into an involvement with visual designs and

Figure 3.5 (a) A typical jazz dance movement with bent knee and lowered center of weight. (b) Lyric-style movement. Note the softened, or curved, use of the arms.

Figure 3.6 (a) Typical movement from a comic choreography. (b) Geometric action emphasizing line, shape, and design. (Geometric dance is sometimes known as dance in an abstract style. The word "geometric" is used here to avoid confusion with dances that are based on an abstraction from reality.)

with impulses and control of energy. The main concern in geometric style dance is how the choreographer manipulates these factors in the dance space. Figure 3.6b shows an example of the geometric style.

As the choreographer, you may decide to compose a literal dance that tells a story, or one that is strictly nonliteral. You may even mix some of the dance styles described so that your jazz or lyric composition also communicates a story to the audience. Whatever your motivation in creating a choreography, make the dance form you choose fit your intent.

*E*xperience in Action

1. View a videotape of a choreography and decide if the work is choreographed in either a jazz, lyric, comic, or geometric style. Make a list of the movement traits or characteristics that you believe place this dance in one style category or another.

2. If you concluded that the dance in exercise 1 does not fit any of the style categories defined in this text, decide how you could describe the style of this choreography, and put this analysis in your journal for future reference.

3. View a videotape of a second choreography that you feel has a contrasting style to that in the previous exercise. Compare the style of the first dance with that of the second. In what ways are these two pieces the same? How are they different? Use the elements of movement—space, time, energy, and shape—as the basis for your comparison.

Developing Your Skills

Style

1. Select a single movement such as a walk and perform it in the jazz, lyric, comical, and geometric styles.

2. Do the preceding exercise using other movements. Be aware of the different kinesthetic feelings that accompany the performance of each movement style. Observe your movements in a mirror so that you can see how each style differs visually. Note your observations in your journal.

3. Create a longer sequence of movements— one that is several phrases in length and that could be a movement theme in a dance. Then try to perform this theme in each of the four movement styles.

Dance Subject Matter

The choice of appropriate subject matter greatly affects the development of a successful composition, because form grows from the motivating idea. Dance is very ephemeral. The nature of its media—movement—causes it to be so. Movement is seen, and then it is gone. It must be remembered through the images of the mind so that each mental picture adds up in the viewer's memory to form a whole dance that is a complete work of art.

Complex subjects are usually inappropriate for choreography. Simple, action-oriented ideas provide much better motivation for dance composition because they can be presented and developed more easily. The audience also understands and remembers action-oriented ideas, while philosophical ideas can be described more effectively through words or a combination of words and actions. Humphrey (1987) advises that in dance (a) the idea of propaganda or social reform can be overwhelming; (b) cosmic themes such as the creation of the world are too vast; (c) mechanical ideas lead to very mechanical, technique-oriented compositions; and (d) literary stories are too complex in terms of the interpersonal relationships involved to be easily translated into movement, particularly by the beginning choreographer.

1. View a number of dances on video, and try, if possible, to identify the subject of each.

2. Compare and contrast the form and development used in the dances in the preceding exercise. See if you can write a description of these forms. Notice whether these choreographers have chosen a traditional form such as the AB or ABA.

3. Try to describe the style in which each dance in exercise 1 is choreographed.

4. If a dance you have viewed in the exercise is a nonliteral work, identify what traits or what thread of development hold this work together and give it the sense of being a whole.

Developing Your Skills
Dance Subject Matter

1. Select a specific feeling such as happy, sad, or angry. Choreograph several phrases of movement that you believe express this feeling.

2. Continuing exercise 1, have a classmate observe your movement phrases to see whether you have been able to communicate the desired feeling.

3. Rework your movement phrases from the previous exercise if you were not successful in communicating the desired feeling. Think about how you could change your use of the elements—space, time, energy, and shape—in order to communicate more successfully.

4. Repeat the exercises, but use another motivation for movement—perhaps one that is movement or action oriented.

5. Select a more complex idea for a dance, and write a description of the development of this choreography. (You might try to work with one of the ideas attributed to Doris Humphrey in this section on dance subject matter, page 69.)

Finishing Touches

Choreographers must learn to look at the total picture that is created in their work. Spatially, dancers form groupings at any single point in time to make ever-changing formations throughout the whole piece. Each of these groupings must be dynamic, not static, creating an interesting picture for the eye so that one part of the dance leads into the next section. Between sections, choreographers should use transitions to give the whole piece continuity and development.

You can begin teaching your movement to your dancers once you have found some phrases through improvisation, have worked with varying these phrases, and have formed an idea for the development of your work. It is possible that the dancers will perform your movements exactly as you visualized, although this is usually not the case. In most circumstances, the choreographer must nurture the execution of the movements by carefully coaching the dancers. The main idea is to make your dance and your performers look as good as possible.

Communicating With Your Dancers

Projection is one aspect of the dance performance that requires coaching. If a dance is to reach an audience, it must *project*. Dancers must perform with sensitivity and awareness; they must learn to direct their energies toward the audience. To aid projection, suggest that your dancers breathe with their movement and allow their energy to flow freely between the center and extremities. In addition, encourage your dancers to reach, stretch, and focus outward while moving.

Choreographers must also communicate with the dancers about the intent of the choreography. This communication can enhance performance quality, enabling performers to get involved in the motivation of the composition and understand the choreographer's ideas. Appropriate imagery can be a helpful coaching tool here. Try to think of many images that relate to the intent of your choreography, and keep them in mind as you work with your dancers. It may even be helpful to keep

a record of specific images you experienced during the choreographic process. Describe these images to your dancers, particularly when a problem arises concerning the performance of a phrase or sequence. If one image does not connect, try another. Attempt to use both visual and kinesthetic imagery. Be persistent and creative in coaching your performers, and don't give up until execution fits your original intent.

When you've finished setting your work, take time to observe the performance of your dance. A videotape of the presentation can be a useful learning aid at this point. Make a video of the entire choreography, and have the performers watch it immediately. You can point out specific performance problems as the tape is reviewed, but the dancers themselves will notice points at which they have done movements incorrectly. One viewing of a tape usually produces marked improvement in performance quality. Videotapes also provide an excellent method of keeping a record of each of your dances. Store the tapes in a dry, cool place away from heat, light, or electromagnetic sources such as a television, loudspeaker, or microwave oven.

Developing Your Skills
Communicating With Your Dancers

1. You can learn about projection from the following exercise. Watch a dancer perform a simple action such as extending the arm diagonally forward from the shoulder. Then have the dancer do this same movement again, this time letting the arm extend as far away from the center of the body as possible. You should notice that the movement appears larger the second time.

2. Another way to enhance projection is to learn to breathe with a movement. In general, dancers breathe in as movement progresses up or out, and breathe out as movement comes down or inward. Again, watch a dancer perform a simple action while the breath is held. Then contrast this performance with one in which the same

movement is done while breathing. The second performance should appear more full, free, and alive.

3. Use of appropriate imagery can also improve movement performance. Give a dancer a specific movement, and watch as this movement is performed. Then suggest an image that would change and refine the performance of the movement. Experiment with many different images and how each affects the performance of the same movement (see table 1.2 in chapter 1 for examples of various types of imagery).

The Critique and Assessment

As you learn to choreograph, you will put together many dance studies. Your teachers will select appropriate motivation for these studies and will guide you through the steps of development. Listen carefully to the suggestions about your work, and relate these suggestions to your developing knowledge of the choreographic craft. Remember that improvement comes gradually and that a critique of your choreography is not a criticism of you as an individual. Creating an artistic work can be intensely personal, but try to interpret an evaluation objectively and constructively, not in a negative manner.

The use of a structured assessment form can make a critique more meaningful. Concrete suggestions should make it easier to change and improve your choreography. Assessment sheets can include categories that fit your goals and match the components generally found in a successful piece of choreography (appendix B contains a sample Choreographic Assessment Sheet). You can fill out an assessment sheet after you have viewed the presentation of your dance. Ideas concerning each of the choreographic components can be written on these sheets along with other suggestions to improve the dance. Any ensuing discussion of your choreography then flows from the assessment components, and not from purely personal reactions of those who have viewed your dance.

You can also use these or other assessment forms to help you think about your choreography as it develops during the creative process. When you feel that specific components need work, make a note of this fact. Think over possible solutions to the problem, and try to visualize your dancers as they move through each solution. You may need to do more improvisation to solve some choreographic problems.

Through an assessment process, you can take a more positive and active part in the discussion and evaluation of your work. You should find that using assessment forms encourages learning, because you have to understand choreographic components in order to fill out the sheet.

Developing Your Skills
Critique and Assessment

1. Watch a videotape of a dance created by an established choreographer. As you watch, attempt to see how the choreographic components discussed in this book were incorporated into the work. Write your observations in a journal.

2. Use the process described in the first exercise to analyze works that you see in live concerts.

3. Watch the same videotape you used in the first exercise, and fill out the Choreographic Assessment Sheet in appendix B.

4. Review the list of choreographic components found in an effective dance (see "Dance Characteristics to Watch For," pages 57-59), and then write an explanation of each one using your own words. You will probably discover that your understanding will develop gradually.

Learning to Choreograph

Hawkins (1988) has said that developing your choreographic abilities takes time and occurs in

developmental stages. It is a trial-and-error process of seeing, experiencing, and learning. Early dances frequently lack clear form and definition. As a novice choreographer you may find that you create strong beginnings without being able to follow through to a logical conclusion or that you tend to string separate movements together rather than forming the movement into sequences or phrases. Viewing the work of established choreographers in performance or on videotape is one way to heighten your sensitivity and gain a better understanding of how to mold and give form to your work (see appendix A for a list of videotape distributors). Learning to choreograph is a skill that takes years of practice. The choreographer should learn perseverance, gain worldly experience, and be able to put aside enough time to create and rehearse a dance. Lavender (1996) states that an authentic dance composition process, particularly at the beginning level, involves experiencing a struggle to get beyond imitating what other choreographers have done in the past.

You will probably be asked to put together many short dances in your choreography class. Each of these short pieces, or studies, usually deals with some aspect of the composition process. In each study you will be working on the forming and shaping process in order to gain a better sense of what makes up a whole dance. Some specific suggestions for exploring and improvising have already been described. The first step in creating either a study or a dance is to discover appropriate movement through exploration and improvisation, as chapter 1 explains. The shaping or forming of your dance should follow such experimentation. Your teacher can also provide you with many helpful suggestions concerning choreographic development.

Review Questions

Think about a piece of choreography that you consider to be a successful work. Describe the form and development of this dance. Try to apply some of the criteria of effective dance form described in this chapter to this choreography.

Select a second dance that you feel is an effective piece, and analyze the form and development of this work as well. Are both this and the preceding piece developed and shaped in the same way?

What is a dance phrase? Is there a relationship between a dance phrase and the whole dance? If so, describe this relationship.

How should the phrases that make up a whole dance compare one to the other? Draw a diagram of several different movement phrases.

Describe two contrasting motivations that you could use as a stimulus for improvising. Would dances developed from these two motivations differ in appearance? If so, what might be some of the qualities or traits of each choreography? How might these two dances be similar?

What is a transition? How could you provide a transition between two phrases? Is the use of transition important to other parts of a dance? Explain.

Name three traditional dance forms and describe the characteristics of each. Also compare the shape or overall development of each of the three forms. Describe how you might use one of these dance forms to help you create your own choreography.

Describe the choreographic technique known as canon. Do the same with ground bass. Compare the appearance of dances or sections of dances that were developed using each method.

How does abstraction in art relate to reality? Give some examples of choreographic abstractions. Explain how you could use abstraction to motivate movement improvisation.

What is a nonliteral choreography? Describe how you could create a dance using nonliteral methods. How would this nonliteral work compare with a literal dance?

What is organic form? Answer this question by using specific examples, and explain how these examples could relate to making a dance.

What is dance style? Name and describe two possible dance styles. What factors make these two movement styles different?

The concepts geometric and abstraction are defined in this book. According to this text, what is the difference between these two artistic concepts?

Would it be a good idea for a beginning choreographer to create a dance based on sociological, psychological, or cosmic themes? Why or why not? If your answer is no, describe a more appropriate motivation.

Your ability to coach your dancers can be an important part of creating an effective choreography. Name a coaching method you could use. Explain a performance problem, and then describe the coaching technique you would use to solve this problem.

What is a choreographic assessment sheet? How could you use assessment to help develop and refine your choreography?

Learning to choreograph occurs in developmental stages. Explain this statement by describing some of these stages. What techniques could you use, as a beginning choreographer, to help you move through these stages?

Staging the Performance

*P*lanning a dance performance can be an awesome task, but you can minimize the challenge by arranging the production process into a series of smaller, more digestible tasks. Each of these individual tasks can be scheduled by beginning with the date of the performance and working backward to the audition.

Several years ago, I choreographed and designed the costumes for a five-part dance based on Mayan artifacts and mythology. In many ways I attribute my ability to complete that project to the fact that I had planned when the choreography, costume designs, and costume and mask construction needed to be ready. By organizing my schedule, I was able to treat each task as one step in producing a large creative work.

A successful dance concert is well organized. This means that you have considered all aspects of production from the audition to the closing performance. This chapter begins with an introduction to the audition and the process of scheduling rehearsals. Blocking and technical and dress rehearsals are discussed next, followed by information about dance floors and the printed program. As the technical aspects of a dance concert can enhance or detract from the production, you'll find many suggestions about how to record the accompaniment, design the costumes and lighting, and use props and sets. At the end of this chapter, you will also learn how to stage informal concerts and lecture-demonstrations.

Planning and Organization

You should plan the content of a performance carefully, whether the concert is formal or informal. Program content should be based on the interests and needs of both the dance students and the audience. You won't build an audience unless you attempt to connect with the needs and ideas of potential audience members. For example, it wouldn't be wise to produce an experimental dance concert in a conservative community. Similarly, dance concerts presented in ethnic neighborhoods should include some representation of the dance forms derived from the predominant culture or cultures. If you're living in a community where dance is not understood, you may need to do some audience education. The information that serves to inform the audience about dance usually takes the form of program notes, program inserts, or a lecture-demonstration. (The lecture-demonstration is discussed later in this chapter.) A community that is knowledgeable about dance will be able to appreciate a dance concert without the aid of explanations, but program content should still be planned to suit community tastes.

You should also consider program variety when planning a concert—particularly with respect to choreographic styles and the number of performers in each dance. Try to alternate the order of light and serious compositions, and of small and large groups. Other suggestions you could try include placing an entertaining but short dance first to allow late arrivals to be seated fairly quickly; presenting another entertaining dance immediately before intermission to make the audience want to come back for the second part of your show; and saving the best for last so the concert builds in energy toward the end. Program order should be based on practical considerations as well. For instance, it may be necessary to have some quick costume changes when the same dancer or dancers perform in one piece right after another. Try to accomplish these costume changes rapidly and smoothly, but if you are able to arrange your concert to avoid quick changes, do so.

Holding Auditions

The audition—the first step in producing a dance concert—is a process that has made many a dancer nervous. Learning new movement materials, performing in an unfamiliar space, and dancing in front of strangers can all contribute to a case of nerves. Encourage dancers to arrive at your audition early. This will give them time to warm up and also allow them to relax, select a dance space, and get a feeling for the space in which the audition will be conducted.

You can do many other things as well to make auditioning less hectic and better organized. One is to have each dancer fill out an information sheet

and assign him or her a number (see appendix B for a sample Dancer's Audition Form). Two of the most important pieces of information for you on this sheet are the phone number and the times when the dancer is available for rehearsals. Have dancers attach their numbers to their dance costumes, so that you'll be able to identify each dancer by number if you do not know the person's name. This is important because dancers are often cast during a meeting that follows the audition session. Dancers should audition in numerical order throughout the entire session.

The audition begins by teaching your movement pattern(s) to the whole group. Each movement sequence you present should be relatively short but representative of the type and style of movement found in the choreography. The dancers will need time to practice each sequence and to ask questions if necessary. Finally, you can watch while the dancers perform the sequence. This performance should be done in small groups so that you're able to see each dancer. You can watch the first 10 dancers, then the next 10, and so on. You'll need to repeat this process for additional dances to be included in the concert. Select those dancers who perform your movements with a sense of clarity, accuracy, understanding, and aliveness—they will contribute most to the success of your work.

If you're composing more than one dance, try, if possible, to distribute the performers among the choreographic works so that no one dancer is in an excessive number of dances, and so that all or most dancers will get some performing experience. The cast list should be posted as soon as possible— preferably the morning after the audition. Dancers should read this list and put a check after their name so that you will know they have read the cast list. It's also helpful to include on the cast list the date and location of the first rehearsal of your dance.

1. Select the movement sequence or sequences you will use to audition dancers for this work. Practice each sequence with everyone who is auditioning. Supply other movement cues to enhance understanding of the performance of this pattern. Use images or ideas that describe the desired movement quality or qualities in the sequence.

2. Design a sample audition information sheet, making sure the sheet includes space for all necessary information.

3. Prepare the dancers' numbers on small squares of paper. These should be sized so that they do not interfere with dancers' movements but so that the numbers are large enough to be seen from the front of the room. You'll need small safety pins for attaching the numbers to each dancer's clothing. Do not use straight pins for this purpose.

4. Visualize how you want the dancers positioned in the audition space. For example, in which direction should they face, and on which pathways will they move across the floor? Decide on how many dancers you want to view in each group.

Scheduling Rehearsals

A well-organized rehearsal schedule is essential for a successful performance. Try to schedule two or more rehearsals each week. The rehearsals should be long enough to allow sufficient progress but not so long that the dancers become exhausted. You will have many rehearsals before your dance is moved into the theatre. One thing you can do to make the transition from studio to theatre easier is to tape the stage dimensions on the dance studio floor. It's also helpful to mark dancers' beginning or ending positions and the placement of sets.

Blocking Rehearsals

You should schedule theatre rehearsals by beginning with the performance and moving backward

to the date on which you first have use of the theatre. The first theatre rehearsal is for blocking. Usually, there will be time for only one blocking rehearsal, which is used to *mount* the dance onstage. You should try to leave more time to block a long dance, but bear in mind that the blocking time will depend on the total time you are allowed in the theatre.

Begin blocking rehearsals by having the dancers run through the entire piece. As you do this, decide where you need to reposition dancers. Next, go through the choreography slowly, and direct the placement of each dancer; be clear about the floor patterns to be followed by each dancer throughout the progression of the piece. You should also indicate how performers are to relate to each other in the stage space, and where each dancer enters and exits. As a safety precaution, clarify the position of all onstage technical equipment. The dancers must know the placement of all *masking*, wiring, lighting, and sound equipment so that there are no dangerous surprises during the program! All loose wires should be taped down, and pieces of carpet should be placed over sharp or protruding equipment to prevent injury. This is also the time to warn dancers about *sight lines*, since performers should not be visible until they are part of the action onstage. A good rule is to have your dancers stand very close to and behind the *leg* or side curtain when awaiting an entrance. Generally, if dancers can see members of the audience from where they are standing, then these audience members can probably see them too.

In some concerts you might be able to close the front curtain after each dance, but in theatres in which this may be too time consuming it is advisable to have dancers enter the darkened stage with the front curtain open. In the course of an entire performance, then, the curtain would be closed before the concert, at intermission, and after the last dance. If the curtain remains open between dances, entrances should be made in a calm and collected manner; also, dancers will find their starting positions more easily if the stage floor is marked with fluorescent tape.

It is customary to have the performers take a bow after a dance. The bow puts a professional and finishing touch on the choreography. After the dance is ended, the performers come back onstage as quickly as possible; the lights are brought back up; the dancers bow; the lights go down; and the dancers exit. In most bows, the performers stand in one line and bend forward from the waist, with the dancer on the far right or left leading the line. A large bow with a flourish of movement down to the floor is not considered in good taste. On the other hand, a bow in which the performers assume a pose from the choreography rather than taking a traditional bow can be effective (see figure 4.1a-c). You should have your dancers practice the bow during the blocking rehearsal, and be sure to include a bow for the accompanists if your work is performed to live music.

Technical Rehearsals

Technical rehearsals usually follow blocking rehearsals. In these rehearsals, the technicians have a chance to set and practice lighting cues, and the performers in turn become familiar with these cues. Technicians, particularly those who are not familiar with dance, may need to see a movement several times before they are able to connect it with the appropriate lighting cue. For this reason, it is helpful to have the *lighting designer* attend rehearsals before the concert is moved into the theatre.

In the technical rehearsal, have the performers mark through the entire piece of choreography, stopping at each point at which there should be a change in the lighting. This is the time to experiment with use of different *gel* colors and with instruments located in different positions (see the section on Color, pages 93-94, for an explanation of how to use gels). The lighting designer must write down each cue, indicating which instruments (such as spotlights, striplights, or floodlights) are needed to produce the desired effect. All cues must be numbered from the beginning to the end of the concert and should note how a particular cue can be used to enhance the choreography and how it relates to specific changes in the dance. Cues should also include information about how to control lighting changes at the *dimmer* board and, if necessary, the duration of the cue. Never recommend that cues be

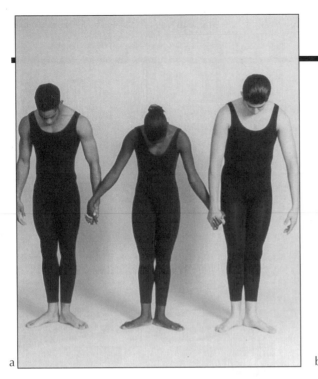

Figure 4.1 (a) A simple bow with clean lines. (b) A bow that is too distracting. (c) A choreographed pose can be used instead of a traditional bow at the conclusion of a dance.

memorized; the large number of cues required during a dance performance makes memorization extremely difficult.

You or your technicians may have to rerun certain segments of a dance a number of times until the lighting is done correctly. Later, you will practice each lighting cue again as the dance is rehearsed during the dress rehearsals. If you have time during the technical rehearsal, run the dance together with the lighting cues immediately after these cues are set. Try to allow a long block of time for the technical rehearsal of your dance, since you'll usually have only one session in which to set the cues.

Dress Rehearsals

Dress rehearsals are conducted immediately preceding the concert and should be run more than once if time in the theatre permits. During dress rehearsals, you have a chance to give lighting and costumes a final check. This is also when the pace of the entire program can be brought up to speed. Remember that audiences get restless at dance concerts that have long breaks between each piece. Dancers should be encouraged to make entrances and exits as quickly and smoothly as possible; performers who dance in two or more successive dances should practice changing costumes. Sometimes the flow of a concert can be accelerated by providing *dressers* to help with quick changes. A dresser has a costume ready and helps undress and dress a performer; a small portable dressing room can be set up behind a screen in the *wings* to facilitate quick costume changes. All rehearsals, including the choreographer's rehearsals, should be written on a calendar and posted where the entire cast can check the schedule (see appendix B for a sample Performance Organization Checklist to help you organize audition and rehearsal scheduling).

Developing Your Skills
Planning Rehearsals

Use a block calendar to organize the following schedule. This will be your *master calendar*.

1. Begin with the date of your performance to determine when you should hold the audition for your dance. (This block of time may already be determined by your school.) The audition date should immediately precede the onset of rehearsals, so that you have several months in which to create your dance. However, if you're given less time in which to rehearse, organize your rehearsal schedule accordingly. Be practical, but try not to sacrifice the quality of your dance.

2. Next, schedule your weekly rehearsals. At least two rehearsals per week are recommended in order to provide continuity and to help your dancers remember the choreography. Check the audition forms for the best rehearsal time for each dancer, and then post this rehearsal schedule.

3. Mark off the time in which you will be allowed to rehearse in the theatre. Then divide this allotment of time into the blocking, technical, and dress rehearsals.

   - Blocking a choreography usually requires one to two hours, but it can take less time for a short dance.

   - Technical rehearsals usually require more time. A long dance with many cues could take an entire evening, since the technical rehearsal involves experimenting with the lighting and writing down the cues.

   - Dress rehearsals should take place immediately before the performance. Again, the number of dress rehearsals is determined by the total amount of time you have in the theatre. It is ideal to have three dress rehearsals, but sometimes this may not be possible. Use full makeup only in the final dress rehearsal.

4. If you can, leave some theatre rehearsal time for changing the lighting, for additional rehearsals if there are problems, and for taking record photographs. Mark all these events on your master calendar.

5. Use the Performance Organization Checklist in appendix B to help organize your rehearsal schedule. Put a check in front of each item as you include it in your schedule; then record the dates on which you plan to conduct each type of rehearsal on your master calendar.

6. Briefly explain your organization of the master calendar, telling how this arrangement fits your situation. For example, why were the blocking or technical rehearsals arranged as represented?

A Word About Dance Floors

The ideal dance surface is a *suspended floor* that is smooth, unblemished, and free of splinters. Theatres that have a cement stage floor are not appropriate for dance and should be avoided if possible. Check the surface of your stage floor carefully. Look for nails, screws, or other sharp objects that could injure a dancer's feet. Cover splintered areas in the floor with masking tape, and then paint the tape the same color as the floor so it will not be noticed. Clean the stage floor with a damp mop before each rehearsal and performance to remove dust that could soil costumes. For your future reference, a listing of some of the companies that sell *portable dance floors*, along with additional information about these floors, is provided in appendix A.

Developing Your Skills
Checking the Dance Surface

1. Find a space in which you could present your dance. This should be a stage or studio space to which you have access. Walk slowly back and forth across this space, inspecting the surface of the floor for splits, splinters, or small objects that could injure your dancers or interfere with their performance. Decide where you might put tape to cover rough areas or holes.

2. Determine whether the surface of the floor needs to be mopped.

3. Inspect the areas located on the edge of the performance space. Make sure that no chairs, ladders, or other equipment block your dancers' ability to make entrances and exits. If such equipment is in the way and cannot be moved, decide how you could alter your choreography so that the obstructions are no longer a problem.

4. Mark your master calendar to indicate an appropriate time in which you could conduct the above inspection of the performance space. The inspection should take place before blocking rehearsals begin.

The Printed Program

The printed program should include the following information:

- Dance title
- Grants/funding sources
- Choreographer
- Musical artist(s) and composer(s)
- Music title
- Recording company label
- Credits (costume designer, props construction, etc.)
- Dancers (in alphabetical order)
- Program notes

The title of a dance is a guidepost for the audience. Choreographers should use dance titles that hint at the nature or content of the dance. This sets the stage and points the way, indicating in general what is to come and what the audience can expect from a choreography. At the same time, a title should leave some of the mystery about a dance intact, allowing members of the audience to explore their imagination concerning the work and to experience the choreography on their own terms.

Good names for dances are often suggested by the title or style of the accompaniment, the style of the choreography, or a relationship created between the performers. Dance dramas can bear names that hint at the story told in the dance, or that relate to some of the major characters. Both the dance title and the program notes should grow from the motivating materials with which you have been working, rather than serve merely to describe the action of the dance. Turner (1971) indicates that titles for nonliteral dances are used as a *metaphor* or point of identification to help the spectator get involved in the choreography and provide a point of reference or a place to begin viewing the work. Often such titles are based on choreographic concepts such as imagery, movement quality, or dance form (see table 4.1 for a brief analysis of dance title and content).

Table 4.1 Dance Titles and Content

Dance title	Dance content
Legends of the Maya	A five-part choreography dealing with Mayan legends. These legends include stories of Mayan gods and the Mayan creation myth.
Under-Currents	A three-part dance in which the three sections portray the following themes: (1) searching; (2) aggression; and (3) harmony.
Electronic Terpsichore	A three-part dance choreographed to a whimsical, electronic score.
Ritual Dance	A two-part dance based on the movement themes of tribal peoples.
Three Episodes	A three-part lyric dance in which each part has a theme or thematic element. For example, in part one the dancers attempt to upstage each other, and in part three small balls are exchanged among the dancers.
Kinetic Rhythm	A fast-paced jazz-style choreography.

On program copy, the dancers' names are usually listed in alphabetical order, although you may also list performers in the order of their appearance in your dance. Sometimes the major dancers and the roles they perform are grouped separately. For legal or copyright protection, list the label on the tape or compact disk so that the music publisher receives credit in the program. Under credits, list the names of others who have made contributions to your work, such as designers, props people, and visual artists. If you received a grant or donation to produce your work, make sure to note this source in the program; consult a representative of the benefactor or foundation to make sure the organization is credited correctly. You may need program notes to explain characters and/or meanings in your dance; if so, try to keep them clear and brief. Some programs also list a rehearsal director if there is one. Dance concerts that are collaborative performances by different groups or companies should include some information about each group. Provide the name of the contact person, an address, a phone number, and some background information about the group. This information helps publicize these groups. Appendix B includes both a sample Printed Program Information Sheet, used to collect and organize information for the printed program, and a sample program entry.

Developing Your Skills
Creating the Printed Program

1. Create a title for your dance by reviewing the information in the preceding section. A few potential titles may have occurred to you during the creative process, and you may still feel that one of these titles is the "right" one. (It's a good idea to make note of all potential titles as they come to mind.)

2. Explain your choice of title for your choreography.

3. Use the Printed Program Information Sheet in appendix B to compose other information concerning your dance that will appear in the printed program.

4. Format the program entry for your dance, and produce a printed copy for your records.

5. Return to your master calendar and select the dates for creating and printing program copy.

Technical Considerations

A considerable amount of finishing needs to be done even after a dance is choreographed and the movement is set or taught to the dancers. Some of this polishing is accomplished by coaching the dancers, but presentation of the final product requires that the director go through several other steps, including:

- Recording the music
- Designing and executing the costumes
- Planning the lighting
- Creating sets and props

Organizing the rehearsal schedule—including blocking, technical, and dress rehearsals—is also part of the final stages of performance production.

Preparing the Accompaniment

Dance accompaniment is best when performed live. This is true of both classroom accompaniment and accompaniment for dance performances. However, while live accompaniment provides better quality and greater flexibility than recorded sound, the cost of paying musicians is usually beyond the budget of most choreographers.

If recorded accompaniment is used, it must be of high quality. The director or sound person should use new tapes, discs, or records for the *master tape*. Old recordings are likely to produce a tape with many pops and cracks, and these extraneous sounds are magnified when reproduced over a loudspeaker system. When making recordings, keep the volume at a uniform but high level, since the use of different audio levels requires constant adjustments in volume during the performance. Use cables and plugs to produce recordings, because microphones allow extraneous sounds to be picked up by recording equipment. Do not cut music or change the speed of the original score. Also, make sure that the format used for recording matches the format of the playback unit, so that both units are either stereo or *monaural*. Audio cassettes can be

used for the master tape, but it is more difficult to locate specific points on a cassette than on a reel-to-reel tape. Use of a reel-to-reel tape recorder allows the sound person to view the tape during the performance in order to locate specific points on the tape more easily (see figure 4.2).

When recording master tapes, splice a light-colored leader between each musical selection. This will allow you or your audio technician to see where you've stopped the tape and also to stop only at a point between the accompaniment for specific dances. It's a good idea to write the name of each choreography on the leader preceding the accompaniment to prevent mistakes in pausing the tape during the concert. Labeling each piece also enables you to cope with last-minute problems such as the need to delete a dance from the program. So you'll be prepared in case of emergency, make a copy of your master tape and have it available during all performances. Extra tape recorders should also be on hand for a show.

If you are using a cassette player for your performance, you could have the music for each dance recorded on a separate cassette. In this way, you could still alter the order of the concert or remove a dance if necessary. Label each tape clearly, and do not record on the back side of any of the cassettes.

Figure 4.2 A reel-to-reel tape recorder.

The audio technician should attend some of the early rehearsals to learn the sequence of movements that make up each composition and to take notes concerning each cue or change in accompaniment. Sound cues include changing volume, fading sound in or out, and turning accompaniment on or off.

Check the speakers to be used during the performance, and if they produce poor-quality sound replace them with better equipment. When possible, use a stereo rather than a monaural sound system, and always check sound quality from different areas in the house. Sometimes it is necessary to place a portable speaker on each side of the stage to provide adequate sound for the performers, but if you do, make sure this sound doesn't bleed into the theatre. These speakers should be placed downstage and directed on upstage diagonals. Schlaich and Dupont (1988) recommend placing microphones onstage to amplify the voices of speaking dancers, or to pick up foot sounds such as taps.

Developing Your Skills
Preparing the Accompaniment

1. Listen carefully to the tape or compact disc track(s) that you have chosen for your music. Notice if there are extraneous sounds.

2. If you can hear extraneous sounds on your tape, get a new copy of your music if possible.

3. Record your accompaniment on quality equipment. You may require a skilled technician for this.

4. Listen to your master tape and repeat the recording process if necessary.

5. Test the master tape and the sound equipment to be used during the performance prior to the dress rehearsals. This is important, since your dancers may need to accommodate to a slight change in tempo. The speed at which tape recorders reproduce sound can differ, even though each recorder is put on an identical setting. Find other equipment if the difference in tempo is excessive.

6. Mark your master calendar to indicate recording dates.

Costuming the Dance

One of the first rules of dance costuming is to make sure the costumes complement the choreography, not detract from it. A dance costume should enhance the movement. The most effective costumes, therefore, are simple in design. You have defeated your purpose if the audience focuses on costumes rather than the dancing. You should begin to visualize costuming as soon as you have a movement sketch or basic outline of your choreography.

The costumes for a dance should be developed from the same idea or ideas that motivated the creation of the choreography. As you consider costume designs, review the feeling, intent, or style that you are trying to create in your piece. Clarify this intent and keep it in mind while you decide on appropriate costumes. Then make some sketches of the proposed costumes. Remember that costumes help create mood. Notice that in figure 4.3, the costumes are playful and comical, whereas in figure 4.4 the costumes project a more serious mood. The costumes in figure 4.5 place the dance in a specific historical period. Also consider the following features with respect to dance costumes:

- Costume color or colors
- Flow and weight of materials
- Style and decoration

Color

Costume color plays a major role in setting the feeling of a piece. Colors such as red, yellow, brown, orange, pink, and rose are considered warm, while green, blue, gray, purple, lavender, and black are cool. You must also think about your dancers when selecting costumes and take into account their coloring, body build, and respective heights. Choose costume colors that are

Figure 4.3 Unitards put together with colored wigs, tops, and leg warmers create simple but comical costumes.

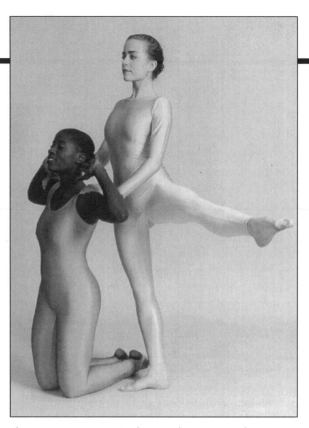

Figure 4.4 Here unitards provide costumes for a more serious dance.

Figure 4.5 A costume from a period in American history. Doris Humphrey (center) in her choreography *The Shakers.*

complimentary to your dancers' coloring, and remember that dancers appear more slender when clothed in darker colors. Lighter or more brightly colored costumes should be worn by dancers with trim figures. If it is necessary to costume a less trim dancer in a light or brightly colored costume, select costumes that camouflage wide hips or other imperfections. This can be done by adding stripes or patches of a darker color in strategic places on a costume (see figure 4.6). Bear in mind that white costumes tend to produce a glare under stage lighting, although the glare can be reduced by dipping the costumes into tea. This process will produce a more subdued shade of off-white that will reflect less light.

Sometimes the choreographer or costume person will have to dye costumes that are white. Dyeing costumes a light shade is usually more successful than trying to achieve vibrant or deep shades; if you desire costumes in those shades, you should purchase them. It is also difficult to dye one part of a costume to match another part.

The texture and type of material also affect the way a costume will accept a dye. In general, synthetic materials do not accept dye as well as organic fibers such as cotton; when in doubt, test a swatch of the material in the dye before immersing the entire costume. Attempts to remove color from a costume and dye it another hue are usually not successful—a rather gray shade of the desired color results and can be difficult to correct.

A choreographer can use costuming to enhance the overall effect of a grouping of dancers, even though individual dancers are of a different height and structure. Dressing all dancers in one color creates unity, although a more interesting effect can be created by using more than one shade of the same color within a group (see figure 4.7a). In this way, unity is maintained, but the stage space appears to have greater depth and more interest. On the other hand, if you place each performer in a different color or in a different style garment, harmony is lost because the audience focuses separately on each dancer (see figure 4.7b). If possible, the soloist should be costumed in a style or color somewhat different from those worn by other performers (see figure 4.7c). Avoid the use of large, bold prints, plaids, and stripes because they tend to distract the audience from the dance.

Flow and Weight of Materials

You can select materials for dance costumes from a fabric store. When you find a material in the right color, unwind some of it from the bolt and move it around to see how it flows. Stiff materials, for example, will stand away from the body and hide and inhibit a dancer's movements. Instead, select materials that will flow with a performer's actions. If possible, test a material by draping some of it on one of your dancers and watch the dancer move in the material. Also consider the material's weight. Very lightweight materials, such as nylon chiffon, create a floating effect when a performer moves, while materials that have more body, such as jersey, flow with the dancer but tend to cling even as the dancer moves.

Figure 4.6 Vertical panels and stripes have a slimming effect.

Figure 4.7 (a) Group unity and design are heightened through use of the same color costumes. (b) Audiences tend to focus individually on each dancer in a group when they are costumed differently. (c) The use of a different color calls attention to the downstage dancer.

Unoccupied spaces around the body (negative spaces) are frequently part of the dance design and should not be covered or filled in with material. Long skirts, for example, can fill in negative spaces. In addition, certain textures are more appropriate for some types of costumes than for others. For example, roughly textured materials should be used to clothe dancers portraying lower-class characters, while plush materials are reserved for

royalty. Shiny materials reflect light and should be employed sparingly, since reflected light attracts attention and should be used for this purpose.

A costume can also help to extend and vary movement. A long, flowing skirt heightens the effect of actions performed with the legs; the choreographer can even use such a skirt to help find movements during the improvisational process. A flowing cape, long sleeves, headgear, or fabrics

that stretch can enhance dance movement and become part of the choreographic design as well (refer again to figures 1.4-1.6).

Style and Decoration

A basic leotard is the best costume for most student performances. It is a good idea to build up a stock of plain leotards in many different colors. They can then be paired with tights of the same or a contrasting color for use in different concerts. Leotards in unusual colors or of an unusual design cannot be adapted as readily for use in later performances.

Give careful consideration to the style and cut of your costumes. Figures 4.8 illustrate examples of poorly designed dance costumes. In figure 4.8a, the costume is too intricate and would divert attention from the choreography. This costume would also inhibit movement by getting in the way.

The garment shown in figure 4.8b cuts the body horizontally, making the dancer appear short and stocky rather than tall and lean, and figure 4.8c shows a leotard that cannot be adapted for use in many separate concerts because the design is not easily used in combination with other costume pieces or decorations.

The *unitard* or body suit has become a popular dance costume in recent years. Unitards are made in one piece to cover the entire body. Decorations can be added, and they are available in styles with or without sleeves and with various necklines. Unitards are made of an elasticized material that fits the body closely and thus are not flattering to some dancers. A unitard costs about the same as a pair of tights and a leotard together but is not as versatile (see figure 4.9).

Choreographers can add various decorations to unitards and leotards, but decorations should be used sparingly and should fit the overall design

a b c

Figure 4.8 (a) Highly detailed and intricate costumes distract from the movement. (b) A costume with horizontal panels or stripes would not be appropriate for a short, stocky dancer. (c) This leotard could not be adapted easily for use in later performances.

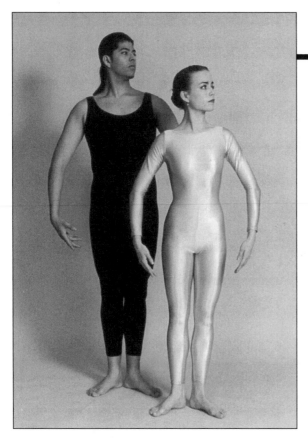

Figure 4.9 These dancers are wearing unitards.

ℰxperience in Action

1. Watch a videotape of a performance by a well-known dance company. Select one dance on this tape and note how the choreographer has used costuming to enhance the style or mood of the work.

2. Make a descriptive list of the choreographer's use of color, material, costume style, and decoration throughout the dance chosen in exercise 1. Then explain how each costume element complements the structure, mood, or message of the choreography. If you find some costume elements to be wrong or distracting, explain.

3. Look at a videotape of a second dance and analyze the choreographer's use of costumes in the same way as in the preceding exercise. Compare and contrast the costume choices made for each piece. Why do the costumes differ in these two works?

concept. Decorative costume pieces could include collars, necklaces, armbands, leg bands, belts, and sleeves—all of which can be made more durable by applying an iron-on fabric stiffener. Costume parts can be held to the underlying garment with hooks or snaps, but small pieces of Velcro fabric are recommended as fasteners for quick changes because they are easy to open and close. Velcro strips can be purchased in most fabric stores in sew-on and iron-on forms. Make sure, however, that the ripping sound made by large Velcro strips cannot be heard by the audience, and that such fasteners are positioned so as not to come loose during partnering work. Test all costume parts during the dress rehearsals.

The look of plain unitards and leotards can also be changed by having dancers wear skirts, pants, or various kinds of tops over the undergarment. You might want to experiment with dyed or painted decorations as well. Dye can be spattered, streaked, dripped, painted, or sprayed onto a costume to create abstract designs, but paint should be used to create more detailed images. Schlaich and Dupont (1988) suggest acrylic latex paints for use on fabrics because they remain flexible, adhere to most surfaces, and can be laundered.

Developing Your Skills
Envisioning the Costume

1. Review the mood or style of your choreography. Try to picture the basic color that you believe complements this mood.

2. Browse through a fabric store. When you find material in an appropriate color, unwind some of it from the bolt and test it for movement quality.

3. Buy a small piece of material of the "right" color and movement quality. The piece should be large enough to cover part of a dancer's body. Drape this material on one of your dancers, and watch how it moves as the dancer performs your choreography.

4. Visualize various costume possibilities that might be suitable for your choreography, and sketch these costumes on an outline of the human figure. (Trace the human figure from a book or magazine if your drawing skills leave something to be desired.) As you

Lighting the Dance

You should keep two main concepts in mind when you're planning the lighting of a dance: stage space and lighting direction. It is also important to understand the controllable qualities of light: intensity or brightness, distribution, movement, and color. The intensity of the lighting depends on the number of instruments used, the distance between the instruments and the dancer(s), and how light is filtered before it reaches the stage. The direction of the instruments and how light is spread over the stage space determines distribution, while movement refers to alterations in the qualities of the light. The color of the lighting also requires careful thought and planning. Color is determined by the color of the gel, or *color media*, placed in the instruments. Lighting can be used to make some stage areas visible, direct the eye to important dancers, create depth and dimension, and enhance style or mood (Brockett, 1992). Lighting enhances the overall composition or series of pictures created in a choreography.

Equipment

Among the most common types of lighting equipment are *spotlights*, *striplights*, and *floodlights* or *scoops*. Spotlights can be of two basic types: Fresnel and ellipsoidal. Fresnel spotlights have a fairly short *housing* and produce soft light, while ellipsoidal spotlights have a much longer housing, are more focused, and can throw light longer distances. The PAR 64 lighting instrument, also in frequent use today, produces light that is similar in quality to the effect produced by a Fresnel. The PAR has an oval beam of light and can provide good side light. Striplights consist of a series of *lamps* set in a long trough; usually every fourth lamp is on the same circuit and is covered with *media* of the same color. Striplights are used to light the backdrop, and on small stages they can provide general illumination. Scoops have no lens but contain a single lamp in a housing with a large opening. They are also designed to provide general lighting. Bear in mind that some lighting equipment must be burned with the *lamp base* pointed up; other instruments require the lamp base to be pointed downward; and some lamps can be placed in either a base-up or a base-down position. Check the instructions for proper positioning of these instruments.

Positioning

Your lighting designer will need enough instruments to cover the stage area with overlapping *pools* of light. Performers cannot be seen when they dance in the dark, so it is paramount that all important stage areas be illuminated. Ellfeldt and Carnes (1971) note that, as a rule, six pools of light are sufficient for general lighting on a small stage (a stage approximately 20 feet wide). Each pool of light should be about 9 to 10 feet in diameter. The instruments that create these pools are positioned either in front of and above the stage, or to the back or side of the stage. The angle of each beam of light is about 45 degrees vertical to the stage floor, so that body shape and form are revealed. This 45-degree angle can be altered to some extent when conditions do not allow for proper location of lighting instruments, but you or your lighting designer will have to judge whether or not the desired effect is being achieved. The six pools of light must overlap by about two feet, although more overlapping is better and will ensure that there are no dark spots onstage.

Each of the six pools of light is created by two spotlights, one coming from stage right and the other from stage left. Ellfeldt and Carnes (1971) propose that pool or area 1 receive its illumination from instruments numbered 1 and 4, pool 2 from 2 and 5, and pool 3 from 3 and 6 (see figure 4.10). The lighting instruments used to create these three

downstage areas are either positioned in the *beams* or are attached to a balcony rail located above the audience and in front of the stage. The three upstage areas (pools 4, 5, and 6) receive their illumination from instruments placed on a *pipe* proportionally closer to the performance area above the *apron* or front of the stage (Ellfeldt and Carnes, 1971).

To cover a larger stage, your lighting designer will need to use more instruments to produce more pools of light. The number of area pools used depends on both the number of lighting instruments available and the size of the stage (see figure 4.11). When more pools are used, each pool is also created with two instruments. The main point in using overlapping pools of light is to provide good general illumination onstage. This type of lighting does little, however, to sculpt the body or pull the figure out from the background. Remember also that all instruments must be secured according to proper safety regulations.

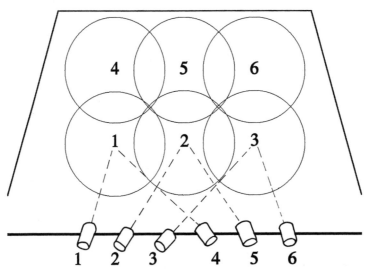

Figure 4.10 The six basic pools of light. Notice how the two beams of light come from opposite directions and blend to create one pool.

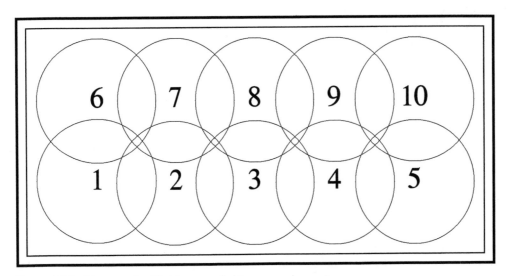

Figure 4.11 More pools of light are needed to cover a larger stage.

You can check for dark spots by having someone walk slowly from one side of the stage to the other. This check is done while all lighting instruments are on and without color media in the instruments. Check for dark spots in both upstage and downstage areas; if dark spots exist, add more lighting instruments or adjust the focus of instruments already in use to make an even effect.

Front lighting has a tendency to flatten the face and body, making illumination from the side important. Dance is a very sculptural art form, and the audience must be able to see the shapes made by the dancer's body. Cunningham (1993) describes how the lighting designer uses side lighting to mold and accent the body, particularly movements of the arms and legs. Side lighting also adds depth and form to the total picture.

To create side lighting, put the instruments on *light trees* placed in the wing or other side positions. These instruments are hidden from view by curtains (the legs) and should not be seen by the audience. The type of instruments you or your designer use for side lighting will be determined by the number and variety of instruments available and by the size of the stage. Remember that side lighting should illuminate the entire body of each dancer, not just the head or any other single part. You'll find that side lighting mounted at a low level gives dancers a lifted quality; side lighting mounted at middle level provides a clean edge to the dancer's form; and high side lighting adds more shadowing and pulls the dancer out from the background. A beam of light from a high side position also goes over the heads of the dancers and cannot be blocked by a performer positioned close to the light source (see figure 4.12 for an example of the effect created by side lighting). Dark spots can be filled in with additional instruments located in the front positions already described.

Providing lighting from both front and side positions is advantageous, but it may not be possible in certain situations. In such cases, it is advisable to use the basic general light *plot* involving areas or pools. A good rule of thumb is to begin by locating lighting instruments so that dancers can be seen, and then to add available instruments as needed to give shape and color to the individual dance compositions.

Figure 4.12 Side lighting molds and shapes the body.

Backgrounds

In many cases, a *cyclorama* (or "cyc") provides the background for a dance concert. A cyc is a large piece of light-colored material that is suspended from a pipe or *batten* upstage of the dancers. It is sometimes curved forward at each end to mask the upstage corners. Lighting instruments are used to throw light on the cyc so that a flood or *wash* of light covers the whole cyc from top to bottom. Brockett (1992) suggests that striplights located in front and above the cyc can produce illumination from the top, while additional striplights can be laid on the stage floor behind masking to create a wash of light from below. The only problem with the use of masking upstage at floor level is that it creates a dark band at the lower edge of the cyc, making it difficult for the audience to see the dancers' feet. Thus, if possible, it is preferable for the designer to create a smooth wash of light on the cyc using striplights placed at the top of the cyclorama. Scoops can also be used to produce a wash of color over the cyc if necessary.

Sometimes a dark curtain can make an effective background for a dance, provided that enough light is still available to illuminate the performers. Frequently when a dark background is used, the

audience sees what is known as a tracer effect, or *afterimage*, in which it appears as though each dancer produces a trail or stream of light. If you can integrate this effect into the visual design of the dance, it can enhance your choreography. The dancers will also be more visible if they wear light-colored costumes.

Color

Color is created in stage lighting through the use of a color media called a gel. Gels are manufactured in many different colors and are made of transparent, nonflammable polyester. Never use cellophane to create colored light, because cellophane burns. The color media is placed in front of the beam of light and is held in place by the frame located at the front of the lighting instrument (see figure 4.13). The lamp of each instrument gives off white light containing all the colors of the spectrum; when a gel is placed in front of white light, it absorbs all color except for the color of the gel. When a red gel, for example, is put in front of a beam of light, only red light passes through. This effect is called *subtractive lighting*.

Red, green, and blue are considered the *primary colors* in stage lighting. In general, gels in primary colors are not used to light dance because they are too intense and absorb too much light. According to Lippincott (1956), gel colors suggested for dance are amber, "bastard" amber, straw, surprise pink, no color blue, moonlight blue, lavender, red, green, magenta, midnight blue, and frost, which is really not a color. *Secondary colors* can be created from the primary colors through a process known as *additive mixing*. For example, a beam of light filtered through a red gel and a second beam filtered through a green gel create the secondary color amber when the two beams of light are focused on the same area.

Lighting color should be selected to enhance the quality or mood of a choreography. As a rule, blues, greens, and lavenders are cool, and reds, pinks, and ambers are warm colors. One suggestion is to have warm colors come from one side of the stage and cool colors from the other side; then other colors are blended in to heighten the mood. When in doubt about color, follow this suggestion, because the use of opposing warm and cool colors molds the body and produces a three-dimensional rather than flat effect (Bentham, 1976). If you do not have sufficient lighting instruments to use opposing warms and cools, use a predominance of one color with some other colors blended in; never use only one color by itself. Also keep in mind that when lighting is done straight on without the appropriate 45-degree angle, it is sometimes better to use a gel that reflects both warm and cool color properties. Such neutral colors include special lavender, surprise pink, and chocolate. The primary colors red, blue, and green plus the secondary color amber can be blended or used alone to create an effective wash on the cyc.

It is essential that you or the designer see all costume colors under the lighting, since colored light changes costume color. Blue light, for instance, can turn a red costume or red makeup black, whereas red light on a red costume will intensify its shade. Lighting a dance is much easier if you use only one or a few different costume colors in the number. The best test for lighting color is to have the dancers put on their costumes and move around under the lighting. This should be done during the technical rehearsal.

Note that green light and green costumes can be particularly difficult to work with. Green lighting

Figure 4.13 A lighting instrument. The "C" clamp is at the top of the instrument and attaches it to the pipe. The gel frame is at the front.

creates an otherworldly effect and should be reserved for dances in which such ambience is desired. Parker and Wolf (1987) advise that green costumes should be used under green light because they appear muddy under other lighting colors.

Special Effects

The designer can augment general lighting through the use of special effects, or *specials*. Specials accentuate a specific dancer or dancers and can be created by directing a more intense spot of light to the desired area onstage. Specials are usually wired to a different dimmer or electrical source so that each can be operated separately from the general lighting. A particularly dramatic effect can be achieved by positioning a special directly above the performers' heads to produce a pool of light that floods down onto the dancers (see figure 4.14). Performers should dance in specials and position themselves so that they are in the *hot spot*, or

Figure 4.14 Overhead lighting can create a dramatic effect.

brightest portion, of the pool of light. This placement of dancers is especially important during any movement in elevation because the dancer must be illuminated throughout the entire movement sequence.

Another kind of special effect can be created through the use of a *gobo*, a cutout pattern that throws a patterned pool of light onto the stage or cyc. Patterns of light can enhance a dancer's movement by making small movements look larger and by creating an onstage environment. Gobos are used only with ellipsoidal spotlights, in which they are placed at the *gate* or metal baffle at the perfect center of the instrument. This placement allows the pattern to be projected without distortion. Gobos can create a star-studded sky, a city scene, or a forest. Gobos can be purchased from companies that sell lighting equipment or can be selected from catalogs containing small black and white pictures of the gobo patterns (see appendix A for a list of some of these companies). Cunningham (1993) suggests that gobos can be constructed by cutting a pattern in sheet metal or even in a pie tin. Never make a gobo out of a flammable material.

You can use many other special lighting techniques, such as *back lighting* and cast shadows, to enhance your choreography. In back lighting, the designer places the light source behind the dancers to produce a silhouette. This effect can be easily achieved by lighting the cyc and leaving the remainder of the stage area dark. To cast shadows, the designer positions the light source in a downstage area or areas to create a shadow of each dancer on the cyc or stage floor. The size of the shadow changes as dancers move closer to or farther away from the light source. Sometimes it is necessary to locate the light source on the apron or front of the stage; you or your lighting designer will have to experiment with the placement of lighting instruments to create the desired effect.

The *followspot*, *black light*, and *strobe* can be used to design additional special effects. The followspot is operated by a technician and is usually located in the light booth at the back of the theatre; when used in an informal setting, it is placed above and behind the audience. Followspots are frequently part of musical theatre productions or ice skating shows. Black light causes costumes

or costume parts that are treated with special paint to fluoresce or glow. For best results, everything else should be black except the treated materials (Reid, 1987). For example, it is very entertaining to see dancers' hats or gloves without being able to see the rest of their bodies. A strobe light produces intermittent bursts of light and makes the dancers appear to be jumping from one pose to the next. Black light and strobe light create powerful visual effects and should be used sparingly. Also, you should know that strobe lights have been linked to epileptic seizures, so it is important to warn the dancers, crew, and audience when such devices will be used in a performance (McGrath, 1990). Individuals susceptible to such seizures should avoid the performance or shield their eyes when the strobe light is used.

As discussed in the post-modern section of chapter 2, you may wish to use slides and/or films in your choreography. Slides and films can be projected on the cyc, and as dancers move around the stage space they become a part of the projected design. Projections can also be used as side light. For the best results, the dancers should wear simple, light-colored costumes.

The designer must consider the availability of lighting instruments when planning specials. If enough instruments are not available to create the effects described, a few extra pieces of equipment can be used for different specials by changing gel colors or by placing a gobo in an instrument. An assistant can make such changes between dances. The choreographer may also need to reposition dancers to accommodate the placement of instruments used for specials.

Creating a Light Plot

You can help your lighting designer by putting together a *rudimentary light plot*. The light plot should begin with a general description of each dance, especially the mood or changing moods throughout each piece. Other factors to be included in the general light plot are:

- A floor plan of the choreography
- Placement of scenery or sets
- Costume colors

- Lighting colors
- Special effects (particularly as they relate to dance movement)

These suggestions should be supplied for each dance, since the lighting designer makes the final light plot from this information. Ellfeldt and Carnes (1971) define the final plot as a *hanging plot* that includes:

- The placement of each instrument
- The instrument type
- The color with which each instrument is gelled
- The number of the channel connecting each instrument to the control panel or dimmer board

A sample Planning Sheet for Lighting Design is included in appendix B. You can use this form to describe the mood or moods of the dance and the desired visual effects. You may want to design your own forms, but be sure to give the designer a very clear picture of how the lighting should relate to and enhance your choreography. Remember that the hanging plot must be completed before theatre rehearsals begin. Your lighting designer will use this plot to determine the placement of each instrument.

If you do not have a lighting designer, you may be able to hire one, or you could enlist the help of a knowledgeable theatre student. If you end up doing all of the lighting yourself, keep your design and plot simple. Sometimes a custodian can familiarize you with the location and operation of equipment.

Lighting is supposed to be an integral part of a dance performance; its purpose is to enhance the choreographic illusion, not to distract from it. Lighting changes that occur at unplanned points in a dance are disconcerting for both the performers and audience. In addition, when the audience notices the lighting rather than the dancing, something is wrong. The designer's job is to blend the two components of dance and lighting together to form a single entity. It is customary to employ very little scenery in dance concerts, so excellence in lighting is essential.

1. Look at a videotape of the same choreography that you viewed in the previous exercises in this chapter. As you play the tape, focus on the use of lighting throughout the dance. How does the lighting complement and enhance the mood or message portrayed? Notice the use of area lighting, background lighting, color, and special effects.

2. Can you suggest other possible lighting for use in the work in the preceding exercise? Give a detailed description of how you would use lighting areas, background, color, and special effects.

3. View a second dance on videotape. Compare the use of lighting in this choreography to the lighting design used in the first piece.

Developing Your Skills
Lighting the Dance

1. Place a light in an otherwise darkened room. (If you are using a table lamp, remove the shade during this exercise.) Notice the area of light that surrounds the light source. Watch while a dancer walks throughout the room. Does the dancer have a different appearance while moving through various areas of the room? Explain why the visual effect changes as this dancer moves.

2. Continuing the previous exercise, place a second light source in the darkened room. Gradually move one light toward the other until the illumination from the two lights blends together. Then reverse the blended effect by moving the lights apart.

3. Now place the two lights so that each reads as a separate lighting area. Watch a dancer move throughout the space, and again notice the effect produced when the dancer is positioned near or far from a light source. Can you see the dark areas? What effect does this have on the dancer's movements?

4. Use a single light source in a darkened room and ask the dancer to stand near this light. Experiment with the exact location of the dancer, trying positions above, below, and to the side of the source of illumination. How do these changes in the location affect the appearance of the dancer? Could such changes in the direction of light be used to complement the mood or message of your choreography? Explain.

5. Place a dancer in front of first a light-colored and then a dark background. Why is one color more effective as background? Would a light or dark background be most effective for your dance?

6. Return to the light source in a darkened room. Hold a square of color media in front of the light and notice how the light changes color as it passes through the media. (See the list in appendix A for names and addresses of companies that sell color media.)

7. Hold a piece of your costume material under illumination of different colors. Which color media produces the desired effect?

8. Use two lamps to mix light filtered through media of different colors. What colors are produced by mixing the light?

9. Experiment with back lighting by placing the light source behind your dancer. Could you use such a silhouette effect in all or part of your choreography?

10. Cut out a pattern in a piece of cardboard—a snowflake, a cloud, or any other shape. Hold the pattern in front of your light source. The cutout should cast a shadow that outlines the same shape as the original pattern.

11. Project a slide on a bare, light-colored wall. (Photographs of scenery or of abstract paintings work well in this exercise.) Watch while several dancers move in front of this projection. What effect does use of the projected image produce? Is this an effect you might use for your dance?

12. Fill out the planning sheet for lighting design found in appendix B. Consider each part of your dance carefully when you use this sheet.

13. Use the completed lighting plan sheet to design a rudimentary light plot. Include the floor pattern used by each dancer and the placement of scenery. Locate each pool of light so that important dance action receives illumination. Be sure to decide on the color media to be used for each pool, and indicate the placement of specials. This light plot could be realistic, based on the type and number of lighting instruments available to you, or it could be the ideal, designed without considering the limitations in your situation.

14. Record your observations and ideas concerning lighting in your journal.

15. Mark your master calendar to indicate the date for completing the light plot and for hanging lighting equipment.

Sets and Props

In most instances, choreographers use props and sets in a minimal way, although many of the classical ballets from the 19th century are an exception to this rule. Musicals incorporate more detailed sets as well. Sets used for jazz and modern dance are more sparse and provide only a suggestion of the performance environment (see figure 3.3 for an example of such a set). The design of sets and props should begin several months before the concert, although simple sets may take less time to construct. Dance sets are usually lightweight and fairly flat so that they can be attached to a batten and flown in and out of the stage area. Many sets are made of soft material and can be taken down and folded for storage. Dance sets are usually placed upstage to provide a backdrop for the dance, but they can also be used as a border to frame the stage space. Some choreographers have used sculptural sets on which dancers can move or pose (see figure 3.4, page 65). Such sets allow

dancers to perform on or between parts of the sculpture. Props can also be worn or carried by the dancers, but they must contribute to the design or meaning of a dance. You can use props to help create a story, and they may even be part of the movements.

ℰxperience in Action

1. Watch a videotape of a dance that includes sets and props. Describe the choreographer's use of the sets and props. Do you feel that they contribute to the effect or meaning of the choreography? Why?

2. View another dance in which the choreographer uses sets and props. Compare the contribution or the importance of sets and props in each dance.

Developing Your Skills
Sets and Props

1. Select a prop that you could use during the process of composing a dance (see chapter 1 for a list of suggested props). Experiment with the movement qualities of this prop, and then begin to choreograph phrases that incorporate the prop into the movement design.

2. Select a larger object that could serve as all or a part of your set, such as a bench or a box. Stand or sit on your set, and begin to move. Design several movement phrases in which the set is an integral part of the choreography.

3. If your dance is already complete, visualize how you could incorporate a set or set pieces into the movement design. Decide whether the use of a set would enhance the overall effect.

4. Mark dates on your master calendar for design and execution of sets and props.

Informal Concerts

A stage may not be available in some communities or in some educational institutions. In such cases you can transform a gymnasium or large studio into a relatively professional looking stage for an *informal concert*. First, however, make sure that an informal performance space has wiring that can accommodate stage lighting equipment. Usually you will need to connect your equipment to a 220 volt outlet to provide adequate power, or you can tie into a breaker box to protect circuits from an overload.

Lighting the Dance Space

Illumination can be provided by attaching lighting instruments to volleyball standards or poles used as light trees. The *"C" clamp* is used to attach each instrument to the pole, but care should be taken to place instruments so that the lamp inside is positioned correctly (see Lighting the Dance, pages 90-97). The standards, with the lighting instruments attached, can supply light from front and—particularly—side positions, but the goal is to come up with a performance area that is evenly illuminated and does not block audience sight lines. Experiment with the placement of the lighting equipment and standards until you obtain the desired effect.

Before you attach the lighting instruments to the poles, make sure each standard is stable and heavy enough to counterbalance the heavy instruments, and for safety reasons, avoid moving the standards after the instruments are attached. The diameter of the pole on each standard must also be checked to make sure the clamp on the instrument fits around it.

Framing the Dance Space

You can frame the dance space with *flats* (see figure 4.15). A flat is easy to build and can be made by constructing a wooden frame; inexpensive muslin is then stretched over the frame to provide the surface of the flat (see figure 4.16). Two widths of muslin may have to be double-stitched together to get a piece of material that is wide enough to cover each flat. The muslin is held in place with staples applied with a gun, and the corners of the muslin are folded under and secured with additional staples. The wood used in the flats should be lightweight, because the flats will be moved into and out of the storage area for different performances. Generally, 3-1/2 inch by 3/4 inch wood cut in desired lengths is recommended for the construction of flats. Use wood that is not warped and that is strong enough to withstand bending after the muslin is stretched in place. The frame for the flats must be high and wide enough to hide dancers from view while they are

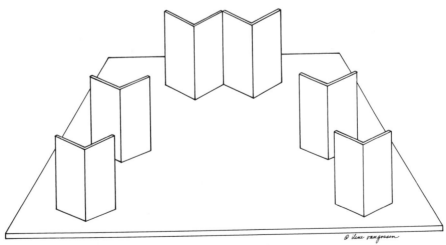

Figure 4.15 Strategically placed flats can give the appearance of a stage in an informal setting such as a gymnasium.

Figure 4.16 Back view of a single flat. Notice how the muslin is folded along the edges of the back of the flat and secured in place with staples.

Figure 4.17 A more detailed photo of the back of a flat showing two of the loose pin hinges.

waiting to enter the stage area. A single flat should be approximately five feet wide and seven feet high.

You can paint the flats once the muslin is stretched over the frames. The paint should be water-based, easy to spread, and of a light color. A beige surface is easy to light, but white surfaces appear too stark onstage, and black flats absorb too much light. Beige is a warm color that can be used under many lighting colors, and one that won't clash with costume colors.

Construct your flats to be freestanding, since those that need supports take longer to set up. Freestanding flats can be made by putting *loose pin hinges* between each flat. Two single flats are then attached together by inserting a pin into each hinge (see figure 4.17). These flats can stand without added supports when opened at an angle of less than 180 degrees. You can place such flats anywhere in the stage area, or use them to outline the space in upstage and stage right and left positions.

Holding a Lecture-Demonstration

The *lecture-demonstration* is usually presented as the first part of an informal dance concert, although it can be effective as part of a formal concert as well. Your entire production could also be a lecture-demonstration. A lecture-demonstration serves to educate the audience by combining spoken text with dancing; the dancers perform movements and dances that demonstrate or explain ideas and concepts presented in the lecture. You could structure lecture-demonstrations to illustrate many different choreographic concepts—such as style, form, or nonverbal communication—but in each instance movement examples would be used to demonstrate contrasting aspects of each idea.

Developing Your Skills
Holding an Informal Concert

1. Choose a place in which you could hold an informal dance concert. The space should be free of pillars and large enough to accommodate your choreography.

2. Next draw a diagram to indicate placement of flats, lighting, and sound equipment. Make sure that you have enough cabling to

connect the lighting instruments to the electrical outlets. On your diagram, show where the dancers will change costume, and how they are to enter and exit the performance area.

3. Plan a schedule of events leading up to the concert. Include dates for the audition, rehearsals, completion of costumes and audiotape, setup, blocking, and technical run-through.

4. Plan a sample lecture-demonstration by beginning with a dance topic or idea you want to explain to the audience. Write an outline of your text, and then select movement examples that would demonstrate the main points of your outline. Record your ideas for a lecture-demonstration in your journal.

Conclusion

Any creative endeavor is an exercise in problem solving. One of the challenges is to choose a direction and then to persevere—to make the imagined entity a concrete reality. In dance, more than any of the other arts, there is potential for creating something from nothing—molding movement to fit the forms and images emerging from your mind. The preceding suggestions concerning movement discovery and choreographic craft are offered as a series of steps to guide you, particularly in the early stages of choreographic exploration. These ideas can assist you with a creative impasse, should one arise, and help you release your creativity.

Review Questions

Explain how to plan the content of dance concerts in a way that will build audiences. How would you change your approach in different communities? Give some specific examples of the nature of the community and kind of concert you would present.

♦

Describe two important considerations that help determine the order of a dance concert. Why are these considerations important?

♦

How can you make dance auditions proceed more smoothly? Describe a few of these ideas.

♦

There are many steps involved in moving a dance from the studio to the theatre. What is each type of rehearsal called? What activities should take place during each type of rehearsal?

♦

Why is it important to check the stage floor before a performance? What is the purpose of a portable dance floor?

♦

Name the pieces of information usually included in the printed program. What is the purpose of including the recording company label, the credits, and the notes on the printed program?

♦

Describe three suggestions for making the master tape for a dance performance. Why are these suggestions important to the success of the performance?

♦

Where should onstage speakers be placed for rehearsals and performances?

♦

Selection of color, material, and decoration are important in the costume design process. Describe how you would use these elements in two dances that have different styles or meaning.

♦

Explain how to transform a leotard or unitard into a number of different dance costumes.

♦

What are at least three of the goals of dance lighting?

♦

Some common forms of lighting equipment are spotlights, striplights, and scoops. Describe the best use of each type of lighting instrument. (In other words, what is the purpose of each of these instruments?)

A pool of light is an area or circle of light cast on the stage. Two lighting instruments are usually used to create a single pool. Explain the purpose of pools of light. Why is it advisable to use two instruments to create each pool?

♦

Explain how you can light the entire stage space with a minimal number of lighting instruments.

♦

The angle of lighting can also be altered. How can you use the angle of lighting to create mood?

♦

Why is the background important in a dance concert? What type of lighting effect is used to create background? In what setting would you use a dark curtain as background? When would you use a light-colored background?

♦

Explain the relationship between costume color and the color of lighting. How can you determine correct lighting color as it relates to costumes? How can you use lighting color to create mood? Give some examples.

♦

What is a gobo, and how could you use it to complement your choreography? What are some other special effects described in this text? Describe how you could use these effects.

♦

Describe the typical dance concert set, and then explain how such a set can contribute to the overall effect of the choreography. Is this type of set used in all dance performances? Explain.

♦

Describe some situations in which an informal dance concert would be appropriate. In other words, how might such a concert serve your goals and needs?

♦

What is the purpose of a lecture-demonstration? Give some examples of concepts that could be used as subjects in the lecture-demonstration.

Choreography Resources

Sources of Music Copyright Information

The following organizations may be able to supply you with information about the copyright holder for your accompaniment (Topaz, 1995, p. 54).

American Music Center
30 W. 26th St., Ste. 1001
New York, NY 10010

American Society of Composers, Authors and Publishers (ASCAP)
1 Lincoln Center Plaza
New York, NY 10023

Broadcast Music Incorporated (BMI)
320 W. 57th St.
New York, NY 10019

European American Music
2480 Industrial Blvd.
Paoli, PA 19301

New York Public Library for the Performing Arts
111 Amsterdam Ave.
New York, NY 10023

Dance Video Sources

British Broadcasting Company (BBC)
80 Wood Lane
London, England W12 0TT

Dance Horizons Videos
12 W. Delaware Ave.
P.O. Box 57
Pennington, NJ 80534-0057

Dance Notation Bureau
31 W. 21st St.
New York, NY 10018

Elektra Nonsuch Dance Collection
75 Rockefeller Plaza
New York, NY 10019

Hoctor Products
P.O. Box 38
Waldwick, NJ 07463

Kultur
195 Highway 36
West Long Branch, NJ 07764

Pyramid Film & Video
P.O. Box 1048
Santa Monica, CA 90406-1048

Ririe-Woodbury Dance Company
Capitol Theatre
50 W. 200 St.
Salt Lake City, UT 84101

Video Arts International, Inc.
P.O. Box 153, Ansonia Station
New York, NY 10023

Dance Floor Companies

Portable floors are available in strips of material similar to linoleum, and can be rolled out and taped in place. A portable floor can also be transported from one performance location to another if you decide to go on tour. Many companies sell portable, multipurpose dance floors that can be used for many different forms of dance.

The American Harlequin Corporation
3111 W. Burbank Blvd.
Burbank, CA 91505

Floor-Tote
1832 Evergreen St.
Burbank, CA 91505

Norcostco
137 W. 10th Ave.
Denver, CO 80204

Rosco Floors
36 Bush Ave.
Port Chester, NY 10573
(Write to this address for a list of distributors.)

Stage Step
P.O. Box 328
Philadelphia, PA 19105

or

910 Cherry St., 4th Floor
Philadelphia, PA 19107

Lighting Equipment Manufacturers and Distributors

Altman Stage Lighting Co.
57 Alexander Street
Yonkers, NY 10701

Cinemills Corporation
3500 West Magnolia Blvd.
Burbank, CA 91505

Colortran, Inc.
1015 Chestnut St.
Burbank, CA 91506-9983

Kliegl Brothers
5 Aerial Way
Syosset, NY 11791

Olesen Company
1523-35 Ivar Ave.
Hollywood, CA 90028

Rosco
36 Bush Ave.
Port Chester, NY 10573

Strand Lighting
18111 S. Santa Fe Ave.
P.O. Box 9004
Rancho Dominguez, CA 90224

Theatrix, Inc.
1630 W. Evans Ave., Unit C
Denver, CO 80110

Forms and Checklists

Choreographic Assessment Sheet

Each of the following criteria can be worth one or two points depending on the total points desired in the scale. You may use fractional points as well. For example, if you feel that the choreographer has created a dance that has a sense of form throughout, enter the maximum score for item 1 in the appropriate blank. If a sense of form is intermittent, score a fraction of the points, and give no points for item 1 if the dance has no sense of form or development.

If you find use of points bothersome or intimidating, simply use this form as a guide for describing your comments or suggestions concerning a dance. Other components more compatible with your own choreographic concepts can be substituted for some of the items listed.

	Score
1. Overall form—beginning, middle, end	_____
2. Unity, continuity, flow	_____
3. Variety, movement manipulation, sequence, opposition	_____
4. Repetition throughout overall form	_____
5. Development of phrasing	_____
6. Interesting relationship among dancers or articulate and creative use of the body shape	_____
7. Use of stage space: blocking, stage area, pathways, awareness of stage space	_____
8. Facings	_____
9. Communication of intent, idea, or feeling, or successful solution of problem	_____
10. Performance, projection, aliveness of movement quality	_____
Total points	_____

Comments

Dancer's Audition Form

Name: _____ Audition Number: _____

Address: _____

City and Zip Code: _____

Phone Number: _____

Height: _____ Weight: _____

Please list times you will be available for rehearsals. _____

Performance Organization Checklist

_____ Scheduling the audition: _____

_____ Organizing and posting the studio rehearsal schedule: _____

_____ Designing the costumes: _____

_____ Designing the props: _____

_____ Designing the set: _____

_____ Preparing the rudimentary light plot: _____

_____ Collecting information for the printed program: _____

_____ Recording accompaniment: _____

_____ Rehearsal scheduling and posting

    _____ Blocking rehearsal: _____

    _____ Technical rehearsal: _____

    _____ Dress rehearsal: _____

_____ Checking the dance floor: _____

Printed Program Information Sheet

Dance title: _____

Grants/funding sources: _____

Choreographer: _____

Musical artist(s) and/or composer(s): _____

Music title: _____

Recording company: _____

Credits (costume designer, props, construction, etc.): _____

Dancers (in alphabetical order): _____

_____

_____

_____

_____

_____

_____

_____

_____

_____

_____

_____

_____

Program notes: _____

Program Supplement

(To be used for collaborative concerts)

Name of institution, group, or school: _____

Contact address & phone: _____

Choreographer's background information: _____

Sample Entry for Printed Program

Mountain Mystery

This dance was made possible through a grant from the Young Foundation.

Choreographer .... Suzanne Jones

Music .... Ralph Limon, "Sunset Song,"
Methods Recording Company

Costume Design .... Cecile Dawson

Dancers .... Julie Applebee, Margery Stayer, Alice Whimple

Planning Sheet for Lighting Design

1. How many sections are there in your choreography?

2. What is the style of your dance? Is it literal, comic, geometric, etc.?

3. Briefly describe the story line or action in each section of your dance.

4. Describe the costumes and costume colors, and provide samples of the fabric.

5. On the rough plan below, describe and show the stage area(s) to be used in your dance.

6. Dance plan:

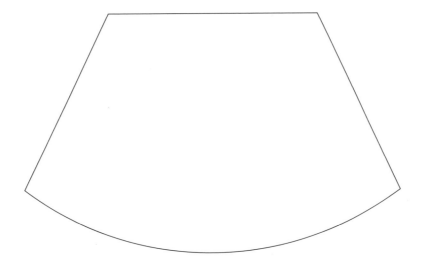

   a. Outline the placement of any set in the diagram, and then describe how your dancers use it.

   b. Use numbers on the diagram to indicate the location of important action in your dance. Then describe how such action can be enhanced with special effects.

   c. Briefly describe the action(s) involved for each special.

   d. Indicate the mood, quality, or focus to be achieved with each special.

7. Will you be using projections on the cyclorama?

8. Would you like any patterns or gobos?

9. How do you see lighting enhancing your dance? Be specific.

10. How do you want the audience to respond to your dance?

Glossary

AB—A simple choreographic form with two sections having two contrasting themes (Blom & Chaplin, 1982).

ABA—A simple choreographic form with three sections having two contrasting themes, A and B, followed by a repeat of the first theme in the third section. In the ABA, the third section may be a shortened version of the original A section (Blom & Chaplin, 1982).

abstract—A type of dance style that communicates no message. May also refer to the process of presenting the core or essence of the real thing in the work of art. (The word *geometric* is used in this text for the word *abstract* to avoid confusion with the second meaning.)

abstraction—The process of removing, separating from, or condensing. Distilling something to its essence (Blom & Chaplin, 1982).

accent—An emphasis or stress on certain musical counts or with specific movements.

additive mixing—The process of producing a new color in stage lighting by mixing beams of light that are different colors from that of the light being created.

afterimage—A visual sensation occurring after the external stimulus is gone.

alignment—The placement of the body's segments one above the other so that the ear, shoulder, hip, knee, and ankle are as close as possible to a straight line that extends at a right angle to the floor.

apron—The front or most downstage areas of the stage.

arabesque—One of the basic ballet poses in which the body is supported on one leg with the other leg extended behind and at a right angle to the support leg. The arms can be held in various positions to create the longest possible line from fingertips to toes (Grant, 1967).

area—A particular extent or portion of the stage space.

asymmetrical—Unbalanced, as applies to a body shape or grouping of dancers (Humphrey, 1987).

auditory—Related to the sense of hearing; descriptive of a type of stimulus for movement.

axial—A movement in which the dancer remains in one spot. Bending, stretching, and reaching are axial movements.

back lighting—A light source positioned upstage or behind the performers.

batten—A metal pipe usually located parallel to the proscenium arch of a stage and from which scenery and lighting instruments are hung (Gillette, 1978).

beam—An opening in the ceiling of the theatre from which lighting instruments are suspended (Gillette, 1978).

black light—A filtered ultraviolet light source that causes specially treated parts of a dancer's costume to be visible, while untreated costume parts are less visible.

blocking—The process of positioning dancers while making a dance; the act of mounting a finished choreography on stage.

brainstorming—A technique used to solve creative problems by coming up with many possible solutions or to find new associations between old things (Shallcross, 1981).

canon—A choreographic form usually providing the movement materials for only part of a dance. A canon is based on the use of one repeated movement phrase performed by different dancers' beginning the phrase a number of counts apart (Blom & Chaplin, 1982). The phrases are danced with and against one another.

"C" clamp—The clamp at the top of a lighting instrument by which it is attached to a pipe, batten, or pole.

chance—A method of choreographic development based on random selection of movement or random organization of actions (Blom & Chaplin, 1982).

character—The basic style, quality, or feeling of a dance or of a section of a dance; also can refer to a dancer who performs a specific role.

choreographer—One who discovers movement for and organizes actions into dances.

choreography—Many sequences of movement that add together to produce a whole dance with a beginning, middle, and conclusion. (Used interchangeably with the term *dance*.)

classical ballet—A dance form that includes the traditional steps, positions, and body carriage that originated before the 20th century; also can refer to a dance presentation choreographed prior to the 20th century.

closure—The act of bringing dance movement to an appropriate ending, as in the conclusion of an improvisation or choreography.

collage—A choreographic form made up of unrelated movements (Blom & Chaplin, 1982).

collapsing—A use of energy in which one gives in to gravity.

color media—The material used to give color to white light.

combination—A grouping of connected movements usually prepared for presentation during the latter portion of a dance technique class. Students are expected to learn and perform combinations as part of the class.

comic—A style of movement that appears funny, odd, or unusual to the viewer.

composition—A dance or choreography that exists as a whole with a beginning, middle, and end. Term is usually applied to modern dance choreography.

concert—A program of separate dances organized into a single performance.

conscious—A state of mind in which the individual is perceiving or noticing with a degree of controlled thought or critical awareness.

contact improvisation—Spontaneous movement drawn from actions done while relating to the environment or while in contact with another moving body (Brown, 1980).

continuity—A principle of choreographic form that provides a natural and organized progression of movement phrases so that one phrase flows naturally into or connects to the next (Hawkins, 1988).

contrast—The use of different attributes of the elements of movement. For example, high movement contrasts with one done at a low level; fast movement contrasts with slow actions.

count—A specific beat among a number of underlying pulse beats that make up a sequence of movements or a measure of music.

craft—The technique of organizing movements into a dance following their discovery through improvisation; the act of designing and shaping a choreography; specific methods or tools used to develop a dance.

cubism—A modern movement in the arts characterized by abstract structure. Cubism fragments visual forms by displaying several aspects of an object at the same time.

cue—The point in a dance at which appropriate changes in lighting or accompaniment need to occur; also can refer to internal or external stimuli that motivate movements.

cyclorama—A plain piece of cloth extending around and above the upstage area to create a feeling of infinite space and to serve as the background for the dancers (Reid, 1987).

dance—Many sequences of movement that add together to produce a whole. A dance has organization, progression, and development, including a beginning, middle, and end. (Used interchangeably with the term *choreography*.)

Dance Content Standards—Seven dance criteria developed to determine what every young American should know and be able to do. The standards cover the areas of dance skills, choreographic principles and processes, aesthetic judgment, cultural and historical concepts in dance, dance and health, and the connection between dance and other disciplines (National Dance Association, 1994).

dance drama—A presentation using movement to express a message or tell a story, usually by showing relationships among the dancer-characters.

dance floor—A portable surface, usually made of a linoleum-like material, that is rolled out on the stage in strips and held in place with tape of the same color.

dance in the round—An arrangement of movement sequences that produces a whole and that is designed to be viewed from all sides rather than from only the front.

design—The overall organization of a dance, including use of space, time, energy, and shape; a pattern traced in space or on the floor; also can mean to organize and structure a piece of choreography.

developmental stage—A degree or level of accomplishment through which a beginning choreographer passes.

dimmer—A device that determines the amount of electricity passed to a lighting instrument, thereby controlling the brightness of that instrument (Reid, 1987).

direct image—The process of mentally visualizing movements before performing them. Direct images are like a mental rehearsal.

direct pathway—The straight line traced by moving across the floor or by moving a part of the body in space.

direction—One aspect of the movement element space. In dance, the eight basic directions in which a dancer can move or face the body are: forward, backward, the right or left side, and the four diagonals.

downstage—Movement toward the front of the stage closer to the audience.

dramatic dance—A choreographic form that tells a story or expresses a message similar to a narrative dance.

dresser—An individual who helps a performer change costume.

dress rehearsal—The practice session(s) or "run-through(s)" immediately preceding the performance in which the dancers wear their costumes.

dynamics—The interaction of force and time (Blom & Chaplin, 1982); the loud and soft aspects of music (Teck, 1994).

electronic music—Accompaniment produced, altered, or reproduced through electronic means, and that uses electronic equipment in a creative manner (Harvard University, 1986).

element—Any one of the three basic components of movement—space, time, and energy or force. (Shape is sometimes included as a fourth element.)

energy—One of the elements of movement. Energy propels or initiates movement, or causes changes in movement or body position. (Used interchangeably with the word *force*.) Six different energy qualities are described in this text.

ensemble—A group of dancers who perform together.

environment—The surroundings or space in which dance movement takes place. Environments can serve as the motivation for improvised movement.

essence—The fundamental nature of a person or thing.

experiment—To try a variety of movement solutions to solve a specific choreographic problem.

experimental—A type of choreography that uses new movement materials or new concepts of form.

exploration—A process producing spontaneous movement based on suggestions made by a leader. Exploration is not as in-depth a process as improvisation (Hawkins, 1988).

expressionism—A modern movement in the arts characterized by the desire to depict the subjective emotions and responses of the artist, rather than the appearance of objective reality.

face—The direction in which the front of the body is turned.

facial expression—A configuration or shaping of features of the face that indicates or projects feeling.

facing—The direction toward which the front of the body is positioned; where one's face is directed.

flat—A wooden frame with muslin stretched over it. Flats provide background and legs (side curtains) in an informal setting.

floodlight—A lighting instrument that has no lens and that casts a broad beam of light. It usually has a metal housing, reflector, and single lamp (Brockett, 1992).

floor pattern—A pathway traced on the floor using locomotor movements.

flow—To transmit energy from one part of the body to another; to move a costume in relation to the actions in a dance.

focal point—A place where the audience readily looks onstage or within a group of dancers.

focus—A place where dancers direct their faces and eyes. Also, a point of concentration or attention for the audience.

follow—To simultaneously copy the movements of another dancer.

followspot—A lighting instrument used to highlight and follow a dancer around the stage or performance area (Reid, 1987).

force—One of the elements of movement. Force propels or initiates movement, or causes changes in movement or body position. (Used interchangeably with the word *energy*.)

form—The overall shape, organization, or development of many movement sequences.

framework—A description or suggestion that limits movement materials discovered during exploration or improvisation.

gate—A metal baffle located just before the focal point in ellipsoidal spotlights. At this point light rays are still converging, and the gate cuts off stray rays to provide a controlled light beam (Parker, Smith, & Wolf, 1985).

gel—The media used to give color to white light. (Used interchangeably with *media*.)

geometric—Descriptive of dances that do not communicate feelings or messages. The emphasis is on movement variation, line, and design. (In this text, the word *abstract* means the same thing.)

global image—A suggestion or motivation for movement that is general and directed at the whole body.

gobo—A mask placed at the gate of a spotlight to project a pattern by blocking out portions of the light beam (Reid, 1987).

ground bass—A choreographic form, usually providing the movement materials for only part of a dance. In a ground bass a phrase or phrases are repeated throughout while a more complex series of movements is performed by

another dancer or dancers (Lockhart & Pease, 1982). The more complex actions play against the simple movements.

hanging plot—The final form of the light plot indicating type, location, gel color, and circuiting for each instrument used in a concert.

hot spot—The most intense place in a pool of light thrown by a spotlight. For good visibility, a dancer should perform in the hot spot.

house—The area of the theatre in which the audience is seated.

housing—The outside portion of a lighting instrument that surrounds other components.

idea—A motif, motivation, or stimulus for movement.

illumination—A stage of the creative process in which a solution or solutions arise. It is the insight into a solution (Weisberg, 1986).

image—A mental picture or body/kinesthetic feeling (see table 1.2).

improvisation—A process producing spontaneous movements stemming from a specific stimulus; a more complete and inner-motivated spontaneous movement experience than exploration (Hawkins, 1988).

impulse—A burst of energy greater than what came before or after.

incubation—A stage of the creative process in which the problem is put aside to germinate.

indirect image—A motivation for movement that is outside the body. Indirect images are like a metaphor. An example is to move like a feather floating on the breeze.

indirect pathway—The curved line traced by the whole body as it travels across the floor, or by a part of the body in space.

informal concert—A program of separate dances performed for the public in a setting such as a gymnasium or dance studio, rather than on a stage.

intent—The motivation that stimulates movement.

involvement—The process of focusing on movement and body sensations. It requires more than a superficial level of attention.

inward focus—The process of paying specific attention to stimuli that come from within oneself.

isolation—Movements restricted to one area of the body such as the shoulders, rib cage, or hips. Isolations are important in jazz dance.

jazz—A dance form that developed along with jazz music. Jazz dance has appeal through its energy and variety (Kraines & Kan, 1990).

kinesthetic—Pertaining to sensations from the body that relate information about body position, movement, or tension.

kinesthetic image—A motivation that describes the body feeling stimulated by the resulting movements.

kinesthetic sense—A mode of receiving information from body sense organs that provides information about body position, tension, movement, and so forth.

lamp—The illuminating device within a lighting instrument (Reid, 1987).

lamp base—The bottom of the light source within the instrument. Care must be taken to burn all lamps in the proper position, whether base up or base down.

learning style—The favored or preferred mode of understanding information. Some people are visual, some are auditory, and others are kinesthetic learners.

lecture-demonstration—An informal performance, including verbal explanations of dance elements and theories together with movement demonstrations of these theories.

legs—Curtains at the sides of the stage that hide dancers waiting to enter the performance area.

level—One of the aspects of the movement element space. In dance there are three basic levels: high, middle, and low.

lighting designer—The individual who creates the final or hanging plot.

light tree—A vertical, freestanding pipe with side arms to which lighting instruments are attached (Gillette, 1978). Light trees are usually placed in the wings behind the legs.

line—A spatial aspect of dance movement; lines are created in space as dancers move, or through the placement of parts of the body. Line can be curved, straight, or a combination of these two.

literal choreography—Choreography that communicates a story or message to the audience (Turner, 1971).

locomotor—A term used to describe dance movements that cross space.

loose pin hinge—A type of hinge in which the central pin can be easily removed.

lyric—A term describing a movement style characterized by actions that are smooth, calm, and controlled.

manipulation—Varying of movement, particularly in terms of space, time, energy, or shape.

masking—Neutral materials defining the performance area or concealing technical equipment (Reid, 1987).

master calendar—A block calendar used to organize a performance. Specific dates for the completion of costumes and other details can be indicated on this calendar.

master tape—The main or original tape recording used to provide accompaniment for a dance concert.

media—The material used to give color to white light. (Used interchangeably with *color media* and *gel*.)

mental image—A picture created in the mind.

metaphor—An image or movement motivation that is likened to an outside object. To collapse like a pat of melting butter is a metaphor for how to move to the floor.

meter—The divisions of music into small groups of pulse beats. Usually each grouping has the same number of underlying pulse beats.

mind-body connection—The concept that thoughts in the mind can affect the body, and that changes in the body can alter the mind.

minimalism—A movement form based on the repeated use of the same movement or movement phrase with only slight changes.

mirror—To copy the movements of another while facing that individual.

mixed meter—A metric division of beats in which the separate groupings differ in terms of the number of underlying pulse beats per measure.

mode of sensing—One of the various channels or ways of receiving information from the outside world. Sight and touch are two modes of sensing.

modern ballet—A choreography that maintains elements of traditional ballet but that was created during the 20th century. Many modern ballets are abstract and nonliteral.

modern dance—A performance movement form that evolved at the beginning of the 20th century. Modern dance can be contrasted with the dance forms ballet, tap, or jazz. Creative work or choreography is an important part of the learning experience in modern dance.

monaural—A sound transmission or recording that has a single transmission path.

motivation—The starting point or stimulus for creative movement. (Used interchangeably with the word *stimulus*.)

mount—To place and position a dance onstage after the completion of the choreography.

movement ideas—A motivation or stimulus for movement that exists in the mind as a thought or concept.

movement manipulation—A method of changing an action, movement, or phrase so that it looks and feels different. The elements space, time, energy, and shape can be used to manipulate movement.

movement potential—The range or degree of motion possible in a joint of the body.

narrative—A choreographic form that tells a story similar to a dance drama (Humphrey, 1987).

negative space—Spaces surrounded by parts of the dancer's body or between two or more dancers. Negative spaces are part of the overall visual design of a choreography including the space between props, sets and the stage environment.

nonliteral choreography—Choreography that emphasizes movement manipulation and design without the intent of telling a story. Nonliteral works communicate directly through movement and need no translation (Turner, 1971).

nontraditional—Choreography created with experimental rather than established methods and forms.

opposition—The act of moving or facing the body in a different direction from the movement direction or facing used by another dancer or dancers (Humphrey, 1987).

order—The sequencing and organization of movements, phrases, and themes within a dance.

organic—Pertaining to a dance or sequence of movements that has an interrelationship of parts similar to the form or organization of parts in nature.

outcome assessment—The measurement or evaluation of achievement in relation to a set of criteria. In creative work, a decision is made to stop because the outcome appears successful or unsuccessful (Amabile, 1989).

overall development—The form or development of an entire sequence of movements as it progresses from beginning to end. (Also known as *overall shape*.)

pantomime—A nonverbal but realistic use of action and gesture as a means of expression. Dance is more abstract than pantomime.

path or pathway—The designs traced on the floor as a dancer travels across space; the designs traced in the air as a dancer moves various body parts.

pattern—The organization of movements into recognizable relationships (Ellfeldt, 1967). Also refers to the organization of sounds into identifiable groupings.

pedestrian—Descriptive of movements from daily life that are not traditionally done in dance, such as sitting, standing, eating, or typing.

perceiving—Achieving an awareness or understanding based on sensory information.

percussive—Use of energy that is powerful and explosive.

phrase—The smallest and simplest unit of dance form (Blom & Chaplin, 1982).

phrasing—The building block of dance form. In music, it is a melodic building block equivalent to parts of a complete sentence unit in language.

pipe—A long, cylindrical piece of metal usually suspended parallel to the proscenium arch of the stage and from which scenery and lighting instruments are hung.

pitch—The high and low aspects of music as determined by the frequency of sound waves (Teck, 1994).

plot—A drawing showing the location of each lighting instrument used in a concert in relation to the physical structure of the theatre. May also refer to a general description of lighting changes throughout a choreography.

pool—A circle of light thrown onstage by a lighting instrument. Most pools are actually not a perfect circle due to location of the lighting instrument and the angle at which the beam of light hits the stage. (Theatrical technique recommends the use of two instruments focused to create one pool of light.)

post-modern dance—A form of modern dance that evolved in the 1960s and 1970s in which choreographers experimented with concepts and forms that challenged more traditional ideas.

potential—The number or kinds of movements possible in each of the joints of the body.

preparation—The actions or processes one goes through to get ready to do creative work.

primary colors—The three most basic colors in stage lighting—red, green, and blue. These colors produce white light when all three are mixed together.

project—To throw one's energy out toward the audience; to make movement onstage more visible or alive; or to be exact in terms of movement expression.

prop—An object that is separate from the dancer's costume but that is a part of the action or spatial design in a choreography or that contributes to the meaning of a dance.

proscenium—The arch that frames the stage area and through which the audience views a performance.

pulse—The underlying and steady beat in dance or music. The pulse is divided into groupings or measures with a specific number of beats per measure; a rhythmic pattern is created over and in relation to the pulse.

quality—Movement characteristics determined by the specific use of energy (Ellfeldt, 1967). Sustained, percussive, and vibratory are movement qualities.

realism—A movement in the arts characterized by a faithful representation of nature or life without distortion or idealization.

repetition—A principle of choreographic form based on using movements or phrases again in a work. Repetition adds closure because the audience feels familiar and more involved with repeated movements.

rhythm—A structure of patterned movement through time (Ellfeldt, 1967).

rhythmic pattern—The organization of movements or sounds into recognizable groupings or relationships. A rhythmic pattern is created by moving more slowly or faster than the underlying pulse or by leaving silences in the movement (Hawkins, 1988).

rondo—A choreographic form with many different sections. There is a return to the original theme in alternation with contrasting sections (Blom & Chaplin, 1982).

rudimentary light plot—A general description of a dance as related to any and all possible lighting to be used in that dance. The hanging plot is developed from this description.

scoop—A lighting instrument that contains no lens and that is used primarily to throw a wash of light on the cyclorama (Gillette, 1978).

secondary colors—The colors in stage lighting produced by mixing beams of light of two primary colors. The secondary colors include cyan, magenta, and amber.

section—Part of a dance smaller than the whole that contains many phrases.

semblance—An object or work of art that has the appearance of or that resembles something else. An abstraction is the semblance of the real thing.

sensory mode—A method of receiving environmental stimuli by means of the different human sense organs such as the eyes and ears.

sequence—A series of movements longer than a phrase but much shorter than a section of a dance; similar to a combination. Also refers to the ordering of movements and phrases in a choreography.

sequential—An arrangement of movements or phrases producing an overlapping effect in time (Hayes, 1955).

shape—An interesting and interrelated arrangement of body parts of one dancer; the visible makeup or molding of the body parts of a single dancer; the overall visible appearance of a group of dancers. Also the overall development or form of a dance. When used as a verb, shape means to give form and development to a choreography.

sight lines—Lines of visibility between the audience and the stage.

silence—An absence of movement in which dancers hold a position.

size—One of the aspects of the movement element space. Size can vary from the smallest possible performance of a movement to the largest.

space—One of the elements of movement. The dancer moves in and through space. Dance movement takes up space, and a dance is performed in a space. Direction, level, size, focus, and pathway are the aspects of space described in this text. An altered use of the aspects allows the choreographer to use space in different ways.

spatial design—A pattern traced in space with the whole body or a part of the body.

special—The use of lighting onstage to draw attention to a dancer or create a particular feeling. (Used interchangeably with the term *special effect*.)

specific image—A motivation for movement that creates a mental picture or a body feeling, and that is directed at one part of the body.

spotlight—Any of a number of types of lighting instruments containing a lens for controlling or condensing a beam of light.

stage left—A direction indicating movement to the performer's left side while that performer is facing the audience.

stage right—A direction indicating movement to the performer's right side while that performer is facing the audience.

stage space—The stage area in which a performance usually takes place. On a traditional stage, this space is framed by the proscenium.

step—A codified or set movement in dance that has a specific name.

stimulus—The starting point or incentive for creative movement. (Used interchangeably with the word *motivation*.)

striplight—A lighting instrument consisting of a series of lamps usually mounted in a trough, and used for general illumination (Brockett, 1992).

strobe—A lighting device that gives off a fast series of short flashes, and that appears to freeze the action onstage (Reid, 1987).

structured improvisation—Spontaneous movement based on predetermined rules or within a predetermined framework.

study—A short dance having a beginning, middle, and end, and that deals with only one or a few aspects of choreographic craft.

style—A personal or characteristic manner of moving or choreographing. In both dance and music, style can refer to the time period in which the work originated, the specific developmental procedures used, or the cultural context of the work (Teck, 1994).

subconscious—A term describing a state of mind in which information or ideas exist below the threshold of conscious awareness.

subject matter—The theme or ideas dealt with in a choreography.

subtractive lighting—A lighting technique that involves placing a color media in front of a beam of light to filter out all light colors except those in the media.

suite—A choreographic form with a moderate first section, second slow section, and lively third part (Humphrey, 1987).

surrealistic—A modern movement in the arts and literature characterized by the representation of dreams or irrational and unusual arrangement of materials.

suspended—A term that describes a use of energy that gives a feeling of stopping temporarily or hovering in mid-air.

suspended floor—A floor of wooden slat construction that gives with and cushions dancers' movements, particularly movements in which the dancer lands from elevation.

sustained—A use of energy that is slow, smooth, and controlled.

swinging—A use of energy that traces an arc in space. In a swing, one must relax and give in to gravity on the downward part of the arc and apply energy during the upward action.

symmetrical—A visually balanced body shape or grouping of dancers (Humphrey, 1987).

syncopation—Placement of accents where they usually do not occur in the metric organization of both music and movement.

tactile—Related to the sense of touch; a type of stimulus for movement.

technical rehearsal—A performance "run-through" during which lighting cues are set in relation to dance movement and the accompanying music.

technique—The learning of movement skills; the ability to use specific methods to create a dance.

technique class—A dance class that focuses on the development of movement skills such as alignment, balance, and coordination. There are many styles and forms of dance technique.

tempo—The speed of movement as it progresses faster, more slowly, or on a pulse beat (Ellfeldt, 1967).

texture—The density or sparseness of a piece of music (Teck, 1994). Can also be used to describe dance movement.

theme—One or several movement phrases that fit together and are developed from the same idea or intent. Can also mean the basic idea of a whole dance.

theme and variations—A choreographic form developed from altering and varying a movement theme (Humphrey, 1987).

time—One of the elements of movement. A choreography develops a form through time. The aspects of time discussed in this book include movement speed, accents, silences, and rhythm. Altering the aspects of time provides changes in a dance.

timing—The rate of speed at which movement is performed, particularly with reference to the underlying pulse or beat.

tone—The quality or feeling in a movement or movements. The quality, pitch, or modulation of a musical sound.

transition—An aspect of choreographic form that provides a bridge from one phrase of movement into the next, or between sections of a choreography. Transitions should fit with dance movements and not be noticeable.

unison—Movement exactly the same as other movements in a group.

unitard—A one-piece, close-fitting dance costume that covers the entire body, including the legs. Unitards may or may not have sleeves.

unity—A principle of choreographic form in which phrases fit together, with each phrase important to the whole (Hawkins, 1988).

upstage—A term indicating movement toward the back of the stage away from the audience.

validation—One of the stages of the creative process. In this stage, the movements discovered in the previous stage are tested and evaluated (Amabile, 1989).

variety—A principle of choreographic form that involves sufficient variation of movement to keep audience interest, while still maintaining unity of the whole (Hawkins, 1988).

verification—The part of the creative process during which movement solutions are tested (Weisberg, 1986).

vibratory—Use of energy that involves shaking or trembling actions.

virtual entity—The illusion that the audience sees when viewing a dance. This visual apparition is different from the physical moving bodies of the dancers. It encompasses elements that do not exist in physical reality, but rather are created artistically by the choreographer (Langer, 1957).

visual—Related to the sense of sight; descriptive of a type of stimulus for movement.

visual image—A motivation for movement that is like a picture in the mind.

visualize—To see or form an image in the mind.

wash—An even blending of light beams from separate instruments; especially an even flooding of light to cover the cyclorama.

wing—The areas at the sides of the stage.

References

Amabile, T.M. 1989. *Growing up creative: Nurturing a lifetime of creativity*. New York: Crown.

Banes, S. 1993. *Democracy's body: Judson dance theatre, 1962-1964*. Durham, NC: Duke University.

_____. 1987. *Terpsichore in sneakers: Post-modern dance*. Middletown, CT: Wesleyan University.

Bentham, F. 1976. *The art of stage lighting*. 2d ed. New York: Theatre Arts.

Blom, L.A., & L.T. Chaplin. 1982. *The intimate act of choreography*. Pittsburgh: University of Pittsburgh Press.

Brockett, O.G. 1992. *The essential theatre*. 5th ed. Fort Worth: Harcourt Brace.

Brown, B. Fall 1980. Is contact a small dance? *Contact Quarterly* 6(1):7.

Bry, A. 1978. *Visualization: Directing the movies of your mind*. New York: Barnes & Noble.

Charlip, R. 1992. Composing by chance (1954). In R. Kostelanetz (Ed.), *Merce Cunningham: Dancing in space and time*, Pennington, NJ: A cappella.

Cunningham, G. 1993. *Stage lighting revealed: A design and execution handbook*. Cincinnati: Betterway.

Dilley, B. Summer 1981. Notes from improvisation, open structures. Boulder, CO: Naropa Institute.

Dowd, I. Summer 1981. Notes from alignment of the axial skeleton. Boulder, CO: Naropa Institute.

Ellfeldt, L. 1967. *A primer for choreographers*. Palo Alto, CA: National Press.

Ellfeldt, L., & E. Carnes. 1971. *Dance production handbook or later is too late*. Palo Alto, CA: National Press.

Gillette, M. 1978. *Designing with light*. Palo Alto, CA: Mayfield.

Grant, G. 1967. *Technical manual and dictionary of classical ballet*. 2d ed. New York: Dover.

Hanrahan, C., & J.H. Salmela. 1990. Dance images—Do they really work or are we just imagining things? *Journal of Physical Education, Recreation and Dance* 61(2): 18-21.

Hanstein, P. Summer 1980. Notes from improvisation workshop. Denton, TX: Texas Woman's University.

Harvard University. 1986. *The new Harvard dictionary of music*. Cambridge, MA: Harvard.

Hawkins, A. 1988. *Creating through dance*. Rev. ed. Princeton, NJ: Princeton.

Hayes, E. 1955. *Dance composition and production*. New York: A.S. Barnes.

Horst, L., & C. Russell. [1963] 1987. *Modern dance forms*. Republication. Princeton, NJ: Princeton.

Humphrey, D. [1959] 1987. *The art of making dances*. Reprint. Pennington, NJ: Princeton Book.

Jacobson, E. 1976. *You must relax*. 5th ed. New York: McGraw-Hill.

Kraines, M.G., & E. Kan. 1990. *Jump into jazz*. 2d ed. Palo Alto, CA: Mayfield.

Kreemer, C. 1987. *Further steps: Fifteen choreographers on modern dance*. New York: Harper & Row.

Langer, S. 1957. *Problems of art*. New York: Charles Scribner's Sons.

Lavender, L. 1996. *Dancers talking dance: Critical evaluation in the choreography class*. Champaign, IL: Human Kinetics.

Lippincott, G., ed. 1956. *Dance production*. Washington, DC: American Association for Health, Physical Education and Recreation.

Lockhart, A., & E. Pease. 1982. *Modern dance: Building and teaching lessons*. 6th ed. Dubuque, IA: Brown.

McDonagh, D. 1990. *The rise and fall and rise of modern dance*. Rev. ed. Pennington, NJ: A cappella.

McGrath, I. 1990. *A process for lighting the stage*. Needham Heights: Allyn & Bacon.

Minton, S.C. 1989. *Body & self: Partners in movement*. Champaign, IL: Human Kinetics.

Minton, S.C. 1991. *Modern dance: Body and mind*. Englewood, CO: Morton.

National Dance Association. 1994. *National standards for dance education: What every young American should know and be able to do in dance*. Pennington, NJ: Princeton Book.

Overby, L.Y. 1990. The use of imagery by dance teachers—development and implementation of two research instruments. *Journal of Physical Education, Recreation and Dance* 61(2): 24-27.

Paivio, A. 1971. *Imagery and verbal processes.* New York: Holt, Rinehart & Winston.

Parker, W.O., H.K. Smith, & R.C. Wolf. 1985. *Scene design and stage lighting.* 5th ed. New York: Holt, Rinehart & Winston.

Parker, W.O., & R.C. Wolf. 1987. *Stage lighting: Practice and design.* New York: Holt, Rinehart & Winston.

Reid, F. 1987. *The stage lighting handbook.* 4th ed. New York: Theatre Arts.

Rossman, M., & D. Bresler. 1983. *Guided imagery: An intensive training program for clinicians* (seminar workbook). Pacific Palisades, CA: Institute for Advancement of Human Behavior.

Rugg, H. 1963. *Imagination.* New York: Harper & Row.

Samuels, M.D., & H. Bennett. 1973. *The well body book.* New York: Random House/Bookworks.

Schlaich, J., & B. Dupont, eds. 1988. *Dance: The art of production.* 2d ed. Princeton, NJ: Princeton.

Schneer, G. 1994. *Movement improvisation: In the words of a teacher and her students.* Champaign, IL: Human Kinetics.

Shallcross, D.J. 1981. *Teaching creative behavior: How to teach creativity to children of all ages.* Englewood Cliffs, NJ: Prentice Hall.

Siegel, M.B. 1977. *Watching the dance go by.* Boston: Houghton Mifflin.

Studd, K. 1983. Ideokinesis, mental rehearsal and relaxation applied to dance technique. Master's thesis, University of Oregon, Eugene.

Taylor, S., & C. Taylor. 1995. *Psychology of dance.* Champaign, IL: Human Kinetics.

Teck, L. 1994. *Ear training for the body: A dancer's guide to music.* Pennington, NJ: Princeton Book.

Topaz, M. 1995. Whose right: How to get the rights to choreograph copyrighted music. *Dance Magazine* 69(5): 52-55.

Turner, M. 1971. *New dance.* Pittsburgh: University of Pittsburgh Press.

Weisberg, R. 1986. *Creativity: Genius and other myths.* New York: Freeman.

Index

A

AB form, 60
ABA form, 60
Abstraction, 64, 66-67
Abstract style. *See* Geometric style
Accents, 28
Accompaniment (music)
   copyright issues, 19-20, 82, 103
   determining structure of, 20
   improvising with, 20-21
   live vs. recorded, 83
   as motivation source, 12
   at performances, 83-84
   phrasing and, 57
   for post-modern dance, 43, 47-48
   relations with composers of, 20
   research on, 3
   selection of, 19
   songs as, 19
   titles for dances and, 81
Acrobatic movements, 43
Acrobats of God (Graham), 64, 65
Additive mixing, for lighting, 93
Afterimages, 93
American Sign Language, 43
Appalachian Spring (Graham), 64, 65
Areas of stage, use of, 34
Assessment, of dances
   Choreographic Assessment Sheet
     for, 106
   guidelines, 71-72
Asymmetry, 38, 39, 40
Audience, interaction with dancers,
   48
Audience building, 76
Audience involvement
   choreographic form and, 58
   with geometric style dance, 67, 69
   titles of dances and, 81
Audiotapes, for performance
    accompaniment, 83
Audio technicians, 84
Auditions
   Dancer's Audition Form, 107
   guidelines for holding, 76-77

B

Backgrounds
   for informal concerts, 98-99
   on stage, 92-93
Back lighting, 94
Backwater Twosome (Paxton), 45

Ballet, classical
   accompaniment for, 19
   lyric style compared to, 67
   sets and props for, 97
Ballet, modern, accompaniment for,
   19
Batten, for hanging lights, 92
Black lights, 94-95
Blocking
   basic principles, 35, 36
   inspection of stage before, 81
   at rehearsals, 77-78, 80
Blocks, to creative process, 17-18
Blueprint (Monk), 46
Bows, at conclusion of performance,
   78, 79
Breathing
   phrasing and, 56
   for relaxation, 5, 6

C

"C" clamps, 93, 98
Canon dance form, 61
Cassette tapes, vs. reel-to-reel, 83
Chance, dance by (choreographic
   method), 43-44, 61-62
Choreographic form, 53-73. *See also*
   specific forms
   building skills for development of,
    54-55, 63
   content and, 63-64
   elements described, 55-59
   forms defined, 60-62
   motivation and, 64
   selection of, 64
   titles for dances and, 81
Choreography
   developing skills for, 17-19, 54-55,
    72
   solving challenges in process of,
    17-19
Circle Dance (Dean), 45
Classical ballet. *See* Ballet, classical
Closure
   improvisation of, 11
   repetition and, 58
Coaching, of dancers, 70-71
Collage dance form, 61
Collapsing movement, defined, 30
Color
   for costumes, 84-86, 87, 88, 93-94
   for lighting, 92, 93-94

Comic style
   collage form and, 61
   costume for, 85
   described, 67, 68
Comic subject matter, 69
Communication, through dance, 32-42
   basic principles, 32
   nonliteral choreography and, 64
   space and, 38-40
   staging process and, 34-38
   total picture in, 32-34
Communication, with dancers, 70-71
Composers, relations with, 20
Concentration
   basic guidelines, 4-5
   exploration and, 6
   improvisation and, 11, 14
Concerts, informal, 98-100
Conclusion, of dance, 59
Contact improvisation, 49-50
Content. *See* Subject matter
Continuity, 58
Contrast. *See* Variety
Copyright, 19-20, 82, 103
Costumes, 84-90. *See also* Dress
   rehearsals
   changes during performances, 80
   color for, 84-86, 87, 88, 93-94
   decoration for, 88-89
   fabric for, 86-88
   lighting and, 87, 93-95
   as motivation source, 12
   style of, 88
Counterbalancing, 50
Counting, and phrasing, 56
Creative act, defined, 4
Creative process, 2-6
Credits, in printed programs, 20, 82
Cues, for technical staff
   lighting cues, 78-79
   sound cues, 84
Cunningham, Merce, 43, 44, 61, 64
Curtains
   as background, 92
   at front of stage, 78
Cyclorama, 92, 94

D

Dance by chance, 43-44, 61-62
Dance floors
   inspection of, 81
   portable, 81, 103-104
   requirements for, 81

M

Manipulation of movement, 24-31
  energy and, 29-30
  purpose of, 24
  shape and, 30-31
  space and, 24-28
  timing and, 28-29
Media, color, 78, 93-94, 95
Memory skills, 18
Mental blocks, 17-18
Meter, 20
Minimalism, 43, 45
Mirroring
  for exploration, 7, 9-10
  improvisation with, 7
Mixed meter music, 20
Modern dance
  accompaniment for, 19
  sets and props for, 97
Monaural recordings, 83, 84
Monk, Meredith, 46, 47
Motivation (stimulus)
  for abstract dance, 64
  accompaniment and, 19
  costumes and, 84
  exploration and, 6, 7
  form and, 64
  improvisation and, 6, 7, 10-14, 15-16
  selection of, 13-14, 15-16
  sequence of, 16
  sources of, 12-13
  style and, 67
Mounting the dance, blocking rehearsals for, 78
Movement potential, exploration of, 8, 9
Multimedia, 43
Music. *See* Accompaniment (music)

N

Naming, of dances, 81-82
Narrative dance form. *See also* Literal choreography
  defined and described, 61
  difficulties with, 69
  props and sets for, 97
  return to, 43
  titles for dances, 81
National Dance Content Standards, viii, 2, 24, 54
Negative spaces, 40
Nikolais Dance Theatre, 13, 14
Nonliteral choreography
  defined and described, 64
  for geometric style, 67
  titles for dances, 81

O

Opposition, 41-42

P

Painting
  for decoration of costumes, 89
  of flats, 99
PAR 64 lighting instrument, 90
Paxton, Steve, 44, 45
Pedestrian movement
  as motivation source, 12
  in post-modern dance, 44-45
Percussive movement, defined, 29
Perez, Rudy, 45
Performances, 75-100. *See also* Costumes; Lighting; Programs, printed; Rehearsals
  accompaniment at, 83-84
  auditions, 76-77, 107
  checklist for organizing, 107
  copyright issues, 19-20, 82, 103
  dance floors for, 81, 103-104
  informal concerts, 98-100
  locations for, 81, 98
  selecting theaters for, 81
Permissions. *See* Copyright
Phrasing
  basic principles, 55-56, 59
  defined, 55
  in specific dance forms, 61
  techniques for developing, 56-57
Pipe, for hanging lights, 91, 92, 93
Pitch, defined, 20
Pools of light, creation of, 90-91
Portable dance floors, 81, 103-104
Post-modern dance, 42-50
  chance method for, 43-44, 61-62
  defined and described, 42-43
  environments for performances, 46-47
  group size in, 45-46
  improvisation in, 48-50
  interaction of dancers with audience in, 48
  pedestrian movement in, 44-45
  repetition in, 45
  technical skill level in, 46
  timing in, 45
Programs, printed, 20, 81-82
  information sheet, 108
  sample entry for, 109
Progressive Relaxation, 5
Projection, of dance movements, 70, 71
Projection, of slides or videos, 47, 95
Props
  basic guidelines, 97
  as motivation source, 12
Proscenium arch, 32-33, 48
Proxy (Paxton), 44

Q

Qualities of movement
  defined, 29-30
  titles for dances and, 81

R

Rainer, Yvonne, 47
Rainforest (Cunningham), 44
Recorded accompaniment, 83
Reel-to-reel tape recorders, 83
Reflective costumes, 87
Rehearsals, 77-80
  blocking rehearsals, 77-78, 80
  dress rehearsals, 80
  planning and scheduling ot, 80, 107
  technical rehearsals, 78-79, 80
  technical staff at nontechnical rehearsals, 78, 84
Relaxation techniques, 5-6
Repetition
  in ground bass form, 61
  importance of, 58
  in post-modern dance, 45
  variety and, 59
Research process, 3-4
Rhythm
  basic guidelines for use of, 28-29
  style and, 67
Rondo dance form, 60
Ross, Bertram, 65
Royalties, for use of music, 20
Rudimentary light plot, 92, 95

S

Safety
  dance floor maintenance for, 81
  with lighting, 91, 95
  during rehearsals, 78
Sanctum (Nikolais), 14
Scenery. *See* Sets
Scoops (floodlights), 90, 92
Scooters, 12, 13
Sculptural sets, 97
Sequential movement
  basic principles, 41-42
  in canon form, 61
Set movements, and phrasing, 57
Sets (scenery), 97
Shadows, 94
Shakers, The (Humphrey), 85
Shape
  basic guidelines for use of, 30-31
  defined, 30
  exploration of, 7, 10
  in geometric style, 67
  improvisation with, 7
  in lyric style, 67
  style and, 67
  symmetry of, 38, 39, 40
Side lighting, 92
Size, of movements
  basic principles, 25-27
  exploration of, 8
Slide projections, as special effect, 47, 95

About the Author

Sandra Cerny Minton coordinates the dance program at the University of Northern Colorado (UNC) in Greeley. She has taught and choreographed dance for more than 25 years and has directed numerous concerts.

Minton has been an active member of both the Colorado Dance Alliance and the National Dance Association of the American Alliance for Health, Physical Education, Recreation and Dance, for which she was publications director for two years. She also has devoted her energy to scholarship and to grant writing at UNC.

Minton earned her master's degree in dance education from the University of California at Los Angeles and earned her PhD in dance and related arts from the Texas Woman's University. She has written numerous articles, a book chapter, and other books on dance choreography and has presented at conferences across North America.

Minton also enjoys reading, hiking, and spending time with her husband and friends.

*You'll find
other outstanding
dance resources at*

www.HumanKinetics.com

In the U.S. call

800-747-4457

Australia 08 8277 1555
Canada 800-465-7301
Europe .... +44 (0) 113 255 5665
New Zealand 09-523-3462

HUMAN KINETICS

The Premier Publisher for Sports & Fitness
P.O. Box 5076 • Champaign, IL 61825-5076 USA